Bed & Breakfasts, Country Inns, and Other Weekend Pleasures

THE UPPER GREAT LAKES REGION

Michigan

Minnesota

Wisconsin

Fodor's Travel Publications, Inc.
New York • Toronto • London •
Sydney • Auckland

ISBN 0–679–02354–2

First Edition

Fodor's Bed & Breakfasts, Country Inns, and Other Weekend Pleasures: The Upper Great Lakes Region

Editor: Caroline Haberfeld
Editorial Contributors: Robert Blake, Karen Cure, Holly Hughes, Andrea Lehman, Larry Peterson, Saul Rosenberg, Melanie Roth
Creative Director: Fabrizio La Rocca
Cartographer: David Lindroth
Illustrators: Alida Beck, Karl Tanner
Cover Photograph: Zane B. Williams
Design: Rochelle Udell and Fabrizio La Rocca

Special Sales

Contributors

Richard Bak, *who lives in suburban Detroit, wrote the Southeast, Southwest, and Upper Peninsula sections of the Michigan chapter.* He has written three books and contributed to The Wall Street Journal Guides to Business Travel: USA & Canada.

Anne Gasior *lives in the suburbs of Chicago, Illinois, and wrote the Door County section of the Wisconsin chapter. She is a feature writer for the* Daily Herald, *a correspondent for* People, *and a contributor to* Chicago *and* Northshore *magazines.*

Deborah Hawkins *is a freelance writer whose articles appear regularly in various regional newspapers; an editor of the* Traverse City Area Entertainment and Leisure Guide; *and the co-founder of* Traverse, The Magazine. *She lives in Traverse City and wrote the Little Traverse Bay Region, Grand Traverse Region, and Mackinac Island sections of the Michigan chapter.*

Lynette Lamb, *who wrote the sections on the Twin Cities Area, Duluth and the North Shore, and Mississippi River Valley and Historic Bluff Country, lives in Minneapolis. She is managing editor of* Utne Reader *magazine and has written travel pieces for a variety of midwestern publications.*

Gene Rebeck *is a Minneapolis-based writer and editor and a frequent contributor to* Utne Reader *magazine. He wrote the Dakota Country and Northwest Cuy-*ana Iron Range sections of Minnesota.

Carla Waldemar, *a native midwesterner, wrote the Hiawatha Valley, Hidden Valleys, Madison and Environs, and Milwaukee and the Southeast Wisconsin sections of Wisconsin. She writes about food and travel for publications including* Food and Wine, Passport, Eating Well, *and the* Chicago Tribune.

Contents

Foreword

While every care has been taken to ensure the accuracy of the information in this guide, the passage of time will always bring change, and, consequently, the publisher cannot accept responsibility for errors that may occur.

All prices and listings are based on information supplied to us at press time. Details may change, however, and the prudent traveler will avoid inconvenience by calling ahead.

Fodor's wants to hear about your travel experiences, both pleasant and unpleasant. When an inn or B&B fails to live up to its billing, let us know and we will investigate the complaint and revise our entries where the facts warrant it.

Send your letters to the editors of Fodor's Travel Publications, 201 E. 50th Street, New York, NY 10022.

Introduction

Fodor's Bed & Breakfasts, Country Inns, and Other Weekend Pleasures *is a complete weekend planner that tells you not just where to stay but how to enjoy yourself when you get there. We describe the B&Bs and country inns, of course, but we also help you organize trips around them, with information on everything from parks to beaches to antiques stores—as well as nightlife and memorable places to dine. We also include names and addresses of area chambers of commerce and visitor centers, should properties we recommend be full or should you be inspired to go in search of additional places on your own. Reviews are divided by state and, within each state, by region.*

All inns are not created equal, and age in itself is no guarantee of good taste, quality, or charm. We therefore avoid the directory approach, preferring instead to discriminate—recommending the very best for travelers with different interests, budgets, and sensibilities.

It's a sad commentary on other B&B guides today that we feel obliged to tell you our reviewers visited every property in person, and that it is they, not the innkeepers, who wrote the reviews. No one paid a fee or promised to sell or promote the book, in order to be included in it. Fodor's has no stake in anything but the truth: A dark room with peeling wallpaper is not called quaint or atmospheric, it's called run-down; a gutted 18th-century barn with motel units at either end is called a gutted 18th-century barn with motel units at either end, not a historic inn.

Is there a difference between a B&B and a country inn? Not really, not any more; the public has blurred the distinction—hence our decision to include both in the title. There was a time when the B&B experience meant an extra

*room in someone's home, often with paper-thin walls and
a shared bathroom full of bobby pins and used cotton balls.
But no longer; Laura Ashley has come to town with her
matching prints, and some B&Bs are as elegant as the
country's most venerable inns. The only distinction that
seems to hold is that a B&B was built as a private home
and an inn was built for paying guests. Most B&Bs serve
breakfast, but not all, and some serve dinner, too; most
inns have full-service restaurants. B&Bs tend to be run by
their owners, creating a homey, family feeling (which can
be anathema to those who relish privacy), while inns are
often run by managers; but the reverse is true, too. B&Bs
can cost more than inns, or less. B&Bs tend to be smaller,
with fewer rooms, but not always. The truth is that many
B&Bs are called so only to circumvent local zoning laws.*

*What all places in this guide—B&Bs or country inns—offer
is the promise of a unique experience. Each is one of
a kind, and each exudes a sense of time and place. All are
destinations in themselves—not just places to put your
head at night, but an integral part of a weekend escape.*

*So trust us, the way you'd trust a knowledgeable, well-
traveled friend. And have a wonderful weekend!*

***

A word about the service material in this guide:

*A second address in parentheses is a mailing address that
differs from the actual address of the property. A double
room is for two people, regardless of the size or type of*

beds; if you're looking for twin beds or a king- or queen-size bed, be sure to ask.

Rates are for two in the high season, and include breakfast; ask about special packages and off-season discounts. Mandatory state taxes are extra. Most places leave tipping to the discretion of the visitor, but some add a service charge to the bill; if the issue concerns you, inquire when you make your reservation, not when you check out.

What we call a restaurant serves meals other than breakfast and is usually open to the general public. Inns listed as MAP (Modified American Plan) require guests to pay for two meals, usually breakfast and dinner. The requirement is usually enforced during the high season, but an inn may waive it if it is otherwise unable to fill all its rooms.

B&Bs don't have phones or TVs in rooms unless otherwise noted. Pools and bicycles are free; "bike rentals" are not. Properties are open year-round, unless otherwise noted, although opening and closing times can change with the weather. To be safe, always call and check.

Michael Spring
Editorial Director

The Upper Great Lakes Region

0 ——— 100 miles
0 ——— 150 km

N

Thunder
Bay

Isle Royale

Lake Superior

ONTARIO

Michipicoten
Island

Keweenaw
Peninsula

Keweenaw
Pt.

Calumet

gon

d

Marquette

141 UPPER PENINSULA

2

M
I
C
H
I
G
A
N

Manistique 2

Sault
Ste. Marie

Sault
Ste. Marie

75

St. Joseph Island

St. Ignace

Escanaba

8

141

Green Bay

Makinaw
City

Mackinac I.

Drummond
Island Manitoulin
Island

Petosky

23

*Grand Traverse
Bay*

Northport

*Lake
Huron*

Traverse
City

Grayling

Green
Bay

Elberta 131

75

N S I N

51

*Lake
Winnebago*

Oshkosh

43

LOWER
PENINSULA

75

23

Saginaw Bay

Fond du Lac

Shebaygan

10

31

Midland

Bay City

Saginaw

151

*Lake
Michigan*

Muskegon

27

Flint

Port
Huron

94

Milwaukee

94

Grand
Rapids

96

Lansing

69

75

*Lake
St. Clair*

al

90

Delevan

Racine

Sangatuck

196 131

Battle
Creek

Ann
Arbor

96

Lake Geneva

Kenosha

Kalamazoo

Jackson

94

Detroit

Rockford

94

94

69

127

*Lake
Erie*

on

ILLINOIS

Chicago

Union
Pier

Gary

80 90

South Bend

Toledo

75

80

INDIANA

OHIO

Special Features at a Glance

Name of Property	Accessible for Disabled	Antiques	On the Water	Best Value	Car Not Necessary	Historic Building	Romantic Hideaway
MICHIGAN							
Bay View at Mackinac		✓	✓		✓		✓
Bear River Valley							
The Benson House	✓						✓
Big Bay Point Lighthouse			✓			✓	✓
Birch Brook	✓						
Blanche House Inn		✓	✓			✓	✓
Bogan Lane Inn				✓	✓		
Bowers Harbor Bed & Breakfast				✓			
The Bridge Street Inn		✓				✓	
Brookside Inn							✓
Centennial Inn				✓		✓	
Cherry Knoll Farm							
Chicago Street Inn		✓		✓			✓
Clinton Inn	✓	✓		✓			
Cloghaun Bed & Breakfast		✓			✓	✓	
The Country Inn of Grand Blanc		✓					
Crane House	✓	✓				✓	✓
Dundee Guest House		✓		✓			
Eagle's Nest Bed & Breakfast		✓		✓		✓	✓
Fairchild House		✓					✓
The Gingerbread House	✓			✓		✓	
Haan's 1830 Inn		✓		✓	✓	✓	
The House on the Hill		✓					✓
The Inn on Mackinac	✓			✓	✓		

Luxurious	Pets Allowed	No Smoking Indoors	Good Place for Families	Boating Nearby	Beach Nearby	Cross-Country Ski Trails	Golf Within 5 Miles	Fitness Facilities	Good Biking Terrain	Skiing	Horseback Riding	Tennis	Swimming on Premises	Fishing Nearby	Hiking Nearby
✓		✓	✓		✓				✓		✓				✓
		✓			✓	✓	✓		✓	✓					✓
		✓		✓	✓		✓		✓	✓					✓
		✓		✓	✓	✓			✓			✓		✓	✓
		✓			✓	✓			✓	✓			✓	✓	✓
		✓	✓	✓			✓		✓			✓		✓	✓
		✓	✓	✓	✓	✓			✓		✓				✓
		✓		✓	✓				✓	✓				✓	✓
		✓		✓	✓		✓		✓	✓				✓	✓
✓		✓			✓				✓	✓				✓	✓
		✓			✓	✓			✓	✓				✓	✓
		✓			✓				✓	✓				✓	✓
				✓	✓		✓		✓					✓	
			✓						✓					✓	✓
		✓	✓	✓	✓				✓		✓				✓
✓		✓					✓								
				✓	✓	✓			✓					✓	✓
		✓							✓						✓
				✓	✓	✓			✓					✓	✓
✓				✓	✓	✓	✓		✓			✓	✓	✓	✓
		✓	✓	✓	✓		✓		✓	✓					✓
		✓	✓	✓	✓				✓		✓				✓
✓		✓			✓	✓	✓		✓	✓					✓
		✓	✓	✓	✓				✓		✓				✓

Name of Property	Accessible for Disabled	Antiques	On the Water	Best Value	Car Not Necessary	Historic Building	Romantic Hideaway
The Inn at Union Pier	✓	✓	✓	✓			✓
Kimberly Country Estate		✓					✓
Kingsley House		✓	✓				✓
La Bergerie		✓		✓		✓	
Laurium Manor Inn		✓		✓		✓	✓
Lee Point Inn			✓				
Leelanau Country Inn							
Linden Lea			✓	✓			✓
Main Street Bed & Breakfast				✓			
Maplewood Hotel	✓		✓		✓	✓	✓
Metivier Inn	✓				✓		✓
Michigamme Lake Lodge	✓	✓	✓			✓	✓
Montague Inn	✓	✓				✓	
Murray Hotel	✓				✓		
National House Inn	✓	✓				✓	✓
Neahtawanta Inn			✓			✓	
1900 Market Street Inn					✓		
North Shore Inn	✓		✓				✓
Old Mill Pond Inn				✓			✓
Parsonage 1908		✓				✓	✓
Pebble House	✓	✓	✓				✓
Pine Garth Inn			✓				✓
Pinewood Lodge	✓	✓	✓	✓			✓
Raymond House Inn						✓	
The Reynolds House at Stonefield Farm		✓		✓			✓

Luxurious	Pets Allowed	No Smoking Indoors	Good Place for Families	Boating Nearby	Beach Nearby	Cross-Country Ski Trails	Golf Within 5 Miles	Fitness Facilities	Good Biking Terrain	Skiing	Horseback Riding	Tennis	Swimming on Premises	Fishing Nearby	Hiking Nearby
				✓	✓	✓			✓					✓	✓
✓		✓			✓	✓	✓		✓	✓			✓		✓
		✓		✓	✓		✓		✓	✓	✓			✓	✓
		✓		✓	✓				✓	✓					✓
✓		✓	✓		✓	✓	✓		✓			✓		✓	✓
		✓		✓	✓	✓	✓		✓	✓				✓	✓
		✓			✓	✓			✓	✓				✓	✓
		✓	✓	✓	✓		✓		✓	✓			✓	✓	✓
		✓	✓	✓	✓		✓		✓	✓					✓
		✓	✓	✓	✓	✓	✓		✓		✓		✓	✓	✓
✓		✓		✓	✓				✓		✓				✓
		✓	✓	✓	✓	✓			✓					✓	✓
					✓			✓					✓	✓	✓
		✓		✓	✓				✓		✓				✓
			✓			✓	✓		✓			✓		✓	✓
		✓	✓	✓	✓				✓	✓				✓	✓
		✓		✓	✓				✓		✓				✓
		✓		✓	✓	✓			✓	✓			✓	✓	✓
		✓		✓	✓				✓					✓	✓
		✓		✓	✓	✓	✓		✓			✓		✓	✓
		✓		✓	✓	✓	✓		✓			✓		✓	✓
				✓	✓	✓			✓					✓	✓
		✓	✓	✓		✓			✓				✓	✓	✓
		✓		✓	✓		✓		✓					✓	✓
						✓						✓		✓	✓

Name of Property	Accessible for Disabled	Antiques	On the Water	Best Value	Car Not Necessary	Historic Building	Romantic Hideaway	
Snow Flake Motel	✓					✓		
South Cliff Inn		✓	✓				✓	
The Stacy Mansion	✓	✓				✓	✓	
Stafford's Bay View Inn						✓		
Torch Lake Bed & Breakfast								
Victorian Inn		✓				✓	✓	
Walloon Lake Inn			✓					
Water Street Inn	✓	✓	✓				✓	
Wickwood Country Inn	✓	✓					✓	
William Clements Inn	✓	✓		✓		✓		
Yelton Manor		✓	✓			✓	✓	
MINNESOTA								
The Afton House Inn	✓		✓			✓		
The Anderson House				✓		✓		
The Ann Bean House		✓			✓	✓	✓	
The Archer House	✓		✓		✓	✓		
Asa Parker House		✓				✓	✓	
Barnum House Bed & Breakfast		✓				✓	✓	
Battle Hollow Bed & Breakfast		✓			✓	✓	✓	
Bearskin Lodge			✓				✓	
Braisie House				✓	✓			
The Brunswick Inn		✓			✓	✓		
The Candle Light Inn		✓			✓	✓	✓	
Caribou Lake B&B	✓		✓	✓			✓	

Luxurious	Pets Allowed	No Smoking Indoors	Good Place for Families	Boating Nearby	Beach Nearby	Cross-Country Ski Trails	Golf Within 5 Miles	Fitness Facilities	Good Biking Terrain	Skiing	Horseback Riding	Tennis	Swimming on Premises	Fishing Nearby	Hiking Nearby
			✓	✓	✓	✓	✓		✓				✓	✓	✓
✓				✓	✓	✓	✓		✓			✓		✓	✓
✓	✓						✓		✓					✓	
		✓		✓	✓		✓		✓	✓					✓
		✓		✓	✓		✓		✓	✓					✓
✓				✓	✓	✓	✓	✓	✓			✓		✓	✓
		✓	✓	✓	✓		✓		✓	✓					✓
		✓		✓	✓	✓	✓		✓	✓				✓	✓
✓				✓	✓	✓	✓		✓		✓	✓		✓	✓
✓				✓	✓		✓		✓					✓	
✓				✓	✓	✓	✓		✓					✓	✓
			✓	✓	✓	✓	✓		✓	✓			✓		✓	✓
	✓		✓	✓	✓		✓		✓					✓	✓
✓		✓		✓	✓	✓	✓		✓			✓		✓	✓
	✓		✓	✓	✓	✓	✓		✓			✓		✓	✓
✓		✓		✓	✓	✓	✓		✓			✓		✓	✓
✓		✓		✓	✓	✓	✓			✓		✓		✓	✓
✓		✓		✓	✓	✓	✓		✓			✓		✓	✓
			✓	✓	✓	✓			✓				✓	✓	✓
		✓		✓	✓				✓			✓		✓	✓
		✓		✓	✓	✓	✓		✓			✓		✓	✓
✓		✓		✓			✓	✓	✓	✓		✓		✓	✓
		✓		✓	✓	✓	✓		✓	✓	✓	✓	✓	✓	✓

Name of Property	Accessible for Disabled	Antiques	On the Water	Best Value	Car Not Necessary	Historic Building	Romantic Hideaway	
Carriage House Bed & Breakfast		✓		✓	✓	✓		
Carrington House Bed & Breakfast		✓	✓				✓	
Carrolton Country Inn				✓		✓		
Chatsworth B&B					✓	✓		
Cottonwood Inn				✓		✓		
Dr. Joseph Moses House						✓		
Dorset Schoolhouse Bed and Breakfast								
The Ellery House		✓		✓	✓	✓	✓	
Evelo's Bed & Breakfast		✓		✓	✓			
Fering's Guest House								
Fitger's Inn	✓		✓	✓	✓	✓		
The Garden Gate Bed and Breakfast				✓	✓			
Grandma's Attic			✓					
Hallett House		✓						
The Heirloom Inn		✓		✓	✓	✓	✓	
Historic Scanlan House		✓		✓		✓		
Hungry Point Inn		✓		✓		✓	✓	
The Inn at Palisade Bed & Breakfast			✓	✓			✓	
JailHouse Inn		✓		✓		✓	✓	
James A. Mulvey Residence Inn		✓		✓	✓	✓	✓	
Le Blanc House		✓		✓	✓	✓	✓	
Lindgren's Bed & Breakfast		✓						
Linné Bed and Breakfast		✓		✓	✓			
The Log House on Spirit Lake		✓	✓				✓	
The Mansion Bed & Breakfast Inn			✓	✓		✓	✓	

Luxurious	Pets Allowed	No Smoking Indoors	Good Place for Families	Boating Nearby	Beach Nearby	Cross-Country Ski Trails	Golf Within 5 Miles	Fitness Facilities	Good Biking Terrain	Skiing	Horseback Riding	Tennis	Swimming on Premises	Fishing Nearby	Hiking Nearby
		✓		✓		✓	✓		✓		✓	✓		✓	✓
		✓		✓		✓	✓		✓		✓		✓	✓	✓
		✓	✓	✓		✓			✓					✓	✓
		✓							✓						
		✓		✓		✓			✓	✓				✓	✓
		✓		✓		✓	✓		✓		✓				✓
		✓		✓	✓	✓	✓		✓		✓			✓	✓
		✓	✓	✓	✓	✓	✓				✓	✓		✓	✓
		✓		✓	✓				✓			✓		✓	✓
		✓		✓			✓		✓					✓	✓
			✓	✓	✓	✓	✓		✓	✓		✓		✓	✓
	✓	✓	✓						✓			✓			
				✓	✓	✓	✓		✓			✓		✓	✓
		✓	✓	✓	✓	✓			✓					✓	✓
		✓		✓	✓	✓	✓		✓			✓		✓	✓
		✓		✓		✓	✓		✓		✓	✓		✓	✓
		✓	✓			✓	✓		✓	✓	✓			✓	✓
		✓	✓	✓	✓	✓			✓					✓	✓
✓		✓		✓		✓			✓					✓	✓
		✓		✓	✓	✓	✓		✓				✓	✓	✓
		✓		✓					✓				✓	✓	✓
				✓	✓	✓	✓		✓	✓	✓	✓		✓	✓
		✓		✓	✓				✓				✓	✓	✓
		✓		✓	✓		✓				✓		✓	✓	
				✓	✓	✓	✓		✓	✓			✓	✓	✓

Name of Property	Accessible for Disabled	Antiques	On the Water	Best Value	Car Not Necessary	Historic Building	Romantic Hideaway	
Martin Oaks		✓		✓		✓		
Matthew S. Burrows 1890 Inn		✓			✓	✓	✓	
Mrs. B's Historic Lanesboro Inn			✓	✓		✓		
Naniboujou Lodge	✓		✓	✓		✓	✓	
Nicollet Island Inn	✓		✓	✓	✓	✓	✓	
Nims' Bakketop Hus			✓					
1900 Dupont		✓		✓	✓	✓	✓	
Oakhurst Inn								
Park Row Bed and Breakfast		✓		✓			✓	
Park Street Inn		✓						
Peace Cliff		✓	✓				✓	
Peters' Sunset Beach		✓	✓			✓		
Pincushion Mountain Bed & Breakfast				✓			✓	
Prairie House on Round Lake			✓	✓				
Prairie View Estate		✓		✓				
Pratt-Taber Inn		✓		✓	✓	✓	✓	
Quill & Quilt	✓	✓		✓		✓	✓	
Red Gables Inn		✓		✓	✓	✓		
The Robards House		✓				✓		
The Rose Bed & Breakfast				✓			✓	
St. James Hotel	✓		✓		✓	✓		
Schumacher's New Prague Hotel						✓	✓	
Snuggle Inn				✓				
Sod House on the Prairie		✓						
Spicer Castle		✓	✓			✓	✓	

Luxurious	Pets Allowed	No Smoking Indoors	Good Place for Families	Boating Nearby	Beach Nearby	Cross-Country Ski Trails	Golf Within 5 Miles	Fitness Facilities	Good Biking Terrain	Skiing	Horseback Riding	Tennis	Swimming on Premises	Fishing Nearby	Hiking Nearby
		✓		✓		✓	✓		✓					✓	✓
	✓	✓		✓	✓	✓	✓			✓		✓		✓	✓
						✓	✓		✓		✓	✓		✓	✓
			✓	✓	✓	✓			✓					✓	✓
	✓		✓	✓					✓			✓		✓	✓
		✓		✓	✓	✓	✓							✓	✓
		✓		✓	✓				✓			✓		✓	✓
		✓		✓	✓	✓	✓		✓			✓		✓	
		✓							✓					✓	✓
		✓		✓		✓			✓		✓			✓	✓
		✓		✓		✓	✓		✓				✓	✓	✓
				✓	✓	✓	✓					✓	✓	✓	
		✓		✓		✓	✓		✓					✓	✓
		✓		✓							✓	✓	✓	✓	✓
	✓	✓		✓		✓	✓						✓	✓	✓
	✓		✓	✓		✓	✓		✓	✓		✓		✓	✓
				✓		✓	✓		✓	✓		✓		✓	✓
		✓		✓	✓	✓	✓		✓	✓		✓		✓	✓
		✓		✓	✓	✓	✓		✓		✓	✓		✓	✓
✓		✓				✓	✓		✓			✓			
			✓	✓		✓	✓	✓	✓	✓		✓		✓	✓
			✓			✓	✓		✓			✓			✓
		✓		✓	✓	✓	✓	✓	✓			✓		✓	✓
		✓	✓												✓
✓				✓	✓	✓			✓		✓			✓	

Name of Property	Accessible for Disabled	Antiques	On the Water	Best Value	Car Not Necessary	Historic Building	Romantic Hideaway
The Stone Hearth Bed & Breakfast		✓	✓	✓		✓	✓
Stonehouse Bed and Breakfast							
The Superior Overlook B&B			✓	✓		✓	✓
Thorwood Historic Inn		✓				✓	✓
Tianna Farms			✓			✓	
The Victorian Bed & Breakfast		✓	✓	✓	✓	✓	✓
Walden Woods		✓	✓	✓			✓
The William Sauntry Mansion		✓			✓	✓	✓
WISCONSIN							
Allyn Mansion Inn		✓				✓	✓
American Country Farm	✓	✓				✓	✓
The Arbor Room	✓						✓
The Barbican Guest House		✓				✓	✓
Bettinger House		✓		✓		✓	
The Boyden House		✓				✓	✓
Breese Waye		✓		✓		✓	
Cedar Trails Guesthouse		✓		✓			
The Church Hill Inn	✓	✓					✓
Collins House		✓	✓		✓	✓	
The Country Manor		✓				✓	
The Creamery			✓			✓	
Dreams of Yesteryear		✓			✓	✓	✓
The Duke House		✓		✓		✓	
The Eagle Harbor Inn	✓	✓					

Luxurious	Pets Allowed	No Smoking Indoors	Good Place for Families	Boating Nearby	Beach Nearby	Cross-Country Ski Trails	Golf Within 5 Miles	Fitness Facilities	Good Biking Terrain	Skiing	Horseback Riding	Tennis	Swimming on Premises	Fishing Nearby	Hiking Nearby
		✓		✓	✓	✓			✓					✓	✓
			✓	✓	✓	✓	✓		✓		✓			✓	
		✓	✓	✓	✓	✓	✓		✓			✓		✓	✓
✓		✓		✓		✓	✓		✓	✓		✓		✓	✓
				✓	✓	✓	✓		✓		✓	✓	✓	✓	✓
		✓		✓	✓	✓	✓		✓	✓		✓		✓	✓
			✓	✓	✓	✓	✓		✓		✓			✓	✓
✓		✓		✓	✓	✓	✓		✓			✓		✓	✓
✓		✓		✓	✓	✓	✓		✓	✓	✓	✓		✓	✓
			✓	✓	✓	✓	✓		✓	✓	✓	✓		✓	✓
		✓		✓	✓	✓	✓		✓	✓		✓		✓	✓
✓				✓	✓	✓	✓		✓		✓	✓		✓	✓
				✓	✓	✓	✓		✓	✓				✓	✓
✓		✓		✓	✓	✓	✓		✓	✓				✓	✓
		✓		✓	✓	✓	✓		✓	✓				✓	✓
		✓	✓	✓		✓	✓		✓	✓		✓		✓	✓
✓		✓		✓	✓	✓	✓	✓	✓		✓	✓	✓	✓	✓
			✓	✓	✓	✓	✓		✓	✓		✓		✓	✓
		✓		✓	✓	✓	✓		✓	✓		✓		✓	✓
			✓	✓		✓	✓		✓	✓				✓	✓
		✓		✓	✓	✓	✓		✓	✓		✓		✓	✓
		✓		✓		✓	✓		✓	✓				✓	✓
		✓	✓	✓	✓	✓	✓		✓		✓	✓		✓	✓

Name of Property	Accessible for Disabled	Antiques	On the Water	Best Value	Car Not Necessary	Historic Building	Romantic Hideaway	
Eleven Gables Inn on the Lake		✓	✓		✓	✓		
Elizabethian Inn	✓	✓	✓		✓	✓		
Enchanted Valley Garden								
The Ephraim Inn	✓	✓	✓			✓	✓	
Fargo Mansion Inn		✓				✓	✓	
48 West Oak		✓				✓	✓	
The Franklin Victorian		✓						
The French Country Inn of Ephraim		✓		✓		✓		
The Gallery House			✓	✓		✓		
The Geiger House		✓		✓				
The Gray Goose Bed and Breakfast		✓		✓		✓		
The Griffin Inn	✓	✓		✓		✓	✓	
The Harbor House Inn	✓	✓	✓	✓		✓		
The Harrisburg Inn		✓						
Hill Street		✓						
Historic Bennett House		✓			✓	✓	✓	
The Inn at Cedar Crossing		✓				✓	✓	
The Inn at Wildcat Mountain		✓						
Jackson Street Inn		✓		✓		✓		
The Jefferson-Day House		✓				✓	✓	
Jeremiah Mabie House		✓				✓		
The Jones House		✓				✓	✓	
Just-N-Trails	✓						✓	
The Kaleidoscope Inn		✓				✓	✓	
The Katy May House		✓		✓		✓		

Luxurious	Pets Allowed	No Smoking Indoors	Good Place for Families	Boating Nearby	Beach Nearby	Cross-Country Ski Trails	Golf Within 5 Miles	Fitness Facilities	Good Biking Terrain	Skiing	Horseback Riding	Tennis	Swimming on Premises	Fishing Nearby	Hiking Nearby
				✓	✓	✓	✓		✓	✓	✓	✓	✓	✓	✓
		✓		✓	✓	✓	✓		✓	✓	✓	✓	✓	✓	✓
	✓		✓	✓	✓	✓	✓		✓	✓				✓	✓
		✓		✓	✓	✓	✓		✓		✓	✓		✓	✓
✓		✓	✓	✓	✓	✓	✓		✓	✓				✓	✓
✓		✓		✓	✓	✓	✓		✓	✓	✓	✓		✓	✓
	✓		✓	✓	✓	✓	✓		✓	✓				✓	✓
		✓		✓	✓	✓	✓		✓		✓	✓		✓	✓
		✓		✓	✓	✓	✓		✓	✓		✓		✓	✓
		✓		✓	✓	✓	✓		✓	✓				✓	✓
				✓	✓	✓	✓		✓		✓	✓		✓	✓
				✓	✓	✓	✓		✓		✓	✓		✓	✓
		✓		✓	✓	✓	✓		✓		✓	✓		✓	✓
	✓		✓	✓	✓	✓	✓		✓	✓				✓	✓
		✓		✓	✓	✓	✓		✓	✓	✓	✓		✓	✓
✓		✓		✓	✓	✓	✓		✓	✓		✓		✓	✓
				✓	✓	✓	✓		✓		✓	✓		✓	✓
	✓		✓	✓	✓	✓	✓		✓	✓	✓			✓	✓
		✓	✓	✓	✓	✓	✓		✓	✓		✓		✓	✓
		✓		✓	✓	✓	✓		✓	✓		✓		✓	✓
		✓	✓	✓	✓	✓	✓		✓	✓		✓		✓	✓
✓		✓		✓	✓	✓	✓		✓	✓		✓		✓	✓
		✓	✓	✓	✓	✓	✓		✓	✓				✓	✓
✓		✓		✓	✓	✓	✓		✓	✓				✓	✓
		✓	✓	✓	✓	✓	✓		✓	✓				✓	✓

Name of Property	Accessible for Disabled	Antiques	On the Water	Best Value	Car Not Necessary	Historic Building	Romantic Hideaway	
The Knollwood House		✓		✓		✓		
Lake House on Monona			✓				✓	
Lakeside Manor	✓		✓	✓			✓	
Lawrence House		✓					✓	
M. Plank House		✓		✓		✓		
The Manor House		✓	✓			✓	✓	
The Mansards on-the-Lake		✓	✓	✓		✓		
Mansion Hill Inn		✓			✓	✓	✓	
Martindale House		✓				✓	✓	
Mascione's Hidden Valley Villas	✓						✓	
Middleton Beach Inn	✓	✓	✓				✓	
Nash House				✓		✓		
Nathaniel Treat House		✓		✓		✓		
Oak Hill Manor		✓		✓		✓		
The Oak Street Inn		✓				✓		
The Ogden House		✓			✓	✓		
Parkview		✓		✓		✓		
The Parson's Inn		✓		✓		✓		
Past and Present Inn	✓	✓					✓	
The Phipps Inn		✓				✓	✓	
Pinehaven				✓				
Plough Inn	✓					✓	✓	
Riley House Bed and Breakfast		✓				✓		
Rosenberry Inn	✓	✓			✓	✓	✓	
The Ryan House		✓		✓		✓		

Luxurious	Pets Allowed	No Smoking Indoors	Good Place for Families	Boating Nearby	Beach Nearby	Cross-Country Ski Trails	Golf Within 5 Miles	Fitness Facilities	Good Biking Terrain	Skiing	Horseback Riding	Tennis	Swimming on Premises	Fishing Nearby	Hiking Nearby
		✓		✓	✓	✓	✓	✓	✓	✓			✓	✓	✓
		✓		✓	✓	✓	✓		✓	✓		✓	✓	✓	✓
		✓		✓	✓	✓	✓		✓	✓	✓	✓	✓	✓	✓
				✓	✓	✓	✓		✓	✓	✓	✓		✓	✓
		✓		✓	✓	✓	✓		✓	✓		✓		✓	✓
✓				✓	✓	✓	✓		✓	✓		✓		✓	✓
		✓		✓	✓	✓	✓		✓	✓		✓		✓	✓
✓				✓	✓	✓	✓	✓	✓	✓		✓		✓	✓
✓		✓		✓	✓	✓	✓		✓	✓		✓		✓	✓
				✓	✓	✓	✓		✓	✓	✓		✓	✓	✓
		✓		✓	✓	✓	✓	✓	✓	✓			✓	✓	✓
		✓	✓	✓		✓	✓		✓	✓				✓	✓
		✓	✓	✓	✓	✓	✓		✓	✓			✓	✓	✓
		✓	✓	✓		✓	✓		✓	✓				✓	✓
		✓		✓	✓	✓	✓		✓	✓				✓	✓
			✓	✓	✓	✓	✓		✓	✓		✓		✓	✓
			✓	✓	✓	✓	✓		✓	✓				✓	✓
		✓	✓	✓	✓	✓	✓		✓	✓				✓	✓
		✓	✓	✓	✓	✓	✓		✓	✓				✓	✓
✓		✓		✓	✓	✓	✓		✓	✓		✓		✓	✓
		✓	✓	✓	✓	✓	✓		✓	✓				✓	✓
		✓		✓	✓	✓	✓		✓	✓		✓		✓	✓
		✓	✓	✓	✓	✓	✓		✓	✓		✓		✓	✓
			✓	✓	✓	✓	✓		✓	✓				✓	✓
		✓	✓	✓	✓	✓	✓		✓	✓				✓	✓

Name of Property	Accessible for Disabled	Antiques	On the Water	Best Value	Car Not Necessary	Historic Building	Romantic Hideaway	
The Scofield House		✓				✓	✓	
Stagecoach Inn	✓	✓				✓	✓	
Sugar River Inn		✓	✓	✓				
The Swallow's Nest				✓				
Thorp House Inn and Cottages		✓				✓	✓	
Trillium	✓	✓		✓			✓	
Victoria-on-Main		✓		✓		✓		
The Victorian Belle		✓				✓		
Victorian Garden		✓				✓	✓	
Victorian Swan on Water		✓		✓	✓	✓		
Viroqua Heritage Inn		✓		✓		✓		
Washington House Inn	✓	✓				✓	✓	
Westby House		✓				✓		
The Whistling Swan		✓				✓	✓	
The White Apron		✓		✓		✓	✓	
The White Gull Inn	✓	✓				✓	✓	
White Lace Inn	✓	✓				✓	✓	
William's		✓						

Luxurious	Pets Allowed	No Smoking Indoors	Good Place for Families	Boating Nearby	Beach Nearby	Cross-Country Ski Trails	Golf Within 5 Miles	Fitness Facilities	Good Biking Terrain	Skiing	Horseback Riding	Tennis	Swimming on Premises	Fishing Nearby	Hiking Nearby
✓		✓		✓	✓	✓	✓		✓					✓	✓
		✓		✓	✓	✓	✓		✓	✓	✓	✓		✓	✓
		✓		✓	✓	✓	✓		✓	✓			✓	✓	✓
		✓		✓	✓	✓	✓		✓	✓				✓	✓
		✓	✓	✓	✓	✓	✓		✓		✓	✓		✓	✓
			✓	✓	✓	✓	✓		✓	✓				✓	✓
		✓		✓	✓	✓	✓		✓	✓	✓			✓	✓
		✓		✓	✓	✓	✓		✓	✓				✓	✓
		✓	✓	✓	✓	✓	✓		✓	✓				✓	✓
		✓		✓	✓	✓	✓		✓	✓		✓		✓	✓
			✓	✓	✓	✓	✓		✓	✓		✓		✓	✓
✓				✓	✓	✓	✓		✓	✓	✓	✓		✓	✓
			✓	✓	✓	✓	✓		✓	✓				✓	✓
		✓		✓	✓	✓	✓		✓		✓	✓		✓	✓
		✓		✓	✓		✓		✓	✓				✓	✓
		✓	✓	✓	✓	✓	✓		✓		✓	✓		✓	✓
✓				✓	✓	✓	✓		✓		✓	✓		✓	✓
		✓		✓	✓	✓	✓		✓	✓	✓	✓		✓	✓

Michigan

Southeastern Michigan
Including Ann Arbor and Detroit

First-time visitors to this part of Michigan are surprised to find more than post-industrial forests of cold smokestacks. While the region's two major urban centers, Detroit and Flint, struggle with the same socioeconomic problems that afflict most Rust Belt cities, no other part of the state offers a greater mix of natural, cultural, and recreational resources. Row a boat on a quiet lake in the morning, browse in rural antiques shops in the afternoon, take in a professional sporting event, dine at a world-class restaurant in the evening, even visit another country for a nightcap—all usually within an hour's reach of your lodging.

While one-third of the state's population lives here, an excellent network of freeways and secondary roads allow travelers to zip easily out of city centers and into the surrounding countryside. If you find shopping in the cavernous Renaissance Center in downtown Detroit frustrating, drive northbound on I–75 for 45 minutes until you reach Holly, a pastoral pocket of old stores. Port Huron is an hour away from Flint or Detroit, and once there, you can watch freighters pass so close you can almost touch them. Port Huron is at the base of the largely rural "Thumb" region (Michigan is shaped like a mitten), honeycombed with farms, sleepy ports, and superb county and state parks. U.S. 25 traces the thumb's outline from Bay City to Port Huron and affords exquisite views of Lake Huron and Saginaw Bay.

Detroit, of course, anchors the region. The Motor City, ringed by some of the most affluent suburbs in the country, is dissected by three major interstate highways. Interstate 75 will take you to Monroe (home of General George Custer) in the south and to Bay City, a port town on Saginaw Bay, to the north. Interstates 96 and 94 will

*carry you west to Lansing and Jackson, respectively.
Running north from the Ohio border, U.S. 127 strings these
two cities together and forms a logical southern boundary
to the region. Urban sprawl is minimal here, and the little
there is blends easily into miles of open country.*

*Despite its lunch-bucket reputation, Detroit actually has
a very cosmopolitan feel as befits the oldest city west of the
Appalachians. The flags of three nations—France, Britain,
and the United States—have flown over this onetime
trading post. As a chief port of entry for settlers heading
for the interior in the mid-1800s, then later as a magnet
drawing a multitude of immigrants and South Americans
to its booming auto plants, Detroit has always been
a polytongued community. At one time an exasperated
Henry Ford was obliged to post work signs in eight
languages in his factories.*

*Today, this diversity is evident in the scores of authentic
ethnic restaurants sprinkled throughout the region. Many
are in such ethnic enclaves as Hamtramck, a large
community of Polish-Americans within Detroit city limits,
and Dearborn, a western suburb that has the largest Arabic
population outside the Middle East. A growing colony of
transplanted Japanese—a sign of the increasing inter-
dependence between U.S. and Asian carmakers—has
materialized, resulting in a rash of Oriental restaurants
and karaoke bars. The village of Frankenmuth, an hour's
drive north of Detroit, remains more German than
American. To add to the mix, Canada is just a short bridge
or tunnel ride away. Americans and Canadians move freely
back and forth; passports are not necessary for citizens of
either country. Spectacular annual events such as the
Grand Prix auto race, Montreaux Detroit Jazz Festival (the
largest free jazz fest in the world), Port Huron–Mackinac
Island sailing regatta, North American International Auto
Show, Gold Cup powerboat races, and the International
Freedom Festival draw hundreds of thousands of people
apiece and help maintain the region's international flavor.*

Countless chain motels and luxury hotels have been built to handle the business and convention trade. As a result, historic inns and bed-and-breakfasts are not nearly as numerous in southeastern Michigan as in other parts of the state. Those that do exist, however, typically have been around for a long time and are very good, their owners having learned how to weather the boom-and-bust cycles that are so much a part of this area's history.

Places to Go, Sights to See

Ann Arbor. Home to the University of Michigan, this leafy, liberal community is a 45-minute drive from downtown Detroit via westbound I–94. Ann Arbor is the quintessential university town: drowsy neighborhood bookshops and funky street performers peacefully co-exist with respected arts centers and world-class research facilities. Sidewalk cafés operate past midnight, while the 101,000-seat Michigan Stadium, the nation's largest college-owned stadium, makes Ann Arbor a great place for tailgate parties on football weekends in the fall.

Auto Racing. The *Detroit Grand Prix* (tel. 313/259–5400), held every June since 1981, has evolved into a three-day weekend party interrupted periodically by the main event and support races. The *Michigan International Speedway* (tel. 313/961–1922), 60 miles west of Detroit on U.S. 12 in Brooklyn, features NASCAR stock car and Indy-style races.

Detroit. Once the nation's fourth largest city, Detroit has lost half of its population since the 1950s. The shrinking tax base has caused one of the country's truly great museums, the *Detroit Institute of Arts* (5200 Woodward Ave., tel. 313/833–7900), to juggle hours of operation, so call ahead. But while the core city has struggled as jobs and people have moved elsewhere, downtown and surrounding suburbs continue to offer first-class shopping, dining, cultural, and entertainment experiences. *Belle Isle* (tel. 313/267–7115), a thousand-acre island park, sits in the Detroit River, 3 miles from the heart of the city, connected by a bridge to the mainland. The multipurpose park has facilities for baseball, golf, swimming, cycling, hiking, basketball, tennis, and many other recreational activities. Other attractions are an aquarium, zoo, nature center, conservatory, and the Dossin Great Lakes Museum. The Detroit Grand Prix is held here in June. The *Fox Theatre* (2211 Woodward Ave., tel. 313/965–7100), which opened in 1928 as America's largest movie palace, today showcases big-name musical acts and large-screen movies. The *Henry Ford Museum & Greenfield Village* (Village Rd. and Oakwood Blvd., Dearborn, tel. 313/271–1620) are two world-famous collections of Americana in the western suburb of Dearborn. Especially noteworthy is "The Automobile in American Life," a lavish, upbeat collection of chrome and neon devoted to the evolution of the automobile and roadside culture. Detroit's chapter of the American Dream comes alive in a tour of

Historic Homes of the Auto Barons (tel. 313/644–2060), which includes several mansions that once belonged to auto pioneers such as Henry and Edsel Ford and the Dodge brothers. To round out the experience, you can schedule a guided tour of old factories and other historic sites relating to Detroit's auto and labor past through the *Detroit Labor History Tour Project* (tel. 313/822–6426). *Motown Museum* (2648 W. Grand Blvd., tel. 313/875–2264) is an unassuming two-story house on West Grand Boulevard where Berry Gordy, Jr., started the "Motown Sound" in the late 1950s. It's stuffed with memorabilia, including album covers, costumes, gold records, and, yes, one of Michael Jackson's gloves. You can squeeze into the small recording studio, where such acts as the Temptations, Smokey Robinson and the Miracles, and Diana Ross and the Supremes cranked out hit after hit. The Detroit Tigers and their predecessors have been playing baseball at the corner of Michigan and Trumbull streets in *Tiger Stadium* (tel. 313/962–4000) since 1896, making this professional sports' oldest address. Prices are reasonable and acquiring tickets is almost never a problem, making it easy to enjoy a summer game.

Frankenmuth. "Little Bavaria," founded by German immigrants in 1845, sits just off the I–75 corridor halfway between Flint and Saginaw. The town markets its heritage through scores of gift shops, lodgings, and restaurants that groan under the weight of flower boxes and gingerbread trim. The village's most popular attraction is *Bronner's Christmas Wonderland* (25 Christmas La., Frankenmuth, tel. 517/652–9931), where more than 50,000 lights and ornaments are for sale year-round.

Port Huron. Situated at the confluence of the St. Clair River and Lake Huron, the hometown of inventor Thomas Edison has changed very little since he was young. The 1858 Grand Trunk Depot from which he sold newspapers on the Detroit-bound train has been restored in a riverside park. Here visitors get incredible close-up views of freighters from all over the world passing through the narrow, quarter-mile-wide passageway. Other maritime treats include the 152-foot-high Blue Water Bridge, from which pedestrians can enjoy panoramic views of the water while waiting for freighters to pass underneath; and the Lighthouse Park complex, which includes an 1874 lightkeeper's dwelling, a white clapboard Coast Guard station, and the oldest surviving lighthouse in Michigan.

Tecumseh. This town, about 30 miles east of Jackson on U.S. 50, is the antiques center of the region. Founded in 1824, it has three antiques malls among its many historic buildings and restored train depot. One of the state's largest antiques fairs is held the third Sunday of every month from April to November at the fairgrounds (tel. 313/429–1131) in nearby Saline.

Boating

Michigan has more registered boat owners than any other state, so the Great Lakes and inland waters become crowded playgrounds in warm weather. Most county and state parks offer boat and canoe rentals and have beaches with supervised swimming. Bay City, on Saginaw Bay, a port for Great Lakes freighters, has speedboat and offshore powerboat racing and other water sports. River cruising is gaining popularity. You can cruise, dine, and view the skylines of Detroit and Windsor on _The Detroiter_ (tel. 313/567–1400) or eat while enjoying the breezes of Lake St. Clair on the 100-foot yacht _The Infinity_ (tel. 313/778–7030).

Fishing

With almost 100 lakes in the metro Detroit area alone, you'll never be far from a fishing hole. The Detroit River, especially around Belle Isle, is popular with anglers. Generally, the waters throughout the region are rated good to excellent for trout, yellow perch, bluegills, crappies, bass, walleye, panfish, and northern pike. Charter-boat fishing for salmon, walleye, and lake trout is available on Lakes Huron, St. Clair, and Erie.

Golf

Michigan's golf season stretches from April through October. New courses continue to spring up, including _Marion Oaks Golf Club_ (2255 Pinkey Rd., Howell, tel. 517/548–0050), halfway between Lansing and Detroit on I–96 in Howell. Desmond Muirhead designed the course at _Bay Valley Inn_ (2470 Old Bridge Rd., Bay City, tel. 517/686–5400) near Bay City, while _Cascades Golf Course_ (1992 Warren Ave., Jackson, tel. 517/788–4323) in Jackson is considered one of the best golf values in the state. In the Thumb, _Verona Hills_ (3175 Sand Beach Rd., Bad Axe, tel. 517/269–8132), with an excellent layout, is just east of Bad Axe on U.S. 142. For a complete listing, contact the _Michigan Association of Public Golf Courses_ (Box 612, Plymouth, MI 48170, tel. 313/582–8860 or 800/223–5877).

Skiing

Downhill resorts can be found just off I–75 north of Detroit at _Pine Knob Ski Resort_ (tel. 313/625–0800) in Clarkston and _Mt. Holly_ (tel. 313/582–7256) in Holly. _Mt. Brighton Ski Area_ (tel. 313/229–9581) in Brighton and _Alpine Valley_ (tel. 313/887–4183) in Milford also are popular. Many county and state parks, as well as a growing number of golf courses, have groomed trails for cross-country skiing.

Restaurants

The region is chock-full of good restaurants. The cavernous **Bavarian Inn** (713 S. Main St., tel. 517/652–9941) in Frankenmuth specializes in hearty, homemade chicken dinners. Ann Arbor's most popular restaurant, **Chuck Muery's Gandy Dancer** (401 Depot St., tel. 313/769–0592), serves fresh seafood dishes in an old fieldstone train station. Some of the favorites in Detroit include downtown's **Fishbone's Rhythm Kitchen Cafe** (400 Monroe St., tel. 313/965–4600), home of New Orleans–style gumbo and whiskey ribs;

the classically Italian **Roma's Cafe** (3401 Riopelle St., tel. 313/831–5940), the city's oldest restaurant; and **The Whitney** (4421 Woodward St., tel. 313/832–5700), where American food and music are served inside a pink-stone mansion that once belonged to lumber baron David Whitney. **The Lark** (6430 Farmington St., tel. 313/661–4466) in suburban West Bloomfield is famous for its crisp service, superb Continental cuisine, and genuinely warm hospitality. World travelers Jim and Mary Lark have transformed their interestingly decorated country inn into the best dining experience on this side of the state.

Tourist Information

The umbrella organization for the entire state is the **Michigan Travel Bureau** (333 S. Capitol Ave., Lansing, MI 48933, tel. 800/543–2937). For information on boating, fishing, and hunting, contact the **Michigan Department of Natural Resources** (530 N. Allegan St., Lansing, MI 48933, tel. 517/373–1204). Site-specific tourist information can be found through the **Ann Arbor Convention and Visitors Bureau** (211 E. Huron St., Ann Arbor, MI 48104, tel. 313/995–7281); **Flint Area Convention and Visitors Bureau** (400 N. Saginaw St., Flint, MI 48502, tel. 313/232–8900); **Frankenmuth Chamber of Commerce** (635 S. Main St., Frankenmuth, MI 48734, tel. 517/652-6106); **Greater Lansing Convention and Visitors Bureau** (119 Pere Marquette, Box 15066, Lansing, MI 48901, tel. 517/487–6800 or 800/648–6630); **Metropolitan Detroit Convention and Visitors Bureau** (100 Ren Cen, Suite 1950, Detroit, MI 48243, tel. 313/259–4333); **Port Huron/Marysville Chamber of Commerce** (920 Pine Grove Ave., Port Huron, MI 48060, tel. 313/985–7101); and the **Saginaw County Convention and Visitors Bureau** (901 S. Washington St., Saginaw, MI 48601, tel. 517/752–7164).

Montague Inn

Robert Montague was a respected businessman and civic leader when he built his 12,000-square-foot Georgian house in 1929. He made his fortune developing a way to use sugar beet byproducts to make hand creams and soaps, a process later sold to the Andrew Jergens Company.

Saginaw's historic Grove District was once an enclave of stunning residences. The city bought the house in the early 1960s and demolished several of the surrounding properties. Then a group of five couples bought it in 1985. Eight months later, they reopened the restored mansion and the adjacent carriage house as the Montague Inn. Not only has the three-story brick mansion been named to the State Register of Historic Places, it is also considered one of Michigan's best inns, a designation that's hard to dispute.

The inn's location on 8 gently rolling acres overlooking Lake Linton is a mixed blessing. There is usually a lot of activity on the grounds, and on days when the city park across the water is staging a concert or a raft race, there can be a large volume of traffic in the area. That said, the inn is still a champion. A winding staircase connects the three floors of guest rooms. The Georgian-style quarters typically contain four-poster beds and wing chairs and are tastefully decorated in subtle hues and patterns. The most compelling is the Montague Suite, which features a fireplace, green Pewabic tile, and great views of the impeccably landscaped grounds.

Guests enjoy a Continental breakfast of oatmeal, cereals, juice, and baked goods in either of two dining rooms, one of which has a welcoming fire on cold mornings. Lunches and candlelight dinners are first-class affairs, too, with an expansive (and expensive) menu and wine list. After meals, a fire is lit in the fireplace of the main-floor library, and guests can look for the hidden cabinets inside the library walls, where Montague stashed his expensive supply of liquor during Prohibition, or sink back into couches to smoke and talk. Others sit at the antique writing desk to pen a postcard: Those who scrawl "Wish you were here" know what they're talking about.

Address: *1581 S. Washington Ave., Saginaw, MI 48601, tel. 817/752-3939.*
Accommodations: *16 double rooms with baths, 2 doubles share 1 bath, 1 suite.*
Amenities: *Air-conditioning, phone and TV in guest rooms, restaurant.*
Rates: *$70–$115, Montague Suite $162; Continental breakfast. AE, MC, V.*
Restrictions: *Smoking in library and Riley Room only, no pets.*

Raymond House Inn

A s Shirley and Ray Denison, owners of the inn, enjoy pointing out, there is no McDonald's in Port Sanilac. The 60-ish couple do what they can to keep the golden arches at bay by heading a movement to have this old port village declared a Historic Maritime District, thereby limiting commercial development.

Port Sanilac sits halfway up the eastern edge of the "Thumb" region on M–25, about 30 miles north of Port Huron and less than two hours from Detroit. It was one of Lake Huron's first ports of call during the heyday of the steamship. Its colorful history includes lumberjacks, lake storms, rum-running, and forest fires that more than once destroyed the town. The background of the comfortable, impressive Victorian house, which is listed on the State Register of Historic Places, is a little calmer but nevertheless significant. In 1850, Uri Raymond, the original owner, opened what is reputed to be the first hardware store in the state. (Raymond Hardware, just a block down the road, is still in business.) Raymond built his two-story brick residence in 1871, adorning it with classic Victoriana: elaborate moldings and a winding oak staircase on the inside, a gingerbread facade and white icicle trim dripping on the outside. It stayed in the family for the next 112 years until Ray and

Shirley—he's a lobbyist for the AFL–CIO, she's a restorative artist who had reframed the Constitution for the Bicentennial—bought it in 1983 and moved here from Washington, DC.

The house, set on an acre planted with trees and gardens of wildflowers, was in good condition and is now full of family heirlooms, antiques, and numerous examples of Shirley's considerable artistic and restorative skills. She has recaned the chairs, restored the frames that hold a collection of old family photos in an upstairs hallway, and designed the grandfather clock in the dining room. The upstairs quarters are authentically furnished, down to crocheted lacework on the shades, handmade quilts, and hand-crocheted rugs. Lake Huron, a block away, can be spied from the upstairs porch and, in the winter, from three of the guest rooms.

Address: *111 S. Ridge St., Port Sanilac, MI 48469, tel. 313/622–8800.*
Accommodations: *7 double rooms with baths.*
Amenities: *Air-conditioning, radio/cassette player in rooms, fireplace, cable TV, and phone in parlor.*
Rates: *$50–$75; Continental breakfast. MC, V.*
Restrictions: *No smoking, no pets; closed Nov.–Mar.*

The Reynolds House at Stonefield Farm

There's a distinct counterculture feel to Mary Laurel Reynolds's small farm, which is appropriate, since that citadel of student activism, the University of Michigan, is only 15 minutes away.

Laurel, a thoughtful, extremely likable native of Chevy Chase, Maryland, followed her husband to Ann Arbor in 1972. When her godfather died and left her the Stonefield Farm in Kittanning, Pennsylvania, she sold it and used the money to buy this turn-of-the-century farmhouse in 1987. Two years later, she turned the adjacent guest cottage into a bed-and-breakfast.

The two-story, cozy, white-frame structure, built in the 1950s, is a little oasis of calm on 10 acres of rolling countryside. Maybe it's the sheep munching contentedly in the distance, helping to keep the pasture down, or the variety of antiques that are spread over the wooden floors of the house. Many are family pieces: The feather bed and cherry furnishings in one of the second-story guest rooms, for instance, belonged to Laurel's godfather. The linen covering the painted iron beds in the other bedrooms and the designer wallpaper are English country. Bedside journals are provided for guests to jot down their thoughts.

Downstairs is a full living room and a kitchen, well-stocked with fresh eggs from resident chickens, juices, fruits, and cereals. Hot bread and muffins are delivered daily to the doorstep. On Sundays, breakfast is served in the main house's formal dining room or, weather permitting, on white wicker under the leafy arms of a mature maple tree.

In terms of accommodations and organized activities, the Reynolds House is only a modest retreat. The cottage has no phone or TV, loud noises such as heavy snoring penetrate its thin walls, and close quarters can be claustrophobic. And aside from the old Royal manual typewriter in the gazebo, where would-be bards are encouraged to peck something out, the most strenuous on-site activities involve fishing for blue gill in the pond or borrowing one of the bicycles for some impromptu exploring. But for those who like to fall asleep to singing killdeer and awaken to the call of a bossy rooster, who still value good conversation over "Cosby" reruns, it's a wonderfully comforting place.

Address: *5259 W. Ellsworth Rd., Ann Arbor, MI 48103, tel. 313/995–0301.*
Accommodations: *3 double rooms share 1 bath.*
Amenities: *Air conditioner in 1 room, phone in main house.*
Rates: *$50–$70; Continental breakfast. MC, V.*
Restrictions: *No smoking indoors, no pets.*

The Stacy Mansion

The story of one of the state's grandest homes can be gleaned from a quick look inside its first-floor library. On a desktop, *The 1874 Historical Atlas of Lenawee County* is opened to a sketch of the four-story brick mansion as it looked when Judge C. A. Stacy owned it. Directly above the open book hangs a buffalo head, provided by the current owners, Sonny and Joyce Lauber, who among their other business interests run one of the few bison farms in the country.

Stacy, newspaper publisher, businessman, and the first probate judge in the county, built the 9,000-foot house in the mid-1850s in anticipation of using it as the governor's residence. He lost the gubernatorial election but held on to the house, which has fine examples of 19th-century craftsmanship such as a foyer with marbled wood and a rare cantilevered oak staircase.

"Sonny drove past the house for 25 years and always talked about buying it," says Joyce. When the badly neglected building on the outskirts of Tecumseh came on the market in 1988, the Laubers didn't think twice. The house had been stripped of nearly everything—from the furnishings to the brass doorknobs and gingerbread trim—so restoration has been a slow, expensive process. To their credit, they have taken time to research and spent the money necessary to recall its 19th-century

ambience. They tore out the carpeting and restored the floors and woodwork and replicated the plasterwork and handprinted wallpaper. They were even able to buy back some of the furniture. All told, the house "is about 95% antiques," says Joyce. One bedroom has a double-mirrored wardrobe and another an 8½-foot-high ornately carved walnut headboard. The only incongruous item is the water-filled mattress in the master bedroom. "We couldn't find a mattress that would fit the odd-sized cherry full-tester bed," she explains.

The 3-acre site is expertly landscaped. Judge Stacy, who owned a local brickyard, would certainly approve of the 25,000 bricks the Laubers used to create the paths that wind through the yards and gardens. A 130-year-old pine tree shades a court of geranium-filled stone planters and wrought-iron garden furniture, while old-fashioned street lamps and red maple trees flank the circular drive and help make the outdoors an appealing retreat in itself.

Address: *710 W. Chicago Blvd., Tecumseh, MI 49286, tel. 517/423–6979.*
Accommodations: *5 double rooms with baths, 2 suites.*
Amenities: *Phone in sitting room.*
Rates: *$75–$120; Continental breakfast. MC, V.*
Restrictions: *No smoking indoors, small pets only.*

Victorian Inn

L ynne Secory and Vicki Peterson were neighbors busily renovating their own homes when they got the impulse to breathe new life into what had once been one of Port Huron's most magnificent houses, the old James A. Davidson residence. Davidson, founder of a large furniture company that bore his name, had built the elaborate Queen Anne house in 1896 and lived in it until his death in 1911. In 1983, Lynne and Vicki persuaded their husbands to buy the property. Enlisting the aid of many preservation-minded friends, relatives, and craftsmen, and working from the architectural plans and spec sheets, they managed to accomplish their mission by the end of the year. Halfway through the project, the house was placed on the State Register of Historic Places. The result of their efforts is a harmonious combination of luxurious lodging and fine dining in a neighborhood of well-maintained Victorian-era buildings that has become a travel destination in itself.

Immediately to the right of the foyer as you walk in is the parlor. Its green velvet valances, antique lace window curtains, green-and-gold floral wallpaper, pincushion settee, and hurricane lamps are invitingly elegant. The second-floor guest rooms are similar blends of antique furnishings and little flourishes: a needlepoint headboard, a papier-mâché picture frame. Two rooms have modern private baths, while the Victoria and Edward rooms share a pedestal sink, claw-foot tub (no shower), and pull-chain toilet.

Guests can eat breakfast in the main-floor 50-seat restaurant, also open for lunch and dinner Tuesday through Saturday. The service is attentive, the staff is immaculately attired in crisp white uniforms, and the mainly American menu is well executed. The inventive soups and desserts are especially popular.

The inn is just a couple of blocks from the St. Clair River, carrying its freighter traffic and cool breezes. The Museum of Arts and History is one block over, on Court Street, and houses one of the finest collections of marine lore in the state. Travel the dozen or so blocks to the Fort Gratiot Lighthouse, the first one on the Great Lakes, and return to the inn and cut the dust at the stone-walled Pierpont Pub. Originally a cellar, it features an old red oak bar that used to be a dry-goods counter.

Address: *1229 Seventh St., Port Huron, MI 48060, tel. 313/984-1437.*
Accommodations: *2 double rooms with baths, 2 doubles share 1 bath.*
Amenities: *Air-conditioning, room service, fireplace in parlor, restaurant, pub.*
Rates: *$55-$65; Continental breakfast. AE, D, MC, V.*
Restrictions: *No pets.*

William Clements Inn

This gray Queen Anne–style mansion in Bay City is what eccentric Great-Aunt Emily's house always looked like, at least in the movies: ornately carved staircases and ceilings, heavy oak furniture, voluminous velveteen drapes. There's even a massive pipe organ on the main floor and a third-floor ballroom. But if natural light has a hard time entering even on sunny days, innkeeper Sharon Kleinsmith keeps up the wattage with her charm and bustling efficiency. The house, built by industrialist-inventor-banker William Clements in 1886 during the peak of the lumber era, was bought six years ago by Eldon and Beverly Bender, who own and operate a bed-and-breakfast in nearby Frankenmuth.

The second-floor guest rooms are spacious and filled with period furnishings, including iron or brass beds, marble-topped tables, and oak armoires. In three rooms, claw-foot tubs have been equipped with showers. The most impressive room is the elegant master bedroom. The king-sized brass bed has a Matelasse spread in a classic Elizabethan motif, elegantly complemented by brass fixtures, a cast-iron fireplace, and gold velvet jabots at the windows. The room also includes a queen-sized hide-a-bed. The sunniest guest room is called James' Room after the Clements' youngest son. Light pours through a floral-lace-curtained bow window onto the queen-sized Canterbury brass bed. The private bath across the hall features china tiles bordered with hand-painted morning glories.

As the quintessential 19th-century man of industry and culture, Clements exhibited a respect for music, equipping the music room with a magnificent Steinway grand piano. But Clements's true passion was collecting books. A few volumes of his impressive collection of books and manuscripts, which formed the nucleus of the library at the University of Michigan that bears his name, remain in the richly paneled main-floor library. Tea and pastries are served here every evening at 7. Guests, however, are just as likely to be found in the screened-in back porch, shaded by a 200-year-old beech tree. There they play cards and talk of the sea captains and lumber barons who built the other grand mansions that fill this historic district.

Address: *1712 Center Ave., Bay City, MI 48708, tel. 517/894–4600.*
Accommodations: *5 double rooms with baths.*
Amenities: *Air-conditioning, TV, and phone in rooms; fireplaces in 2 rooms.*
Rates: *$73–$106; Continental breakfast weekdays, full breakfast weekends, evening refreshments. AE, MC, V.*
Restrictions: *No smoking, no pets.*

Blanche House Inn

When Mary Jean Shannon sold her suburban house in 1988 to buy a run-down mansion in Detroit, no one thought that a bed-and-breakfast could make it anywhere in Motor City, much less in the depressed center-city area. Today, there's still only one, but the Blanche House is a beautiful example of Detroit's grand past and inspiration for its eventual renaissance. Designed by Louis Kemper and built in 1905, the Colonial Revival structure once served as a prep school for Henry Ford II, former governor G. Mennen Williams, and other local notables.

Mary Jean, aided by her son, Sean, has done a commendable job restoring the towering porch pillars, 10-foot etched-glass doors, oak wood-work and floors, and ornate plasterwork. The guest rooms, all named after someone who has figured in the inn's history, are fitted with antiques, including an 1850s brass British army bed in the Bell Parker Room. There is a back porch, where guests can relax in hammocks that overlook a marina and the Stanton Canal.

Address: *506 Parkview Dr., Detroit, MI 48214, tel. 313/822–7090.*
Accommodations: *13 double rooms with baths, 1 suite.*
Amenities: *Air-conditioning, cable TV and phone in rooms, hot tubs in 3 rooms.*
Rates: *$60–$115; full breakfast. AE, D, MC, V.*
Restrictions: *No smoking, no pets.*

Chicago Street Inn

If you like auto racing, you can hardly do better than to stay at this bed-and-breakfast at the foot of touristy Irish Hills, just 3 miles from the Michigan International Speedway. On summer weekends, the air is alive with the sound of engines, and the tiny downtown is swamped with young racing fans.

In this casual environment, innkeepers Bill and Karen Kerr have obviously decided that authenticity should take a back seat to comfort. Aluminum siding and a contemporary veranda do nothing for the Queen Anne–style house, especially when compared with the beautifully restored brick residence next door. Your stay, however, is made pleasant by the easygoing atmosphere and an interior graced by hand-wrought oak moldings and fretwork, stained-glass windows, and a striking cherry-wood and ceramic-tile fireplace. Guest rooms are extremely feminine but tastefully done. Shades of rose, teal, cinnamon, peach, and cream bring out the best in the antique beds and accessories.

Address: *219 Chicago St., Brooklyn, MI 49230, tel. 517/592–3888.*
Accommodations: *3 double rooms with baths, 2 doubles share 1 bath.*
Amenities: *Air-conditioning, cable TV in sitting room, phone in entranceway, fireplace in sitting room; basketball court.*
Rates: *$55–$65; full breakfast. AE, MC, V.*
Restrictions: *No smoking upstairs, no pets.*

Clinton Inn

This is basic lodging in a drowsy town that had its heyday nearly a century ago. Settlers from New York came to the region in the early 1800s and named the village after their state governor, DeWitt Clinton. The three-story brick hotel officially opened Thanksgiving Day, 1901, and was a popular way station for salesmen traveling Michigan Avenue, now U.S. 12. Vestiges of the building's former glory can be found in the golden oak staircase and oak trim, which new owners Mark and Laurie Pederson are restoring.

The Clinton Inn is a work-in-progress, and the Pedersons are striving to replace the uninspired modern furnishings in the second-story guest rooms with period pieces. (The third floor is still given over to apartments.) The village is near the antiques meccas of Saline and Tecumseh. The place remains a bargain, especially if you're in town to visit the historic Southern Michigan Railroad, which offers rides between Clinton and Tecumseh on weekends and holidays.

Address: *104 W. Michigan Ave. (Box 457), Clinton, MI 49236, tel. 517/456-4151.*
Accommodations: *6 double rooms with baths, 4 single rooms with baths.*
Amenities: *Air-conditioning and cable TV in guest rooms.*
Rates: *$25-$50; Continental breakfast. AE, MC, V.*
Restrictions: *No pets.*

The Country Inn of Grand Blanc

When Earl Pigeon was living in Europe as a General Motors executive, he and his wife, Neva, traveled extensively across the Continent, stayed in bed-and-breakfasts whenever possible, and learned that comfort is the paramount feature of a good establishment. That philosophy is apparent in their own B&B, a sprawling yellow turn-of-the century Victorian house dripping with gingerbread trim and wrought iron.

Walnut trees line the drive up to the house, which sits back from the road on 10 acres of gentle hills and meadows in an upscale suburb of Flint. There is a wraparound wooden porch with stone steps and foundation; a flower-filled deck encircles a large oak tree behind the house. Inside, the lovely oak woodwork and staircase and antiques such as a Victorian wood screen in the parlor add character to the otherwise contemporary decor. Upstairs, nooks and crannies have been pleasantly incorporated into guest rooms, including a suite that has a microwave and TV with VCR. A Continental breakfast is served in the homey kitchen; for those who want to sleep late, a basket of pecan rolls is left outside the guest-room door.

Address: *6136 S. Belsay Rd., Grand Blanc, MI 48438, tel. 313/694-6749.*
Accommodations: *2 double rooms share 1 bath, 1 suite.*
Amenities: *Air-conditioning.*
Rates: *$45-$65; Continental breakfast. AE, MC, V.*
Restrictions: *No smoking, no pets.*

Dundee Guest House

The greatest asset of Karen and Jerry Glover's gingerbread-trimmed brick house in Dundee is its location. The sleepy village sits on the River Raisin, near wineries, historic sites, and a meandering stream, and is just 15 miles east of Monroe, home of General George Custer. Dundee is also near the university towns of Ann Arbor and Ypsilanti.

The Glovers—who bought the 120-year-old house in 1989—run a friendly establishment. Jerry, forced into early retirement by Eastern Airlines, has time to linger over what is truly a bottomless cup of coffee. (Karen still works at Michigan Bell.) The decor here strives to be Victorian, but undistinguished wallpaper, modern bathrooms, and the plush pink carpet in one of the guest rooms compete with such authentic touches as crocheted lace curtains, a bentwood cradle, carved oak staircase, and Karen's collection of handmade porcelain dolls. Still, there's a good feeling here, the kind of unhurried pleasantness thought to characterize this country back when it was a collection of small towns like Dundee.

Address: *522 Tecumseh St., Dundee, MI 48131, tel. 313/529-5706.*
Accommodations: *2 double rooms with baths.*
Amenities: *Croquet and gazebo in backyard.*
Rates: *$40–$60; Continental breakfast. MC, V.*
Restrictions: *No smoking, no pets; closed Dec. 24–25.*

Southwestern Michigan
*Including Battle Creek, Grand Rapids,
Kalamazoo, Saugatuck*

*The southwest quadrant of Michigan offers travelers a wide
range of entertaining choices, from a leisurely afternoon
drive to pick raspberries in the country to a week of
carefully orchestrated relaxation at a tony lakeside retreat.
In fact, thanks to growing media attention that has
resulted in a number of travel-magazine pieces, the region
is fast becoming recognized as a four-season vacation area.
This "discovery" would have amused such old-time
aficionados as Al Capone and L. Frank Baum, who knew
the Lake Michigan shoreline as a salve for troubled spirits.
Baum wrote some of his Wizard of Oz books here; perhaps
Scarface came here to sort out his thoughts about Bugs
Moran or the Purple Gang.*

*The advent of air-conditioning and affordable air travel to
more exotic places made some of the area's features less
compelling. But southwestern Michigan's cool summers and
mild winters are starting to draw visitors again, thanks to
a blossoming of individual entrepreneurs and increasingly
promotion-minded communities. Along the Red Arrow
Highway, which runs north from the Indiana border
through towns like New Buffalo, Lakeside, and Union Pier,
cottages and storefronts are finding new life as bed-and-
breakfasts, art galleries, and antiques shops. Farther up
the coast, such upscale ports as South Haven and
Saugatuck continue to do land-rush business from
Memorial Day to Labor Day, with a 50-50 mix of
Chicagoans and Michiganders vying for space in the harbor
inns and B&Bs. Nearly everything revolves around sand
and water, from beach volleyball and kite-flying
tournaments to breakneck dune-buggy rides. Saugatuck is
particularly trendy, with a large number of fine
restaurants and shops and a gay community. The
combination of berthed sailboats, ancient shade trees, and*

old houses remind visitors of New England coastal villages. A few miles north from here is the delightful conservative city of Holland, noted for its tulip farms and its streets that undergo daily scrubbing.

Inland, orchards parade across the gently rolling, fertile terrain. Spring produces an explosion of fragrance and color—and numerous festivals. July ushers in picking season. You can drive down just about any back road and come across a U-Pick farm, cider stand, or winery. In the fall, the orange globes of pumpkins and squashes splash the roadsides with color. During the winter, cross-country skiers glide silently up and down the mild, undulating hills, later heading for inns that are nearly always empty in midweek.

The countryside is a jumble of farms, small manufacturing centers, and a few crossroads communities that have yet to recover from the decline of the railroad. If you're lost, don't be afraid to approach someone for directions. Even in the larger cities—Kalamazoo, Grand Rapids, and Battle Creek—people are unmistakably, hospitably Midwestern. Not only do they talk to you; they listen. And for those traveling the area's highways, you should know they trust strangers enough to keep the rest room doors unlocked.

Places to Go, Sights to See

Battle Creek. Dubbed the "Cereal Capital of the World" with Post Cereals, Ralston Purina, and the Kellogg companies located here, Battle Creek is host to a pair of fun annual events: Every June, thousands participate in what is described as *the world's largest breakfast;* in July some 200 hot-air balloonists compete in the weeklong *International Balloon Championship* (tel. 616/962–0592). Ten miles to the east is the well-preserved town of Marshall, whose *Historical Society* (tel. 616/781–5163) presents a tour of nationally recognized 19th-century homes every September.

Cherry County Playhouse. A fixture in Traverse City for many years, the theatrical company moved to the Frauenthal Theatre in downtown Muskegon in 1991. Summer stock productions include children's plays, musicals, comedies, and celebrity concerts. Call 616/727–8888 after April 15 for the schedule.

Flower Festivals. Every spring 30 communities work together to produce the *Blossomtime Festival* (tel. 616/926–7397), which includes a floral parade through Boston Harbor and St. Joseph. More than 400,000 people attend the *Tulip Time Festival* (tel. 616/396–4221) in Holland, held for 10 days every May when the blooms are at their peak.

Grand Rapids. The state's second largest city is a clean, well-ordered manufacturing community 30 minutes east of Lake Michigan. It has an amazing number of churches per capita and is a conservative, friendly place with quite a few things to see. The *Gerald R. Ford Museum* (303 Pearl St. NW, tel. 616/456–2674) traces the life and times of the 38th president. Self-guided walking tours of *Heritage Hill* (tel. 616/459–8950), a historic district of some 1,300 buildings east of the rejuvenated downtown, are well-liked as is the exotic *John Ball Zoological Gardens* (1300 W. Fulton St., tel. 616/776–2591).

Kalamazoo. This pleasant college town, roughly halfway between Chicago and Detroit on I–94 and just an hour's drive from Lake Michigan, is popular as a way station or as a destination in itself. The immaculate *Kalamazoo Aviation History Museum* (2101 E. Milhan Rd., tel. 616/382–6555) features rare, operational World War II aircraft, memorabilia, and restoration work of vintage planes. Aircraft buffs and casual visitors flock to the *Michigan International Air Show* (tel. 616/383–1000 or 616/381–1692), which attracts more than 100,000 people every June.

Michigan's Adventure Amusement Park (Russell Rd. exit off U. S. 31, tel. 616/766–3377), 8 miles north of Muskegon, is the state's largest amusement and water park with more than 20 thrill rides, 10 water slides, a wave pool, a children's activity pool, shows, games, food, and the only two roller coasters in Michigan.

Paw Paw. A dozen miles west of Kalamazoo, the village has several wineries, including *Frontenac Vineyards* (tel. 616/657–5531), *St. Julian Winery* (tel. 616/657–2964), and *Warner Vineyards* (tel. 616/657–3165), Michigan's largest. Each offers free tours and samplings. The *Wine Country Scenic Train* (tel. 616/657–5963) has 90-minute excursions year-round, including autumn-color tours and Santa Trains.

Saugatuck and Douglas. A thriving arts colony has developed in these two lakefront communities, which sit on opposite sides of the mouth of the Kalamazoo River. The *Ox-Bow Art Workshop* in Saugatuck is the Midwest's oldest summer school of painting, but artists are in evidence everywhere—from the tasteful downtown shops and galleries to the boardwalk pier, one of the Great Lakes' longest. Picturesque beaches and the area's alternative lifestyle have helped create one of the state's most fashionable vacation spots.

SS *Keewatin*. One of the last of the Great Lakes' classic passenger steamboats is permanently docked in Douglas as a maritime museum (South of the Saugatuck–Douglas Bridge, tel. 616/857–2151 or 616/857–2107).

Guided tours of this luxuriously appointed 1907 vessel are available from
Memorial Day through Labor Day.

Veldheer Tulip Gardens/DeKlomp Wooden Shoe & Delft Factory. Two
million bulbs exhibit their color every spring at Veldheer's (12755 Quincy at
U.S. 31, Holland, tel. 616/399–1900), making it one of the premier attractions
for Holland-area visitors. At the DeKlomp factory next door, visitors can
watch workers carve wooden shoes and handpaint the famous blue-and-white
Delftware.

Beaches

The best beaches are in state parks such as Grand Haven, Holland, and Van
Buren. The state's longest stretch of beach—2½ miles—is at Warren Dunes
State Park (Red Arrow Hwy., tel. 616/426–4013), south of Bridgman.
However, because of eroding shorelines, some of the area's public beaches
may be partially restricted.

Boating

No one in Michigan is ever more than 6 miles from a lake or stream, so you
won't have to work hard to find a place to either launch or rent a boat.
Marina activity, particularly in major yachting and sportfishing ports like
South Haven and Muskegon, is frenzied through the peak summer months,
but slows down considerably with the cool weather. For those who prefer to
leave the driving to someone else, you can cruise the Kalamazoo River and
Lake Michigan aboard *The Queen of Saugatuck* (tel. 616/857–4261),
a 67-foot-long stern-wheeler, or the *City of Douglas* (tel. 616/857–2107), a 60-
foot yacht.

Fishing

Whether you cast your line from a boat or off a pier, southwest Michigan
offers some reel opportunities. The waters hold panfish, trout, walleye, bass,
northern pike, bullheads, catfish, and, especially, yellow perch. Visiting
anglers will find some of Michigan's finest fishing in the center of Grand
Rapids, where the Grand River is kept stocked with chinook, steelhead, and
coho salmon. Also worth noting are Reeds Lake in East Grand Rapids, which
has bluegills, crappies, and northern pike, and the Muskegon River, popular
for its annual perch and salmon runs. Charter fishing on Lake Michigan is
available at marinas up and down the shoreline.

Golf

The state is known for its large number of fine courses, many on the "Golf
Coast" of Lake Michigan. You can play 18 holes among dunes and pines at
the *Grand Haven Golf Club* (1700 Lincoln Rd., Grand Haven, tel. 616/842–

4040), rated one of the country's top public courses. *Clearbrook* (135th Ave., Saugatuck, tel. 616/857–1766) in Saugatuck is the southwest shoreline's only championship public golf and fine dining complex. Tee off at *Winding Creek Golf Course* (8600 Ottafan St., Holland, tel. 616/396–4516) in Holland or *Grand Island Golf Ranch* (6266 W. River Dr., Belmont, tel. 616/363–1262) in Grand Rapids. A complete listing of all golf courses in the state is available through the *Michigan Association of Public Golf Courses* (Box 612, Plymouth, MI 48170, tel. 313/582–8860 or 800/223–5877).

Restaurants

You can have your steak and scampi prepared tableside at **Churchill's** (3927 28th St. SE, tel. 616/942–0590), an elegant favorite in downtown Grand Rapids. The city features another fine dining experience at **Schnitzelbank** (342 Jefferson St., tel. 616/459–9527), where German fare and paneled rooms transport you to the Old World. In Macatawa, just west of Holland, the sophisticated but unpretentious **Sandpiper Restaurant** (2225 S. Shore Dr., tel. 616/335–5866) offers a full range of reasonably priced American cuisine and a bird's-eye view of the harbor. Orchard country farther south offers more than just roadside cider stands. In Bridgman, sautéed chicken breast with chopped pecan crust is a specialty of the **Tabor Hill Winery Restaurant** (185 Mt. Tabor Rd., tel. 616/422–1161), which overlooks the surrounding vineyards. And "monster" Reuben sandwiches and chunky wedges of homemade pie make **Wick's Apple House** (52281 Indian Lake Rd., tel. 616/782–7306) in Dowagiac a delicious detour.

Tourist Information

The **Michigan Travel Bureau** (333 S. Capitol Ave., Lansing, MI 48933, tel. 800/543–2937) has statewide tourist information. To learn more about boating, fishing, and hunting opportunities and regulations, contact the **Michigan Department of Natural Resources** (530 N. Allegan St., Lansing, MI 48933, tel. 517/373–1204). The following cover more specific areas: **Greater Battle Creek Visitors and Convention Bureau** (34 W. Jackson St., Battle Creek, MI 49017, tel. 616/962–2240); **Greater Grand Rapids Convention Bureau** (245 Monroe NW, Grand Rapids, MI 49503, tel. 616/459–8287); **Holland Area Chamber of Commerce** (272 E. Eighth St., Holland, MI 49422, tel. 616/392–2389); **Kalamazoo County Convention and Visitors Bureau** (128 N. Kalamazoo Mall, Kalamazoo, MI 49007, tel. 616/381–4003); **Muskegon County Convention and Visitors Bureau** (349 W. Webster Ave., Muskegon, MI 49440, tel. 616/722–3751); **Saugatuck/Douglas Chamber of Commerce** (303 Butler St., Saugatuck, MI 49453, tel. 616/857–5801); **Lakeshore Convention and Visitors Bureau** (Box 890, South Haven, MI 49090, tel. 616/637–5252); **West Michigan Tourist Association** (136 E. Fulton St., Grand Rapids, MI 49503, tel. 616/456–8557).

Crane House

Bob and Lue Crane are fourth-generation Fennville fruit farmers whose sprawling homestead takes in 310 acres of apple, cherry, raspberry, blueberry, and peach orchards; a restaurant; and a 120-year-old farmhouse painted white with green shutters. The farmhouse is a large, two-story wood structure that Bob and Lue bought from Bob's cousin and renovated five years ago. "The place was empty and ready to fall down," says their daughter, Nancy Crane-McFarland, who today serves as innkeeper. "To help defray some of the costs of fixing it up, we decided to turn it into a bed-and-breakfast. "

In many ways, the Cranes seem as if they've stepped right off a *Saturday Evening Post* cover—along with the house. The interior is a pleasant mix of farm antiques, Americana, and primitive art. The upstairs guest rooms have stenciled walls, ceiling fans, and wood, iron, and brass beds, each with a handmade quilt and a feather mattress. The rooms overlook the orchards—a truly splendid sight in the spring and fall. The parlor boasts Nancy's great-grandmother's curved-glass oak curio cabinet and a 1900 stove, and the breakfast room has a pine hanging dry sink. "The only other time I've seen one was in an old episode of 'Bonanza,' " says Nancy, whose own young family lives in the house.

The Cranes are genuine, neighborly, family-centered, and industrious. They also have a fair amount of business savvy. Across the highway from the house is their Pie Pantry Restaurant, which Bob and Lue started as an alternative way to make money when American agriculture suffered reverses in the early 1970s.

The restaurant, in an old barn, is a cheerful jumble of worn chairs and tables under a folksy burlap-sack ceiling, with a Round Oak stove and a wall of framed Charles Lindbergh clippings. In summer, the gravel drive becomes a turnstile as pleasure drivers take time out to pick fruit, buy cider, or sample some of the outstanding fruit pies, sandwiches, and soups. The orchards, restaurant, and B&B are truly a family operation, with three generations of Cranes pitching in wherever they're needed.

Address: *6051 124th Ave., Fennville, MI 49408, tel. 616/561-6931.*
Accommodations: *3 double rooms with baths, 2 doubles share shower.*
Amenities: *TV and phone in den.*
Rates: *$60–$90; full breakfast. MC, V.*
Restrictions: *No smoking indoors, no pets; 2-night minimum on holidays.*

Kingsley House

David and Shirley Witt tout their impressive Queen Anne house in tiny Fennville as being "as American as apple pie," an example of truth in advertising if ever there was one. It was built in 1886 by Harvey Kingsley, who introduced fruit trees to this area around Lake Michigan. Tipping their caps to Kingsley, the Witts have placed his picture in the living room and named each of the guest rooms after a variety of apple. The winding oak stairway leads to six second-story chambers dubbed McIntosh and Golden Delicious, among others. The most interesting is the Jonathan Room, a former stableboy's room, with a century-old sleigh bed and an 1850 platform rocker. Nestled in the tower, the Dutchess Room, the brightest with its five windows, is regally decorated in cranberry and antique lace. Immediately above it is Northern Spy, a honeymoon suite that features a fireplace, whirlpool bath, and a calming view of miles of rolling countryside.

Shirley, who was born in the Netherlands, runs the household with smooth efficiency and simple elegance. The guest rooms and common areas are spacious and immaculately clean. The furnishings are a tasteful blend of oak and cherry antiques that harmonize with such family ornaments as the shadowboxes the Witts made.

Breakfast is a fancy affair, served on linens and Royal Dalton china in the formal cherry-wood dining room. The Delftware and silver are typical of Dutch touches throughout the house. Five menus are rotated but meals usually include country ham, farm-fresh eggs, hash browns, and homemade muffins and bread. Coffee and the morning paper are set out by 7:30 AM, and tea, cold drinks, cookies, and snacks are available all day.

With busy M89 close at hand, traffic noise can be a problem in the front rooms. To escape, hop on one of the four 18-speed Peugots the Witts provide and pedal 8 miles south to the Allegan State Game Area, famous as a rest stop for geese and other migrating waterfowl. Once there you can hike, canoe, swim, cross-country ski, or pick wild blueberries, strawberries, and other fruit.

Address: *626 W. Main St., Fennville, MI 49408, tel. 616/561-6425.*
Accommodations: *6 double rooms with baths, 1 suite.*
Amenities: *Air-conditioning, whirlpool tub, TV and phone in 3 rooms, 2 phones, fireplace and whirlpool tub in suite.*
Rates: *$75–$125; full breakfast, refreshments all day. AE, MC, V.*
Restrictions: *No smoking, no pets.*

National House Inn

The National House Inn in Marshall is more than a magnificently preserved and smooth-running period hostel; it's a centerpiece of what many consider the finest cross-section of 19th-century architecture in the country. The oldest operating inn in the state opened as a stagecoach stop in 1835, two years before Michigan was admitted to the Union. For many years it served double duty as one of the final stops on the Underground Railroad that spirited escaped slaves to Canada, 120 miles to the east. In 1878, it was converted into a wagon and windmill factory. The inn was drawing its final breath as an apartment house when a consortium of local business people bought it and restored it for the nation's Bicentennial.

For the past 10 years, innkeeper Barbara Bradley has watched a parade of tourists, business travelers, and honeymooners pass through the rustic entryway, warmed by a massive beam-and-brick open-hearth fireplace. The rough-hewn ceiling beams and aged plank floors are the framework for the selection of country antiques found in every room. There are punched-tin chandeliers; Windsor, ladderback, and herringbone wing chairs in the living room; spindle-legged tables and hurricane lamps in the dining room; and gilt-framed oil portraits throughout. Thanks to a unique warming fireplace set into handcrafted, paneled cabinets, the upstairs lounge is comfortable and inviting, although in warmer weather guests prefer sitting in the back porch and gardens.

Guest rooms are attractively wallpapered and carpeted, with the decor ranging from country style to the Victorian style of the Ketchum Suite, which overlooks a handsome garden and the village circle. There's plenty of elbow room in the dining room, where a Continental breakfast of boiled eggs, fruit bowls, wheat bread, coffee, and a wide variety of fruit juices and teas are served.

Marshall is right off I–94, 10 miles east of Battle Creek. In 1991, the village—frequently referred to as the "Williamsburg of the Midwest"—was designated a National Historic Landmark District. The district encompasses some 850 structures (and nearly 50 historical markers), including striking examples of Queen Anne, Italianate, and Gothic Revival architecture. The town hall itself is a century-old stone livery.

Address: *102 Parkview St., Marshall, MI 49068, tel. 616/781–7374, fax 616/781–4510.*
Accommodations: *16 double rooms with baths.*
Amenities: *Air-conditioning, cable TV and phone in rooms, no-smoking rooms available.*
Rates: *$67–$105; Continental breakfast. AE, MC, V.*
Restrictions: *No pets.*

South Cliff Inn

Five years ago, Bill Swisher left behind a 10-year career as director of the Cassopolis, Michigan Probate Court and opened the South Cliff Inn. "I grew up in the area, and I suppose I was always looking for an excuse to come back," Bill says.

In the pre-air-conditioning days of the early 1900s, St. Joseph ("St. Joe," as it's sometimes called) and its sister city, Benton Harbor, were among the Midwest's most popular lakefront summer resorts. The collapse of the area's manufacturing base led to a decline of fortunes in the 1970s, especially in Benton Harbor, always the more blue-collar of the two. South Cliff Inn, a salmon-colored brick English cottage, is a small but important representative of an economic renaissance that once again is capitalizing on the therapeutic breezes of Lake Michigan.

The 80-year-old inn is perched on a bluff, giving all but one of the six guest rooms superb views of the water. The largest room, the Sunset Suite, is perhaps the most popular. The queen-size bed, sofa, and wing chair are dressed in complementary teal English chintz fabrics, while the private bath features a custom-designed marble tub. Soaking is a spectator sport in the adjacent Harbour Room, where guests can lie back in a bubbling whirlpool bath and watch the sun melt into the lake in the evening. The entire place is decorated in English country style, with plenty of bold prints, chintz fabrics, and a large number of antiques. Drawing the most attention in one of the guest rooms is an imposing 150-year-old oak armoire that is so large it had to be hoisted through the windows.

The trouble was worth it: The inn is comfortable, sun-filled, and, with just one part-time staffer to assist Bill, commendably unhurried. A Continental breakfast includes juice, homemade bread and muffins, and—this being orchard country—plenty of fresh fruit. That's enough carbohydrates to fuel a short walk to the downtown of this pleasant harbor town, whose turn-of-the-century storefronts and monuments, landscaped brick streets, and Lake Michigan backdrop combine to make it perhaps the most picturesque in the entire state.

Address: *1900 Lakeshore Dr., St. Joseph, MI 49085, tel. 616/983–4881.*
Accommodations: *6 double rooms with baths.*
Amenities: *Air-conditioning, cable TV in den, whirlpool bath in 1 room.*
Rates: *$65–$105; Continental breakfast, refreshments all day. AE, D, MC, V.*
Restrictions: *Smoking on main floor only, no pets; 2-night minimum on weekends, 3-night minimum on holidays.*

Wickwood Country Inn

Guests at Saugatuck's oldest bed-and-breakfast are in for a treat, both figuratively and literally. The new owner, Julee Rosso-Miller, is the co-author of *The Silver Palate Cookbook*. With 2 million copies sold, it's the second best-selling cookbook in the history of publishing, behind *The Joy of Cooking*.

Julee came to her new career as innkeeper in much the same way she became a well-known gourmet writer: serendipity. Her mother's heart attack in 1986 forced her to reappraise her own hectic lifestyle as half-owner of one of the first-ever gourmet takeout shops in the country, New York's Silver Palate. She moved to Saugatuck and fell in love with the sunsets over Lake Michigan—and Ray Miller, a local builder. They married, then persuaded their neighbors to sell what has long been regarded as the best B&B in town. Of course, the location doesn't hurt: It's two blocks from downtown's many fine shops and restaurants, and a short walk from the beach and other lakefront attractions.

With its brick floors, cedar walls, and vaulted ceilings, the circa-1940 inn resembles one of those small toasty hotels that dot the English countryside. The main-floor rooms, filled with overstuffed chairs, French and English antiques, fresh flowers, and original art, surround a courtyard blooming with perennials, roses, and herbs. The guest rooms have individual themes but are uniformly captivating, with plenty of antique lace and Ralph Lauren and Laura Ashley fabrics, and cabbage rose patterns on the walls and beds.

Guests are pampered from daybreak to dusk. A buffet breakfast is served and a newspaper is supplied weekday mornings on the old English pine buffet table in the dining area, which is filled with antique toy trains, boats, and trucks. On weekends, a hearty brunch is prepared. Hors d'oeuvres, which might include a light salmon mousse, bruschetta, Chinese ribs, and crudites with low-fat dip, are put out at 6 PM. As if this weren't enough, candies and jars of spiced nuts are placed in each room. Calorie counters can relax, though: most items are selections from Julee's upcoming low-fat cookbook.

Address: *510 Butler St. (Box 1019), Saugatuck, MI 49453, tel. 616/857–1097, fax 616/857–4168.*
Accommodations: *11 double rooms with baths, 2 suites.*
Amenities: *Air-conditioning, phone in guest rooms, fireplace in 1 suite, cable TV in library.*
Rates: *$100–$140; full breakfast, refreshments in the evening. AE, MC, V.*
Restrictions: *No pets; 2-night minimum on weekends, closed Dec. 24–25.*

Fairchild House

In an area fairly bustling with bed-and-breakfasts, Selicia Fairchild's is one of the most intimate and romantic. The two-story white stucco house, built in 1919, has a reputation for thoughtful, personalized service. For Selicia, the phone and TV in the parlor are barely tolerable amenities; her idea of relaxation is classical music filling the house as a backdrop for evening hors d'oeuvres and pleasant conversation in front of the fireplace. There are three distinctive bedrooms, all tastefully done with fine period antiques, cutwork linens, European feather beds, down comforters, and prize-winning quilts. One bedroom set is a replica of Abraham Lincoln's purported wedding suite. Fresh flowers and plush Turkish bathrobes are indicative of the care that goes into everything here, including the elegant champagne breakfasts served in summer in the lacy gazebo in the garden. For special occasions, a romantic breakfast in bed can be arranged with advance notice.

Address: *606 Butler St., Saugatuck, MI 49453, tel. 616/857–5985.*
Accommodations: *3 double rooms share 2 baths.*
Amenities: *Air-conditioning, bathrobes, phone, TV, and fireplace in parlor.*
Rates: *$85; full breakfast. MC, V.*
Restrictions: *No smoking, no pets; 2-night minimum on weekends and May–Oct.*

The Inn at Union Pier

Chicago newlyweds Bill and Madelaine Reinke bought the 1910 main house and two cottages in 1983 and spent the next two years renovating the shuttered lakeside resort on wonderfully landscaped grounds, giving the buildings a light Scandinavian atmosphere. Comfort and thoughtfulness are the buzzwords here. There are plenty of comforters, watercolor pictures, and wallpaper patterned in small print. Towels are provided for those who wish to dip into either the hot tub on the back porch or Lake Michigan, 200 feet away.

Hikers, bicyclists, and cross-country skiers all find tree-lined Lakeshore Road an attractive conduit to several interesting shops and galleries in neighboring New Buffalo. This is where orchard country meets the shoreline, so sunset cruises and wine-tasting are also just a short drive away.

Address: *9708 Berrien St. (Box 222), Union Pier, MI 49129, tel. 616/469–4700.*
Accommodations: *15 double rooms with baths.*
Amenities: *Air-conditioning, hot tub, sauna, beach towels, cable TV and telephone in Great House, fireplaces in 11 rooms.*
Rates: *$95–$140; full breakfast, afternoon and evening refreshments. D, MC, V.*
Restrictions: *No smoking in dining room, no pets; 2-night minimum on weekends, 3-night minimum on holidays.*

Maplewood Hotel

This 1860s Greek Revival has been gradually restored since Catherine and Sam Simon bought it in 1990. Part of the hotel's charm is in its combination of formality and hospitality; it's one of the few in the area that welcomes children. Each of the 15 antique-filled bedrooms has its own bath (five with whirlpool tub), and five of the rooms have working fireplaces. Breakfast is served at 14 small, linen-covered tables in the dining room and on the screened porch.

Those who arrive by train can enjoy the scenery as they're chauffeured to the hotel in a Rolls-Royce. Maplewood's central location puts first-rate shops, galleries, and restaurants within shouting distance—literally—so street noise can be a concern. But the spot has the advantage of nearby golf, tennis, boating, and fishing.

Address: *428 Butler St. (Box 1059), Saugatuck, MI 49453, tel. 616/857-1771, fax 616/857-1773.*
Accommodations: *15 double rooms with baths.*
Amenities: *Air-conditioning, cable TV, phone, fireplaces in 5 rooms, whirlpoools in 5 rooms; lap pool.*
Rates: *$80–$145; full breakfast. AE, MC, V.*
Restrictions: *Smoking on porch only, no pets; 2-night minimum on weekends, 3-night minimum on holidays, closed for 3 days at Thanksgiving and Christmas.*

Parsonage 1908

Once a parsonage, the stunning two-story, white Queen Anne–style house, adorned with black-shutters, geranium-filled window boxes, and tricolor crescent flags, sits on a little rise in an upscale residential section of Holland. Like so many neighborhoods in this heavily Dutch community, there is a palpable sense of order and serenity in the rows of immaculately kept houses, lawns, and gardens.

Bonnie McCoy-Verwys, assisted by her daughters Wendy and Heather, is an outgoing hostess and a very capable gardener and cook. She bought the house in 1974 and 10 years later opened it as Holland's first bed-and-breakfast. Through patience and attention to detail, she has restored the Victorian house over the years.

The oak woodwork and leaded-glass windows are supplemented by less obvious touches of authenticity: lined dresser drawers with a sachet in each, for instance; a bedroom closet holding high-button shoes, hatboxes, and other old-fashioned accessories. In the finely landscaped backyard, croquet wickets share space with a fragrant—and rare—mimosa tree.

Address: *6 E. 24th St., Holland, MI 49423, tel. 616/396-1316.*
Accommodations: *3 double rooms share 2 baths.*
Amenities: *Air-conditioning, TV in sitting room, portable phone in hallway.*
Rates: *$80–$90; full breakfast, refreshments. No credit cards.*
Restrictions: *No smoking, no pets; closed last week in Feb.*

Pebble House

The American Arts and Crafts movement of the early 1900s is faithfully followed inside this simple 1912 concrete-block and river-rock house. Ed and Jean Lawrence, who own the East Road Gallery in town, have meticulously furnished guest rooms and common areas with distinctive clean-lined Mission-style furniture and accessories, including hand-hammered copper bowls and green cut-glass lamps. Dried flowers and pastel accents help soften the lines of the style, which is carried over in the nearby Coach and Blueberry houses, connected to the main house by walkways. The Lawrences work hard to make this a true retreat: phones and children are discouraged, and there's nary a television in sight. Alternatively, some 2,000 books, including volumes of fiction, travel, and design are tucked all over. Outside, a tennis court and nearby beach beckon.

Address: *15093 Lakeshore Rd., Lakeside, MI 49116, tel. 616/469-1416.*
Accommodations: *3 double rooms with baths, 3-bedroom Coach House with bath, 2-bedroom Blueberry House with bath.*
Amenities: *Air-conditioning, phone in guest room upon request, phone in main lounge, kitchenette and wood-burning stove in Blueberry House.*
Rates: *$90–$96, Blueberry House $190; full breakfast, refreshments. MC, V.*
Restrictions: *No smoking indoors, no pets, closed Dec. 24.*

Pine Garth Inn

Guests immediately get a good feeling about this comfortably rumpled summer estate, as unpretentious as its owners, Russ and Paula Bulin. The Illinois transplants bought the 90-year-old yellow frame house in 1988 and dressed it up in what Paula calls country eclectic—a blend of striped and floral linens and wallpaper and family furniture. Russ is a professional woodworker. Samples of his handiwork are everywhere inside the inn and five adjoining contemporary wood cottages: log beds, twig furniture, distressed pine armoires. The inn sits on a bluff overlooking 200 feet of private beach. All but one of the guest rooms have a full view of the water; four rooms have their own private deck. The cottages are good for family gatherings, otherwise the rooms in the house are more desirable.

Address: *15790 Lakeshore Rd., Union Pier, MI 49129, tel. 616/469-1642.*
Accommodations: *7 double rooms with baths, 5 2-bedroom cottages with baths.*
Amenities: *Air-conditioning, TV and VCR in bedrooms, phone in library, hot tubs and fireplaces in cottages.*
Rates: *$105–$140, cottages $195–$225; full breakfast, afternoon refreshments. AE, MC, V.*
Restrictions: *Smoking in Great Room only, no pets; 2-night minimum on weekends, 3-night minimum on holidays.*

Snow Flake Hotel

Students of roadside architecture find it hard to pass this one by, even at 40 mph. The neon-lit, one-story motel on an uninspired commercial strip is important because it's the only one Frank Lloyd Wright ever designed. It opened in 1962, three years after Wright's death, and has gone through a succession of owners. Isobel Magil, who worked at the Detroit Science Center for many years, operates it now with her husband, Calvin.

Isobel's matter-of-fact manner disguises a deep appreciation of the motel's significance. The star-shape layout surrounds a 2½-acre court, with a hexagonal swimming pool featuring an open steel dome and encircled by geometric grillwork. Guest rooms have plenty of the Wright stuff, too: soaring cathedral ceilings and walls of windows, built-in dresser seats and desks. Velour bedspreads are touches Wright never intended, but the staff and patrons make a stay here a pleasurable trip back in time.

Address: *3822 Red Arrow Hwy., St. Joseph, MI 49085, tel. 616/429-3261.*
Accommodations: *32 double rooms with baths, 25 single rooms with baths.*
Amenities: *Air-conditioning, cable TV, and phone in rooms, no-smoking rooms available; heated pool, restaurant, and cocktail lounge.*
Rates: *$38-$48. MC, V.*
Restrictions: *No pets.*

Yelton Manor

Elaine Herbert explains that she and her husband, Robert Kripaitif, are the typical "Yuppie escape story." Two years ago they fled the corporate world and bought this rambling 1873 Victorian house from a Kalamazoo contractor, who had turned it into arguably the finest bed-and-breakfast in South Haven. Elaine, a marketing professional, has actually improved on that reputation. One of the keys is the eight-person staff—they are attentive without being suffocating. For do-it-yourselfers, the fridge in the separate guest kitchen is kept stocked with juices, homemade cookies, and other goodies. The house is elegantly styled in country Victorian, with most of the furnishings new oak reproductions. Third-floor rooms can be turned into suites for honeymoon and anniversary couples. In the heart of South Haven, The Yelton is only a quarter-block from North Beach access. One mile north is the Kal-Haven Trail, a 38-mile bicycle path that is especially pretty in July when the blueberry fields are in fruit.

Address: *140 N. Shore Dr., South Haven, MI 49090, tel. 616/637-5220.*
Accommodations: *1 double rooms with bath, 2 suites.*
Amenities: *Air-conditioning, cable TV in rooms, 3 phones for guests, whirlpool baths in 5 rooms, fireplace in 1 room.*
Rates: *$95-$180; full breakfast, refreshments. AE, MC, V.*
Restrictions: *No smoking indoors, no pets.*

Upper Peninsula

When Ernest Hemingway was writing "Big Two-Hearted River" in the early 1920s, he kept a map of northern Michigan pinned to the wall of his Paris apartment. Such inspiration is almost superfluous for those who have visited Michigan's Upper Peninsula and treasure mental canvases of the region's rugged natural beauty.

Remote and thinly populated, the U.P. (as it's commonly called) is nearly surrounded by Lakes Superior, Michigan, and Huron. It's larger than Massachusetts, Connecticut, Rhode Island, and Delaware combined, but even its largest city, Marquette, has only 22,000 people. It has more in common with Wisconsin, with which it shares a long western border, than with the lower half of Michigan. The U.P. was awarded to the Wolverine State in 1837 as settlement in a boundary dispute with Ohio, which got Toledo. The progress of the various industries that have since shaped the region—copper and iron mining, lumbering, maritime shipping—can be traced by the various museums, ghost towns, and shipwreck preserves that form part of the landscape. Despite the presence of a healthy commercial fishing industry and several fine colleges and universities, today the U.P. is best known as a visually stunning outdoor paradise.

Natives of the region, who proudly refer to themselves as "Yoopers," have historically reveled in their isolationism. Over the years there have been serious attempts to make the U.P. a separate state, and such names as "Cloverland," "Hiawathaland," and "Superior" have been proposed. When the Mackinac Bridge opened in 1957, finally linking the two dissimilar halves of the state, one noted Yooper suggested bombing it. Those south of the bridge were pretty sure he was kidding.

This is not to say that Yoopers, a good many of whom are retired auto workers from the Lower Peninsula, aren't an affable bunch. If anything, they're too busy enjoying their surroundings to worry about a visitor's origin. Spring finds the rivers teeming with spawning trout, salmon, and steelhead, and the forests growing shaggy and fragrant. From Memorial Day through Labor Day the U.P. is filled with vacationers, although even in the peak months of July and August it's easy to find solitude in the region's many state parks or on its numerous lakes. Air-conditioning is unnecessary, as the warmest days dissolve into cool, even bracing, nights. From early September to mid-October there is an autumn color show that rivals anything in New England. With 6 million acres of land open to hunting, the forests and wetlands are filled with orange-jacketed men and women pursuing deer, black bear, ruffed grouse, snowshoe hares, bobcats, raccoons, and coyotes. The long months of winter are thoroughly enjoyed by skiers, snowmobilers, ice fishermen, and participants in the never-ending stream of dogsled races and ice carnivals. Winter is declared over when students at Lake Superior State University in Sault Ste. Marie ceremonially burn a snowman in effigy.

While the Upper Peninsula has many finely furnished places to bed down and eat in, seasoned travelers know not to be critical with the occasionally tacky or threadbare lodgings euphemistically labeled "rustic." Not that anyone looking forward to long evenings discussing trout fishing by a wall paneled with moose heads and mining memorabilia cares enough to compare the U.P. with Newport or Martha's Vineyard: The priority of most travelers to these parts—with apologies to E. M. Forster— remains a view with a room.

Places to Go, Sights to See

Isle Royale National Park (tel. 906/482–0984). This island wilderness, in the northwest corner of Lake Superior, is accessible only by seaplane or boat, and is as rugged a vacation experience as one can find. You won't find any roads here: what awaits you are lots of moose, wolves, and other wildlife, unspoiled forests, and cold, refreshing lakes. The park's small marina and two lodges are open from May through October and reservations are a must.

Lighthouses. For more than 150 years, Great Lakes mariners have entrusted their lives to these beacons. There are more than 40 fully operational lighthouses along the shores of the Upper Peninsula, many of them unmanned. You can explore three in the Hiawatha National Forest near Brimley, including the 65-foot *Iroquois Lighthouse* (tel. 906/437–5272). Built in 1870, it has a museum that focuses on the lives of lighthouse keepers and their families.

Soo Locks. A 21-foot drop-off in St. Mary's River near Sault Ste. Marie forced early settlers to portage from Lake Superior to Lake Huron. The discovery of huge copper and iron deposits in the western U.P. prompted the building of two locks and a canal in 1855 to handle deep-draft vessels. Today viewing platforms give an almost overwhelmingly close-up look at ships from many nations, including super freighters that are up to 1,000 feet long and 105 feet wide.

Tahquamenon Falls. The most spectacular of the U.P.'s 150 waterfalls is also the second largest east of the Mississippi River. They can be reached via M-123 from Paradise, the closest community. Tahquamenon's fame was first secured in Longfellow's "Song of Hiawatha," and tourists haven't stopped coming yet. The surrounding country is magnificent in the autumn, by which time the crowds have dwindled, and breathtaking in the winter, when light bouncing off the water turns giant icicles into rainbows of ice sculptures.

Underwater Preserves. Hundreds of shipwrecks can be found in the cold, clear waters of the Great Lakes. They are accessible to divers at several underwater preserves, including the *Marquette Underwater Preserve* (300 Lakeshore Blvd., Marquette, tel. 906/226–2006 or 800/338–7982), where vessels ranging from iron freighters to wooden schooners sit in the waters of Lake Superior. Dive charters and boat tours are available at the *Alger Underwater Preserve* (Commercial St., west side of Munising Bay, Munising, tel. 906/387–4477) in Munising Bay, the resting place for shipwrecks dating back to the 1850s. Some are visible from the surface, others are 110 feet under. About 60 miles north of the Mackinac Bridge, Whitefish Bay, a notorious stretch of Lake Superior's navigable waters, has been the site of numerous shipwrecks, including the *Edmund Fitzgerald*, which met its end in 1975. These are commemorated at the *Great Lakes Shipwreck Museum* (Whitefish Point Rd., tel. 906/293–3392) at Whitefish Point, about 11 miles north of Paradise. The memorial includes an 1849 lighthouse. For those who'd like a closer look, the *Whitefish Point Underwater Preserve* (tel. 906/492–3445) offers some of the best diving opportunities in North America.

Fishing

Anglers look on the U.P. as nirvana: With its 4,300 inland lakes, 12,000 miles of rivers and streams, and access to three of the Great Lakes, how could it be anything less? Giant Lake Gogebic in the western U.P. and Little Bay de Noc, near Escanaba in the south central part of the region, are famous for their large walleyes. The Sylvania Wilderness and Recreation Area near Watersmeet has a fish population of pike, perch, bass, trout, and walleye. The Great Lakes offer coho, lake trout, steelhead, chinook salmon, yellow perch, northern pike, and small-mouth bass. The shore has numerous marinas and public-access sites from which to launch or charter a boat.

Skiing

Some of the best alpine skiing in the Midwest can be had in the U.P. Vertical drops of 600 feet and runs of 5,000 to 6,000 feet are common at *Marquette Mountain* (tel. 906/225–1155), a mile south of Marquette on County Road 553, and *Big Powderhorn Mountain* (tel. 906/932–4838) in Bessemer and *Porcupine Mountains State Park* (tel. 906/885–5275) near Ontonagon, both in the western corner of the U.P. Cross-country trails are nearly everywhere, running alongside roads and frozen streams and inside forests and state parks.

Snowmobiling

With annual snowfalls exceeding 200 inches in some areas, snowmobiling has long been a popular recreation in the Upper Peninsula. There are hundreds of miles of trails groomed and marked by the state, many of them passing right through the center of towns and others leading to frozen waterfalls, forests, and other scenic overlooks. Rentals can be arranged through snowmobile dealers in most communities.

Restaurants

Dog Patch (820 E. Superior St., tel. 906/387–9948) and **Robin's Nest** (3520 I–75 Business Spur, tel. 906/632–3200) in Sault Ste. Marie are representative of most restaurants in the U.P.: casual and inexpensive, specializing in seafood dishes such as lake trout and whitefish. **The Harbor Haus** (1 block off U.S. 41, Copper Harbor, tel. 906/289–4502), which overlooks Lake Superior in Calumet, breaks out of the mold somewhat by offering a German menu along with the freshest lake catch.

Tourist Information

The **Upper Peninsula Travel & Recreation Association** (Box 400, Iron Mountain, MI 49801, tel. 906/774–5480 or 800/562–7134 for IL, MI, MN, and WI residents) is the central source for travel information in the region. The **Michigan Department of Natural Resources** (530 W. Allegan St., Lansing, MI 48933, tel. 517/373–1204) can answer questions on boating, fishing, and hunting regulations and opportunities. **The Michigan Travel Bureau** (333 S.

Capitol Ave., Lansing, MI 48933, tel. 800/543-2937) has statewide tourist information.

Laurium Manor Inn

Dave and Julie Sprenger were working as engineers in San Jose, California, when, as Julie describes it, they "decided to commit corporate suicide" and trade Golden State's laid-back charms for the ruggedly isolated Keweenaw Peninsula. They shared a dream of owning a mansion they had visited in Laurium, a former copper boom town. In 1988, they bought the vacant three-story neoclassic house. After three years of restoration work, which included attaching showers to a half-dozen claw-foot tubs, they reopened the heavy oak doors as a bed-and-breakfast.

The Upper Peninsula's largest and most opulent mansion was built in 1908 by Captain Thomas H. Hoatson, owner of the Calumet & Arizona Mining Company. At a time when miners were toiling 6,000 feet underground for 8¢ an hour, Hoatson spent $50,000 constructing the 40-room mansion, and an additional $35,000 furnishing it. The copper magnate had impeccable taste, as lodgers and afternoon tour groups ($2 a head) quickly learn.

Every room is a marvel. Silver-leaf overlay draws your eye to the ceiling of the music parlor. The dining room boasts stained-glass windows and gilded elephant-hide wall coverings, while the kitchen has a wall-size, built-in icebox made of marble, tile,

and oak. And then there are the two cedar closets that are big enough to serve as bedrooms in most bungalows.

The bedrooms were built extra-large. The largest, the Laurium Suite, is a majestic 530 square feet and has a hand-carved oak fireplace and private balcony. All the guest quarters are outfitted with queen- and king-size beds, handmade flannel quilts, and period antiques.

During the buffet breakfast of pastries, cereal, and fruit you can plan day trips to the historic Calumet Theatre, where Sarah Bernhardt, Lillian Russell, and Douglas Fairbanks, Jr., performed, or to one of the ghost towns sprinkled throughout the copper region. Lake Superior is just 4 miles away; Fort Wilkins State Park, a mid-19th-century army post on the northernmost tip of Keweenaw, is a short drive up U.S. 41.

Address: *320 Tamarack, Laurium, MI 49913, tel. 906/337-2549.*
Accommodations: *8 double rooms with baths, 2 doubles share 1 bath, 4 suites.*
Amenities: *Fireplace in 2 guest rooms, phone and cable TV in den.*
Rates: *$49–$89; Continental breakfast. MC, V.*
Restrictions: *No smoking, no pets.*

Michigamme Lake Lodge

Everything about this lodge is larger than life, from its location atop a bluff overlooking Lake Michigamme (Indian for "Big Lake") to its massive 2½-story stone fireplace. That's wholly in keeping with the Bunyanesque image of the Upper Peninsula where, according to legend, Babe the Blue Ox's hoofprints created many of the lakes.

The truth is a tad less sensational, but interesting nonetheless. The site was selected by a prominent fruit wholesaler and banker named Sam Cohodas for his summer home. A platoon of Finnish woodsmen spent a year felling, cutting, and fitting giant white pines to build the all-log dwelling. The stone for the great room's fireplace was quarried in the area. The lodge was opened in 1935 and was used for the next 52 years by the Cohodas family. Frank and Linda Stabile, hoteliers in Marquette, bought it in 1988 and reopened it as a bed-and-breakfast.

Deborah Kassis manages the three-person staff. "Our philosophy is to keep the lodge as rustic as it was when it opened," says Deborah, explaining the complete lack of radio or television (although Indian flute music is softly piped in). The range of activities, like the scenery, seems limitless. You can swim along the 1,700-foot private beach, bike along old logging trails, paddle a canoe to explore the giant lake's necklace of jade islands, go fishing for walleye and bass, hike, or look for moose in the nearby 17,000-acre McCormick wilderness preserve.

The cavernous interior is filled with bird's-eye maple furniture. Guest rooms are large and have views of the lake; the beds have down quilts and handcrafted pillows. Arrangements of axes, carpentry tools, and decoys share wall space throughout the lodge with a veritable herd of deer heads and bearskins. The fireplace anchors the large common areas, which have unique cedar chandeliers and a giant 125-year-old mirror. An inside balcony overlooks the main floor, its rails draped with Indian rugs, while a 40-foot sun porch stuffed with antiques and original Adirondack and twig furniture is a favorite of the guests at any time of the day or night.

Listed in the State and National Registers of Historic Places, this may just be the grandest rustic lodging in an area brimming with them—and that's no tall tale.

Address: *Michigamme Lake Lodge Rd. (Box 97), Champion, MI 49814, tel. 906/339–4400 or 800/358–0058.*
Accommodations: *3 double rooms with baths, 6 doubles share 3 baths.*
Amenities: *Phone on first floor.*
Rates: *$69–$125; Continental breakfast. MC, V.*
Restrictions: *No smoking, no pets; closed Jan. 1–Apr. 30.*

Big Bay Point Lighthouse

This 1896 brick-tower lighthouse, 30 miles north of Marquette at the end of a rocky point, is one of only three in the country offering bed and breakfast. Owners Linda and Jeff Ganble were active in historic preservation in Chicago when they purchased the decommissioned but still operating lighthouse in April 1992. "We emphasize a stress-free environment here," says Linda. To that end, television is banned and the phone is off-limits except for emergencies. After breakfast, guests are encouraged to get out and explore the ruggedly picturesque surroundings. You can climb to the top of the tower, which rises 103 feet above the water, or tramp the 53 acres of hardwoods and meadows and 4,500 feet of Lake Superior shoreline.

One guest room is in the base of the lighthouse and the others are in the former lightkeeper's house attached to the tower. There is plenty of log furniture and a large collection of watercolor paintings, photographs, and other works by local artists. In the living room, guests gather every evening in front of the fireplace to drink wine and listen to Linda and Jeff discuss lighthouse history and local lore.

Address: *3 Lighthouse Rd., Big Bay, MI 49808, tel. 906/345-9957.*
Accommodations: *5 double rooms with baths, 2 doubles share 1 bath.*
Amenities: *Sauna.*
Rates: *$95–$165; Continental breakfast, wine served in the evening. No credit cards.*
Restrictions: *No smoking, no pets.*

Eagle's Nest Bed & Breakfast

Eagle's Nest is perched on a 300-foot ridge overlooking Lake Superior and the village of Eagle River on the western edge of the Keweenaw Peninsula. Three-quarters of a mile from the nearest neighbor, the property includes 20 acres of mixed hardwoods and pine, a stocked trout pond, and several hiking trails. Linda LaMotte, a U.P. native who summered here as a child, sold her Atlanta flying school in 1980 and bought the large, two-story cedar-log house, which was built in 1858 at the start of the copper mining boom. She also owns the Eagle River Inn, the sole business in the four-block downtown. Despite the growing presence of snowmobilers and wealthy developers, Eagle River remains a perfect retreat.

The living room, last redone in the 1940s, has mohair furniture, a hardwood floor, stained-glass windows, brass wall lamps, and a hand-carved birch fireplace. In the evening, Popov, Linda's 110-pound half-wolf, half-malamute guardian, plops in front of the 6-foot-tall Royal Oak parlor stove in the adjacent Humboldt Room. The guest rooms' cedar furniture is timeless in design, if not in fact.

Address: *Garden City Rd. (Box 14), Eagle River, MI 49924, tel. 906/337-4441.*
Accommodations: *3 double rooms share 2 baths.*
Amenities: *Phone in hallway.*
Rates: *$55–$65; full breakfast. MC, V.*
Restrictions: *No pets.*

Pinewood Lodge

J erry and Jenny Krieg sold their electronics store in Milwaukee to build this massive three-story log house in 1990. Twenty-seven miles east of Marquette on M28, Pinewood Lodge's greatest asset is its enviable location, one of the most coveted in the U.P. It sits on a private beach bordering Lake Superior in an area surrounded by raw natural beauty. There are volleyball nets set up in the sand and plenty of other recreational options, including swimming, and trails for cross-country skiing, snowmobiling, biking, and hiking.

The large, airy rooms feature pine paneling and the ubiquitous log furniture; a sitting room has a TV, VCR, stereo, and fireplace. A filling breakfast that typically includes waffles, Yorkshire pudding, and baked Finnish pancakes served with fruit is taken in a sun-filled dining room. Of the guest rooms, the two on the third floor are the nicest, offering sweeping views of Lake Superior. A homey loft also overlooks the water and is a favorite gathering spot.

Address: *U.S. 28 (Box 176), Au Train, MI 49806, tel. 906/892–8300.*
Accommodations: *3 double rooms with baths, 3 doubles and 1 single room share 2 baths.*
Amenities: *Hot tub and sauna.*
Rates: *$40–$65; full breakfast. AE, D, MC, V.*
Restrictions: *No smoking indoors, no pets.*

Water Street Inn

F or those infatuated with Great Lakes lore, the Water Street Inn is the perfect place to drop anchor. The sprawling, three-story Queen Anne is in the heart of Sault Ste. Marie, the third oldest city in the United States, and just an hour's drive north of the Mackinac Bridge.

The house, bought by retirees Phyllis and Greg Walker in 1991, has classically elegant accoutrements, including a turret, Tiffany windows, and marble fireplaces. The sometimes whimsical decor is a reflection of the Walkers' travels, with a Columbian sculpture of a rain god sharing space with a Mexican stuffed owl. Phyllis serves "a serious Northern breakfast" of lemon bread, apple butter, oatmeal pancakes, and other delights. The four second-floor guest rooms are comfortable, tidy, and filled with family heirlooms. The front-facing guest rooms have wonderful views of the river and the twinkling lights of Canada. From the wraparound porch or the gazebo, guests can relax and watch freighters slowly pass on the St. Mary's River.

Address: *140 E. Water St., Sault Ste. Marie, MI 49783, tel. 906/632–1900 or 800/236–1904.*
Accommodations: *4 double rooms with baths.*
Amenities: *Portable phone.*
Rates: *$70–$85; full breakfast. MC, V.*
Restrictions: *No smoking indoors, no pets.*

Mackinac Island

In 1780, fearful of an American attack during the Revolutionary War, the British moved an entire town from what is now known as Mackinaw City over icy waters to a remote island. The townspeople could never have envisioned that today nearly 1 million visitors flock to Mackinac Island (pronounced "Mac-i-naw, like the city) each year to absorb its rich history and natural beauty.

Mackinac Island is between three of the Great Lakes (Huron, Michigan, and Superior) in the Straits of Mackinac, where Huron and Michigan join. The region played a vital role in the northern frontier beginning in the 1600s, long before the island was settled by the British. The Chippewa supplied the French with furs in exchange for such items as blankets, cooking utensils, and weapons. Originally called Michilimacinac, after an Indian word meaning "great turtle," Mackinac Island, with its rising bluffs, looks like the back of a turtle.

In 1815, after more than 30 years of military struggles, Mackinac Island became a permanent part of U.S. territory, and in 1875 Congress created the nation's second national park on the island. The land, which now comprises more than 80% of the island's 2,200 acres, was later transferred to Michigan and became its first state park.

The island's military history and late 1800s culture come to life inside the walls of Fort Mackinac. This historic fort has been painstakingly restored (14 of its buildings are more than 200 years old), and a tour is one of the best ways to learn about the island. Be forewarned, however; the fort's cannons are fired numerous times throughout the day as part of dramatic reenactments, and although islanders have learned to take this in stride, more than a few visitors have been shaken by the blasts.

Aside from these noises, Mackinac Island has a romantic and timeless tranquility about it, and visiting is akin to traveling back about 100 years. As you approach the island, a foghorn sounds in the distance, and magnificent Victorian homes overlooking the harbor come into view. The only signs of the 20th century are the catamaran that ferries you to the island or the five-seater airplanes that fly over from St. Ignace. There are no bridges leading from the mainland. The beautiful Mackinac Bridge, an experience in itself to travel over or look at, connects only Michigan's upper and lower peninsulas.

Three different boat companies operate from the towns on either side of the bridge: Mackinaw City on the lower peninsula and St. Ignace on the upper peninsula. The ferry lines are comparable in schedule and price, and competition is stiff—so stiff, in fact, that, after exiting I-75, the main highway leading north from central Michigan, you'll start seeing individual ticket booths a good 10 minutes before you get to the docks.

Plan to leave your car behind when you board the ferry, since no motorized vehicles are allowed on Mackinac Island. (Parking is free for day visits and just a few dollars for overnight.) Once you've landed, step lightly, since the main mode of transportation is the horse-drawn carriage; more than 600 horses inhabit the island during the summer months. Visitors can also rent bikes or walk to almost anywhere on the island. Bicycle valets will deliver your luggage from the ferry docks, leaving you to peruse the island at your leisure.

Main Street winds along the harbor, and although "downtown" is not exactly peaceful, the sounds of clomping horses and bicycle bells add some charm to the noise of the crowds during peak season (July and August). A wealth of tourist attractions, such as fudge shops (an island specialty and source of the name "fudgie," humorously bestowed upon tourists), souvenir and gift shops, galleries, restaurants, bike rentals, and carriage companies, makes this the busiest spot on the island. Watching the hustle and bustle of the ferry handlers is a fascinating reminder of a bygone era, since most everything needed on the island (food, supplies, horses, and so forth) is brought by ferry from the mainland and then delivered by carriage or bicycle to its destination.

The island is only 8.1 miles in circumference, and a paved road circles the perimeter. A bicycle ride or carriage tour around the island is a popular way to enjoy the natural beauty of Mackinac Island State Park, which provides unique limestone formations and breathtaking views of the Great Lakes.

Mackinac Island has an active year-round community of about 600 residents. The tourist season runs from mid-May to mid-October, and most accommodations are booked far in advance for July and August. Known worldwide for events such as the Lilac Festival in June and Stone Skipping Contest in July, Mackinac attracts an international set. September offers a calmer pace, since crowds have diminished and the weather is still warm during the day but cooler at night, wonderful for sound sleeping. Most of the attractions are only open during the tourist season, and until the whole collegiate work force arrives on the island, don't be surprised to find your innkeeper still finishing up some last-minute details.

Places to Go, Sights to See

Beaumont Memorial (Market St., tel. 906/847–3328). Dr. William Beaumont is renowned for his landmark experiments on the human digestive system in the 1820s. Educational displays tell of his experiments and discoveries and the conditions under which he worked.

British Landing Nature Center (tel. 906/847–3328). On the northwest side of the island, the center has exhibits that provide information about the night of July 16, 1812, when 36 British soldiers and hundreds of Indian allies landed and captured Fort Mackinac without firing a single shot.

Colonial Michilimackinac (tel. 906/847–3328). Located in Mackinaw City, this is a reconstruction of the original mainland fort and surrounding frontier fur-trading village, which was founded in 1715.

Fort Mackinac (E. Bluff Rd., tel. 906/847–3328). Costumed interpreters demonstrate 19th-century blacksmithing and stage dramatic reenactments. Also of interest are the exhibits, artifacts, and a Discovery Room for children, where they can try on period clothing and "fire" muskets. Fourteen of the restored buildings are more than 200 years old.

Grand Hotel (Cadotte Ave., tel. 906/847–3331). One of the island's premier landmarks, the Grand Hotel first opened in 1887 and is considered one of the world's finest resorts. Visitors may stroll on its 700-foot veranda, visible from the mainland; partake of afternoon tea; meander through its gardens; peruse the historical photo collection; or even swim in the pool, built especially for the 1946 Esther Williams film *This Time for Keeps.* A special $5 guest pass must be purchased by any visitor who is not a hotel guest.

Indian Dormitory (Main St., tel. 906/847–3328). Native American culture displays and period settings are enhanced by live interpretations of life in the 1800s.

Mackinac Island State Park. A tour of the park, from Arch Rock (a natural limestone arch that stands almost 150 feet above the water and 50 feet across) to Wildflower Trail (a small grove of wildflowers that shows a beautiful array of colors) is a must, especially since it encompasses nearly 80% of the island.

Mill Creek (tel. 906/847–3328). Located on the mainland, in Mackinaw City, this is an authentically reconstructed, operating, water-powered sawmill. Founded in 1790, it supplied lumber for many of the buildings on Mackinac Island.

Ste. Anne's Church (Huron St.). Still an active parish, the church is an architectural beauty built in 1874.

Stuart House Museum (Market St., tel. 906/847–3328). Housed in John Jacob Astor's American Fur Company warehouse, which was built in 1810, the museum depicts the history of the bygone fur-trading era.

Restaurants

The Pub Oyster Bar (Main St., tel. 906/847–3454) serves up seafood chowder, homemade pizza, and, of course, oysters. The elegant, 100-foot-long, lunch buffet served daily at the **Grand Hotel** (Cadotte Ave., tel. 906/847–3331) includes a large selection of entrées and great desserts; dinner is also served, and a $5 discount to offset the guest pass is applied to the restaurant bill. In the Iroquois Hotel, **The Carriage House** (Main St., tel. 906/847–3321) offers gourmet dining overlooking the water; a specialty is Great Lakes whitefish. At **Horn's Gaslight Bar** (Main St., tel. 906/847–6154), you can enjoy burgers, sizzle steaks, and, at dinner, Mexican food accompanied by a piano player and dancing.

Tourist Information

Mackinac Island Chamber of Commerce (Mackinac Island, MI 49757, tel. 906/847–6418); **Mackinac State Historic Parks Visitors Center** (Main St., Box 370 G, Mackinac Island, MI 49757, tel. 906/847–3328); **Michigan Travel Bureau** (333 S. Capitol, Lansing, MI 48933, tel. 800/543–2937).

Bay View at Mackinac

Owner Doug Yoder's great-great-grandfather, Dr. John R. Bailey, a surgeon at Fort Mackinac, would be pleased. Doug, who works in the music industry in Nashville during the winter, has painstakingly restored this 1890s house, which has been in his family for more than 100 years. The two-year renovation, which cost a half-million dollars, has made the most of the home's elegance.

The sitting room's tin ceiling and fireplace and the refinished wood moldings throughout the house have kept their charm. The wraparound porch is decked out in green and white with skirted, glass-topped tables. Panoramic views of the water and abundant bright begonias and geraniums make this a perfect place to enjoy late afternoon refreshments.

Guest rooms feel more modern than Victorian as a result of the renovation, but bright new fabrics, skirted tables, and flower-garden wallpaper borders mixed with authentic period pieces, such as an antique, inlaid mahogany headboard, create a nice blend of old and new. Marble floors and ceramic tile in the bathrooms add a classic touch. All the curtains and bedspreads have been handmade for the inn, as was the carpeting throughout the hallways and stairs. Three different designs were cut and laid together to create a beautiful rose-colored and flowered carpet.

Newlyweds and chronic romantics will enjoy the third-floor Bridal Suite, which has a whirlpool bath and a private balcony overlooking the harbor. There have already been several weddings on that balcony.

Upon arrival you'll discover a sampling of fudge in your room in true Mackinac Island tradition. In the morning you'll awaken to the aroma of Doug's Bay View Blend Coffee and home-baked pastries.

Doug explains that some finishing touches are needed to make the renovation complete, but as you step onto the second-floor balcony, you are greeted by a view of the Straits of Mackinac so spectacular that the finishing touches don't really matter.

Address: *Summer: Main St. (Box 448), Mackinac Island, MI 49757, tel. 906/847–3295. Winter: 920 Cantrel Ave., Nashville, TN 37215, tel. 615/298–2759.*
Accommodations: *18 double rooms with baths.*
Amenities: *Ceiling fans in rooms, TV in sitting room on request, conference room, gallery and marine supply store; short-term docking facilities.*
Rates: *$95–$165; Continental breakfast. MC, V.*
Restrictions: *No pets; 2-night minimum on weekends, closed Oct. 15– Apr.*

Haan's 1830 Inn

The charm of Haan's 1830 Inn is not just in its appearance but in the owners themselves. Vernon and Joy Haan share business responsibilities at the inn with their son Nicholas and his wife, Nancy. Even their three-year-old granddaughter lends a hand by folding napkins before breakfast at the 12-foot harvest table.

The house was built up around the foundations of a log cabin dragged over the ice from the mainland during the Revolutionary War. In the mid-1800s, it was the home of Fort Mackinac officer and onetime island mayor Colonel Preston. The white columns in front give evidence that the inn is the oldest Greek Revival home in what was the Northwest Territory; it was also the first B&B on Mackinac Island.

The Haans have turned what could have seemed old and shabby into someplace warm and inviting. Guest rooms are named after figures from the island's past and are tastefully decorated with a variety of antiques, including an elegant burled-walnut headboard. Taller guests should avoid the Reverend William Ferry and Pere Marquette rooms since the ceilings in that part of the house are unusually low, probably to retain heat in the winter.

A fascinating centerpiece in the sitting room is a large black safe originally used by one of fur trader John Jacob Astor's agents. Original 1830 prints hang on the wall, and there is a large dark cherry desk that was built and used in Fort Mackinac. The second-story porch tucked under the trees is a great place to hide out and absorb the island's atmosphere; for those looking for more excitement, the island's downtown is a mere three blocks away.

The Haans clearly enjoy running the inn. The marble-top breakfast buffet brims with delicious coffee cakes, muffins, and jams to be enjoyed at your leisure in front of a crackling fire in the dining room. Vernon is a history buff with a special talent for bringing history to life. In fact, you won't need to spend money on any of the island tours; Vernon is far more interesting and lively. The Haan in the inn's name, like the 1830, is clearly not just for effect.

Address: *Summer: Huron St. (Box 123), Mackinac Island, MI 49757, tel. 906/847–6244. Winter: 1134 Geneva St., Lake Geneva, WI 53147, tel. 414/248–9244.*
Accommodations: *4 double rooms with baths, 2 doubles share a bath, 1 housekeeping suite.*
Amenities: *Ceiling fans, chocolates, vouchers for cocktails at local restaurants in rooms.*
Rates: *$80–$110; Continental breakfast. No credit cards.*
Restrictions: *No smoking indoors, no pets; closed Nov.–Apr.*

The Inn on Mackinac

Trying to find all 13 colors on the inn's exterior, beyond the purple, pink, green, and peach, is a favorite pastime of guests. Assistant general manager Kelly Irby says that most people can only identify five or six. The bright colors, inspired by Victorian homes like those of 1920s San Francisco, make the Inn on Mackinac one of the more eye-catching houses on the island.

Built in 1867, with the back section added later, the house used to be called the Chateau Beaumont in memory of the fort's famous army surgeon, William Beaumont. In 1988, the inn was remodeled to emphasize its quaint Victorian charm while providing a number of modern amenities.

The larger, more expensive rooms in the front, older section of the house are furnished with charm: cherry armoires, white shutters in the windows overlooking the street, and white lace swags over the beds. Although the rooms in the back section are comfortable and also redecorated, they lack the view and are smaller. Request a room with a bay window (they can be found in both sections) since they add a sense of spaciousness to the room.

Although you are unlikely to meet up with owners Pat and Alice Pulte (they also own the Murray Hotel), a complete staff is on hand to answer any questions you might have about the island or the inn. Because of its size, the inn may lack some of the intimacy of other B&Bs, but it makes up for that in style and convenience. Although not right in the center of town, it is certainly close.

A sense of comaraderie is evident as soon as you step out onto the expansive wraparound porch on the second floor, where guests gather throughout the day. In fact, the outdoor areas at the inn are as enjoyable as the rooms. At street level, a lattice-covered arch leads to a charming brick patio surrounded by gardens. This level, which includes the lobby and dining room, was created during remodeling by digging out the home's basement and adding French doors all the way around. You can eat breakfast inside or on the patio or sample some of the Pultes' homemade fudge, made fresh daily and sold in the lobby.

Address: *Summer: Main St., Mackinac Island, MI 49757, tel. 906/847–6348 or 800/462–2462. Winter: Box 7706, Ann Arbor, MI 48107, tel. 313/665–5750.*
Accommodations: *44 double rooms with baths.*
Amenities: *Air-conditioning, TV in rooms, handicapped accessible.*
Rates: *$88–$160; Continental breakfast. MC, V.*
Restrictions: *No pets; closed Nov.–Apr.*

Metivier Inn

You can't miss the Metivier Inn, located on a quiet section of Market Street one block from the hustle and bustle of Main Street. Beautiful landscaping and a white picket fence along the sidewalk in front of the house make this inn a standout.

The house, built in 1877, was a single-family home until 1984, when it opened as a B&B. Originally it had only 13 guest rooms, but recent renovations have added more on the third floor. The back deck off that floor, overlooking the magnificent Grand Hotel and golf course, is very peaceful and popular for weddings. A side porch, accessible from four rooms on the second floor, is perfect for a group of people looking for some shared privacy. The front porch runs the full width of the house and is nicely furnished with the owners' personal collection of antique white wicker. In fact, soft colors and antique-style furniture throughout give the inn a simple, clean, and tasteful look.

Various names from Mackinac Island's past adorn the doors to each guest room. Because of its larger size and unique view, the John Jacob Astor Room, in the turret at the front of the house, is one of the nicest. An antique sleigh bed adorns one of the main-floor rooms, or, for a romantic night, try one of the four rooms outfitted with a four-poster canopy bed.

A Continental breakfast, brought in from a local bakery each morning, is served in the lobby, which, although somewhat sparse, is nonetheless comfortable; it is furnished with couches, chairs, and a woodstove that adds atmosphere when stoked up on cooler days or in the evenings.

Metivier is efficiently run and quiet, but it lacks some of the personal touches that can make for a unique stay. Although it is owned by two couples, Ken and Diane Neyer and Mike and Jane Bacon, the inn is professionally managed by Michael and Janice Graves, who live on the premises and seem very responsive to their guests needs without being intrusive.

Guests can also enjoy a visit to Biddle House, a restored turn-of-the century home, right next door.

Address: *Summer: Market St. (Box 285), Mackinac Island, MI 49757, tel. 906/847–6234. Winter: tel. 616/627–2055.*
Accommodations: *20 double rooms with baths, 1 housekeeping suite.*
Amenities: *Woodstove and cable TV in sitting room, ice machines on each floor, conference room.*
Rates: *$115–$165; Continental breakfast. D, MC, V.*
Restrictions: *No pets; closed Nov.–Apr.*

Bogan Lane Inn

Trish Martin grew up in this home on Bogan Lane, and, even though the house shows its age in some areas (it was built around 1850), she has made it so cozy that her guests will feel at home as well. The location just off Huron Street, three blocks from downtown, is close enough to enjoy the island and far enough away to hear only the foghorns at night.

Of the guest rooms, the Porch Room, with charming quilts and curtains, offers a cozy retreat, although it has only twin beds. The Rose Room, next door, is furnished with a comfortable antique double bed.

As the only year-round B&B on Mackinac Island, Bogan Lane Inn is perfect for a cross-country-ski weekend or midwinter getaway, and Trish's home-baked pastries warm up even the coldest morning. Whether enjoying a fire in the living room, playing one of the many board games kept on hand, or getting the scoop from Trish on the island's secret spots, you'll feel like you're staying at your grandmother's cottage.

Address: *Bogan La. (Box 482), Mackinac Island, MI 49757, tel. 906/847-3439.*
Accommodations: *2 double rooms with baths, 2 doubles share 1 bath.*
Amenities: *Ceiling fans in guest rooms.*
Rates: *$50-$70; Continental breakfast. No credit cards.*
Restrictions: *No smoking indoors, no pets.*

Cloghaun Bed & Breakfast

Baskets of bright red begonias adorning both balconies are the first things you see at this Market Street B&B. Inside though, it's the century-old family treasures, beamed ceilings, arched windows and doors, the butter churn by the fireplace, and rosebud china set out for breakfast that create the relaxed and charming atmosphere at the Cloghaun (pronounced "Clawhahn").

The original owners, Thomas and Bridgett Donnelly, left Cloghaun in Ireland during the great famine of 1848 and settled here. The house, built in 1884 for their growing family, is still owned by descendants James Bond and his wife. The property is managed by Chris and Ray Clark, who run it in such an inviting manner you'd think it was their own.

All the rooms interconnect and can be turned into suites if desired. Even those without private baths have sinks. The sitting room is full of books, historical tidbits, jigsaw puzzles, games, and even a box of toys for the younger set.

Address: *Summer: Market St. (Box 203), Mackinac Island, MI 49757, tel. 906/847-3885. Winter: 1063 Sunningdale, Grosse Pointe Woods, MI 48236, tel. 313/885-4547.*
Accommodations: *5 double rooms with baths, 3 doubles share 2 baths.*
Amenities: *Ceiling fans in rooms; TV/VCR in sitting room.*
Rates: *$65-$95; Continental breakfast. No credit cards.*
Restrictions: *No smoking indoors, no pets; closed Oct. 15-May 15.*

Murray Hotel

The Murray Hotel, dubbed the "centennial bed-and-breakfast inn," has been providing hospitality to visitors for more than 100 years. Owned by islanders Pat and Alice Pulte (they also own the Inn on Mackinac), it has a distinctly Victorian air, enhanced by the wide balustrade staircase and wicker-filled lobby. The guest rooms are clean but simply decorated with floral wallpaper borders, wicker furniture, and a few antique dressers and headboards.

The Murray is on Main Street, in the heart of Mackinac Island's downtown. This means noise from morning to night during the summer season, but it's a great spot for people-watching and for being at the heart of the comings and goings.

With a professional staff running the daily operations, dining rooms, delicatessen, cocktail lounge, and a more formal check-in procedure, the Murray feels somewhat more like a quaint 19th-century hotel than a B&B retreat.

Address: *Summer: Main St. (Box 476), Mackinac Island, MI 49757, tel. 906/847–3361 or 800/462–2546. Winter: Box 7706, Ann Arbor, MI 48107, tel. 313/665–5750.*
Accommodations: *69 double rooms with baths.*
Amenities: *Air-conditioning and TV in all rooms, whirlpool bath in 2 rooms.*
Rates: *$70–$150; Continental breakfast. MC, V.*
Restrictions: *No pets; closed Oct. 15–Apr.*

1900 Market Street Inn

Facing Marquette Park, this recently renovated turn-of-the-century house was formerly a private home owned by the Triskett family. Island residents and sisters Sandra and Deborah Orr teamed up to convert it into a B&B in 1991.

The downstairs guest room is elegant and romantic, with high ceilings, a fireplace, a piano, and a beautiful four-poster bed. The woodwork up the wide staircase leading to the second-floor rooms was beautifully restored, and each room, from the chintz to the wallpaper, carefully adheres to coordinated color schemes, from soft pastels in one to deep burgundy and green in another.

Although very clean and modern, the inn itself is relatively small, with only a sparse lobby and tiny front porch to gather in. Coffee and danish are served in the lobby each morning, or, for those who want more variety, there's a complimentary Continental breakfast two blocks away at the Pub Oyster Bar.

Address: *Market St. (Box 315), Mackinac Island, MI 49757, tel. 906/847–3811.*
Accommodations: *7 double rooms with baths.*
Amenities: *Ceiling fans, cable TV in rooms, handicapped accessible.*
Rates: *$85–$115; Continental breakfast. MC, V.*
Restrictions: *No pets; 3-night minimum during boat races, closed mid-Oct.–mid-May.*

Grand Traverse Region
Including Traverse City

The Traverse City Convention and Visitors Bureau promotes Traverse City as "a Great Lakes paradise," and it may not be far from the truth. More than 250 miles of Lake Michigan shoreline and numerous inland lakes contribute to this area's natural beauty and recreational opportunities. The region that Chicago businessman Perry Hannah built as a lumber empire in the late 1800s has long been a popular vacation destination for Midwesterners. Over the past 10 years, it has gained national prominence as a convention area. It is also host to the National Cherry Festival.

Its popularity is most obvious during the summer (May through Labor Day), when the population swells from just under 30,000 to 200,000. Traffic jams can be annoying, and reservations for weekend lodging are a must. Winter also attracts visitors, since the terrain is perfect for cross-country skiers and four of the Midwest's top downhill ski resorts are within an hour's drive. Luckily, winter crowds are not overwhelming. Fall, which brings the brilliant foliage to the hardwood trees, and spring, when cherry orchards are in full blossom, also offer a special beauty, and crowds are not as intense.

Three counties, Leelanau, Grand Traverse, and Benzie, make up what Michiganders refer to as the Grand Traverse region. It stretches north from Frankfort, up the east side of Lake Michigan to the tip of Leelanau Peninsula, back down to Traverse City, and east through a town with the unlikely name of Acme. The Old Mission Peninsula juts north from Traverse City, dividing the waters of Grand Traverse Bay into the East and West bays. While East Bay is home to a wide variety of chain motels and restaurants, it also claims some of the cleanest beaches in the area. The growth of West Bay has been more carefully monitored, so

*there are numerous public beaches, marinas, parks, and
a bike path that stretches the full width of the harbor.*

*Traverse City, at the foot of West Bay, is considered the
metropolitan hub of northwestern Michigan and is the
area's central destination point. With a year-round
population of just under 20,000, it offers an unusually
strong mix of cultural activities, and a huge selection of
shops for a town its size. Among the city's entertainment
offerings are a fine-arts museum, professional theater,
symphony orchestra, zoo, steam-power passenger train, ski
area, active arts council and community playhouse, public
recreational center (complete with lighted walking and
biking paths, indoor ice rink, swimming pool, and tennis
courts); it also has a college. Traverse City, however, has
maintained an appealing small-town feel: Tree-lined
historic neighborhoods, a downtown waterfront, regularly
held open-air block parties and street sales, and people
with a well-deserved reputation for friendliness help keep
the city bustling, but accessible.*

*Myriad opportunities for fun are not confined to Traverse
City. Touring Old Mission and Leelanau peninsulas is
a perfect way to spend a day. Acres of generations-old
farms and wineries mingle with art galleries, restaurants,
shops, antiques stores, parks, and beaches. The climate is
favorable for farming, and the area boasts abundant
orchards and five excellent wineries offering free tastings
and tours. Visitors can also play golf in the Grand
Traverse area, on courses designed by Jack Nicklaus and
Arnold Palmer. The nationally renowned Interlochen
Center for the Arts, just south of Traverse City, hosts
a variety of entertainment, which includes the Canadian
Brass, the Tokyo String Quartet, the Red Star Red Army
Chorus and Dance Ensemble, and Peter, Paul, and Mary.*

Places to Go, Sights to See

Dennos Museum Center (1701 E. Front St., Traverse City, tel. 616/922–1055), built in 1991, contains three galleries that hold exhibits from around the country and displays a permanent collection of Inuit art, said to be one of the largest in the United States. There are also hands-on exhibits for children, a small theater, and a 367-seat auditorium, home to the summer stock Michigan Ensemble Theatre.

Grand Traverse Lighthouse (M201, just north of Northport on Leelanau Peninsula, tel. 616/386–5503) was built in 1858, has been restored, and is now a living museum. Descendants of the former lighthouse keeper live in the front half of the building; the remaining space is devoted to pictures and displays—including a Fresnel lens used in the lighthouse—testifying to the rugged life of a keeper.

Gwen Frostic Prints (5140 River Rd., Benzonia, tel. 616/882–5505) is on a 280-acre nature preserve 30 minutes southwest of Traverse City. The stone studio, library, and printing facility were created by popular naturalist, author, and artist Gwen Frostic. Frostic's beautifully simple nature prints and poetry are reproduced in books, stationery, and other paper products and shipped around the world. Visitors may find it fascinating to watch the press at work or take delight in wandering around the grounds.

Interlochen Center for the Arts (M137, tel. 616/276–9221) has earned international recognition as a leading center for the development and training of talented and gifted students and as an advocate of the arts. It operates as a private high school during the school year, with students from around the world, and hosts a music camp for all ages during the summer. Throughout the year, student and faculty exhibits and performances are held along with those of internationally acclaimed artists. The 1,200 acres of scenic forest that make up the campus are on the edge of Green Lake in Interlochen, just south of Traverse City. The campus is open to visitors year-round.

Leelanau Sands Casino and **Grand Traverse Band Bingo Palace** (M22, just north of Suttons Bay, Peshawbestown, tel. 616/271–3538) are operated by the Grand Traverse Band of Ottawa and Chippewa Indians. They offer the only legal gambling opportunity in the region, under the terms of their agreement with the federal government, because they are on an Indian reservation. Visitors can try their luck at anything from blackjack and poker to slot machines and bingo, where stakes can run as high as $25,000.

The **Manitou Islands,** off the coast of Lake Michigan near Leland, offer hiking and camping made enjoyable by the enchanting scenery. Motorized tours are also available. Both North and South Manitou islands are under the jurisdiction of the National Park Service. For information on day trips and evening cocktail cruises leaving from Fishtown, in Leland, call *Manitou Island Transit* (tel. 616/256–9061).

The **Music House** (M31, 2 mi. north of Acme, tel. 616/938–9300) is an
emporium and museum offering a magical experience. Wander through
replica villages and listen to the working displays of automated music
machines, pipe organs, and jukeboxes as well as the Amaryllis, a 30-foot-wide
dance organ from the Victoria Palace Ballroom in Belgium. Exhibits of
record collections, early radios, television sets, and phonographs provide an
amusing and lively history of the sounds of music.

Sleeping Bear Dunes National Lakeshore (tel. 616/326–5134), one of the
world's largest moving sand dunes, towers over the waters of Lake Michigan
and Glen Lakes. The area is part of the National Lakeshore Park and also
includes the Manitou Islands. A scenic drive through the park provides
spectacular views of the dunes, Lake Michigan, and the Glen Lakes. There's
a dune climb, for hearty visitors, and plenty of other areas to explore on
foot. Park information is available at the Philip A. Hart Visitors Center, on
Route M–72 in Empire, which includes a minimuseum and an excellent
multimedia presentation.

Traverse City Opera House (112½ E. Front St., tel. 616/941–8082), built in
1891, is one of only 18 opera houses remaining out of the 127 built in
Michigan. This Victorian landmark is listed on both the National and the
State Registers of Historic Sites. Architecture lovers will appreciate the
meticulously restored vaulted ceiling and elaborate decorative moldings. The
original curtain is still in place, and vintage advertisements and a landscape
mural add considerably to the Victorian ambience. There is no charge to tour
the opera house, which is often host to a variety of community events.

Beaches

In this region known for its attractive shoreline, the beaches are too
numerous to list, but rest assured that there is a beach for everyone and no
charge for enjoying them. Such city beaches as **Clinch Park** and **West End,**
within walking distance of downtown Traverse City, come complete with
lifeguards and refreshment stands, marinas, and nearby establishments
renting out boats. At the remote **Pyramid Point** and **Good Harbor** beaches
(off Route M–22, on southwest side of Leelanau Peninsula), you can enjoy
building a fire while watching the sunset on Lake Michigan. Parks with
beaches include **Interlochen State Park** (M137 via U.S. 31, tel. 616/775–9727)
and **Traverse City State Park** (Munson Ave., tel. 616/775–9727).

Restaurants

On the Old Mission Peninsula are two very different restaurants in the same
big house: **The Bowery** (13512 Peninsula Dr., tel. 616/223–4333), the more
casual of the two, is known for its barbecued ribs and large beer selection,
and **Bowers Harbor Inn** (13512 Peninsula Dr., tel. 616/223–4222) offers
romantic dining overlooking the bay. Visitors may want to inquire about the
resident ghost. **Old Mission Tavern** (17015 Center Rd., tel. 616/223–7280) is
filled with an eclectic collection of works by local artists, which are for sale.

In Traverse City, two elegant restaurants that serve regional cuisine with views of the bay are **Top of the Park** (300 E. State St., tel. 616/946–5000), on the 10th floor of the Park Place Hotel, and **Windows** (7677 W. Bayshore Dr., tel. 616/941–0100), 2 miles north of town. For a taste of the old lumbering era, try **Dill's Olde Towne Saloon** (423 S. Union St., tel. 616/947–7534), home in the summer to the musical Golden Garter Revue, or **Sleder's Tavern** (71 Randolph St., tel. 616/947–9213), in Slabtown, where you are presented a gift if you kiss the moose head. On the Leelanau Peninsula, the **Riverside Inn** (302 River St., tel. 616/256–9971), overlooking the Leland River in Leland, offers fresh whitefish, French cuisine, and an extensive wine selection. In Suttons Bay, you can try cozy **Boone's Prime Time** (102 St. Joseph's St., tel. 616/271–6688) for steak, fish, or burgers, or the gourmet **Hattie's Bar and Grille** (111 St. Joseph's St., tel. 616/271–6222), where diners can enjoy an eclectic menu ranging from risotto to veal chops while sitting amidst an art exhibit that changes monthly.

Tourist Information

Traverse City Area Chamber of Commerce (202 E. Grandview Pkwy., Traverse City, MI 49684, tel. 616/947–5075); **Traverse City Convention and Visitors Bureau** (415 Munson Ave., Suite 200, Traverse City, MI 49684, tel. 800/872–8377, fax 616/947–2621).

Centennial Inn

I n the heart of Leelanau County's rolling farmland, the Centennial Inn was designated a Michigan Centennial Farm by the state's Historical Commission. In the same family for more than 100 years, the farm got its first new owners when Karl and JoAnne Smith bought it four years ago.

The Smiths have carefully restored the two-story clapboard farmhouse, built in 1865. The original barn and two outbuildings are still in excellent condition. The smaller one has been turned into a gift shop, featuring antiques and folk art created by local artisans, as well as JoAnne's baskets and Karl's reproduction furniture. Since the inn is about 6 miles from the small town of Lake Leelanau, guests will need to drive a short way to find restaurants and shops.

As you approach the house, you'll come across a glistening sundial. The lettering around it reads, "Grow old along with me, the best is yet to be." The Centennial Inn is proof that what is old can also be very good. On the front porch, pots of red-blossomed geraniums are placed around a white bench, creating a colorful frame for the entrance.

The Smiths have decorated the farm in Shaker style, yet their loving attention makes what could seem sparse feel warm and inviting. A scattering of Oriental rugs complement the glow of the refinished,

original hardwood floors. A candle chandelier hangs over the rough-hewn pine table in the dining room, and an elaborate pewter collection is displayed above the buffet. The parlor, one of the coziest spots, is perfect for reading, watching TV, or just enjoying the country fireplace.

The guest rooms continue the Shaker theme. The front room downstairs has a four-poster bed with a white lace canopy and homemade white quilt. Every detail harmonizes, down to the blue-and-white checkered curtains in the window and the old crockery on the tables.

A deluxe Continental breakfast is more than enough to fill you up. In the cooler months, breakfast can be enjoyed in the cozy dining room, but during the summer, either of two outside areas makes a perfect eating spot: The deck on the west side overlooks a big birch tree and apple orchards, and, on the east side, there's a red-brick patio with twig furniture. A swing in the back overlooks acres of unspoiled rolling land: The peaceful sight can take you back 100 years.

Address: *Rte. 1 (Box 251), Lake Lee-lanau, MI 49653, tel. 616/271-6460.*
Accommodations: *3 doubles share 1 bath.*
Amenities: *Nordic ski trails.*
Rates: *$55; Continental breakfast. MC, V.*
Restrictions: *No smoking, no pets.*

Linden Lea

A small and enchanting spot on the shore of a crystal-clear inland lake, Linden Lea is, as one of its owners describes it, reminiscent of scenes in the movie *On Golden Pond.* Country roads wind their way to the bed-and-breakfast, and, once you've found it, you won't want to leave.

In 1979, Jim and Vicky McDonnell bought what was a small summer cottage, built around the turn of the century by three Civil War veterans. Vicky remembers, "The original cottage was a mess—rotting floors and everything—but I just kept looking at the view and saying, 'This is it. This is the place.' " Since then, Jim, a former teacher, has skillfully renovated the building and tacked on an addition; five years ago the couple opened their multilevel, contemporary home as a B&B.

The living room, complete with a marble and cherry-wood fireplace from the late 1800s, expansive picture windows, high ceilings, and a large, comfortable sectional sofa, is an inviting place to unwind and enjoy the view. With that in mind, the guest rooms have cushioned window seats that overlook the lake. The rooms, separate from the family quarters, also offer a measure of privacy.

The mix of antiques and treasures creates a warm, eclectic atmosphere. Jim began collecting unusual paperweights on a trip to Scotland, and now more than 30 of the colorful glass pieces adorn a table near the stairway. The handmade dolls and the unusual plates scattered throughout the house are gifts Vicky's mother received while serving as an army nurse. A player piano dating to 1871 is a favorite of guests.

The McDonnells and their daughter, Audrey, are a congenial family. They've been known to offer babysitting services and invite guests to join the family for dinner on a cold winter night when the prospect of curling up in front of the fireplace seems more appealing than braving the elements to find a restaurant.

The breakfast menu varies, and guests may be treated to such delights as quiches, freshly baked peach puffs, chocolate-chip banana muffins, and stuffed French toast. After breakfast, guest can take the rowboat to explore one of Long Lake's many islands.

Address: *279 S. Long Lake Rd., Traverse City, MI 49684, tel. 616/943-9182.*
Accommodations: *2 double rooms share 1 bath.*
Amenities: *TV and VCR in living room; private sand beach.*
Rates: *$60–$70; full breakfast. No credit cards.*
Restrictions: *No smoking, no pets; 2-night minimum May–Oct.*

North Shore Inn

Originally part of a former estate, this rambling, colonial-style home was built in 1946. Dick and Sue Hammersley, who have lived in the area for 20 years, bought the house in 1983, remodeled it, and turned it into their family home. Sue was a preschool teacher at the time, but a few years later, with her family's support, she left her job to convert their home on the shores of picturesque West Bay into a luxurious retreat.

The sit-down gourmet breakfast (Continental buffet if you miss the 9 AM meal) is an experience. Sue varies the menu according to the season, and the portions are generous. There is always a selection of muffins, coffee cake or cobblers, fresh fruit and juice, and a main dish such as pancakes, eggs, or a sausage casserole. Many of the herbs she uses in cooking and the fresh flowers found throughout the house are grown in Sue's English garden, whose colorful accent can be seen from the Wedgewood Suite.

The common room is filled floor to ceiling with books, games, and a collection of old movies for the VCR. A bay window stretches the full height of the room and looks out over the lawn and the beach. The musically inclined can tinkle on a grand piano and a Hammond organ. At the south end of the house, a screened-in porch is a marvelous place to enjoy the outdoors, even on an overcast or rainy day.

All the guest rooms are large; the popular Heritage Room, on the main floor, has a private entrance and a kitchen. Another favorite is the Country Rose Room, which has a pink marble fireplace and a private balcony overlooking the beach. Sue made the Whig Rose quilt that adorns the brass bed. All the guest rooms except the Bayshore Room, which is the smallest, have separate sitting rooms with sofa beds, so two couples may comfortably share a suite. The fireplace in each room has wood laid, ready to light when you arrive.

There is much to enjoy on the premises; but a bonus is the inn's location: only a few minutes' drive from either the restaurants and shopping in the quaint town of Northport or the rugged beauty of Northport State Park.

Address: *12271 N. Northport Point Rd., Northport, MI 49670, tel. 616/386-7111.*
Accommodations: *1 double room with bath, 2 suites, 1 housekeeping suite.*
Amenities: *Morning coffee and tea baskets left outside guest rooms.*
Rates: *$125; full breakfast, afternoon refreshments. MC, V.*
Restrictions: *No smoking, no pets; closed Nov.–Apr.*

Birch Brook

A fieldstone walkway leads to this charming brick ranch, nestled in 2 acres of pastoral land with a brook running through it. Guests fall asleep to the soothing sounds of water just outside their windows. To relax, you may choose among three decks and patios, each with its own view of the woods.

The living room overlooks the back woods and is tastefully decorated with wing chairs, fresh flowers, artwork, and a collection of Hummel figurines. Books and old photos of logging days in the area adorn the rooms. The guest rooms, while small, are warmly furnished with patchwork quilts, a walnut washstand, rocking chairs, and candles. On summer mornings, the green-house is a cheery spot to enjoy breakfast.

Owners George and Lynn Anderson have been Northport residents for many years and are happy to give tips on the best restaurants, places to visit, and fine beaches. The house is within walking distance of Northport, so guests can peruse its shops and galleries and then return easily to the peaceful bed-and-breakfast.

Address: *310 W. 3rd St., Northport, MI 49670, tel. 616/386–5188.*
Accommodations: *2 double rooms share 1 bath.*
Amenities: *Fireplace in living room.*
Rates: *$50–$55; Continental breakfast. No credit cards.*
Restrictions: *No smoking, no pets.*

Bowers Harbor Bed & Breakfast

T his 1870 farmhouse in the heart of the Old Mission Peninsula's cherry country is on 200 feet of private sandy beach on the West Bay. Owners Gary and Mary Ann Verbanic named each guest room in the two-story house after the view seen from its windows: The Harbor View Room looks down on Bowers Harbor; the Pine View Room overlooks 100-year-old white pines. Each is in a classic country style, complete with brass beds, goose-down pillows, and comforters. The living room, which also has a view of the water, contains a large stone fireplace and is a peaceful place to enjoy quiet conversation or a good book.

The house has a wraparound fieldstone porch, a perfect spot to watch northern Michigan's dramatic sun-sets or the morning mist as it rises off the water. You might go for a swim at the beach, though the water can be on the chilly side. For a surer bet, play a game at the tennis courts or have a meal at one of the area's best restaurants, Bowers Harbor Inn, both within walking distance.

Address: *13972 Peninsula Dr., Traverse City, MI 49684, tel. 616/223–7869.*
Accommodations: *3 double rooms share 1½ baths.*
Amenities: *Off-street parking.*
Rates: *$75–$95; full breakfast. No credit cards.*
Restrictions: *No smoking, no pets; 2-night minimum on weekends July–Sept. 15.*

Brookside Inn

Owners Pam and Kirk Lorenz have created a private haven perfect for romantic getaways, and they even promote a couples-only policy to ensure quiet and privacy for their guests.

The guest rooms contain king-size waterbeds, TVs, wood stoves, and whirlpool baths for two. Each also has a different theme: The Garden Room has colorful flowered wallpaper, and the New Orleans Room has wrought-iron window trim and flower boxes.

A full-service restaurant on the main floor of the contemporary, cedar-sided structure offers a large selection of unique dishes, including the popular "stone dinner." Delivered to the table on marble warmed by a square stone heated to 900°, this delicious dish consists of beef or veal, boneless chicken breast, shrimp, and three homemade sauces. A full breakfast is also served in the dining room. The Lorenzes cook all food from scratch, using herbs from their garden and wine from their cellar. Guests are invited to partake in some wine tasting, but alcoholic beverages are not included in the room rate.

Address: *115 N. Michigan Ave., Beulah, MI 49617, tel. 616/882-7271.*
Accommodations: *15 double rooms with baths.*
Amenities: *Saunas, steam baths, and tanning solariums in 3 rooms.*
Rates: *$175-$230; full breakfast and dinner. AE, MC, V.*
Restrictions: *No pets, couples only.*

Cherry Knoll Farm

Dorothy and Percy Cump recently remodeled this 1885 Victorian farmhouse on 115 acres of beautiful rolling farmland a few minutes from Traverse City. The interior is decorated in true country fashion; older furnishings are mixed with authentic antiques.

The family room, with a fireplace, is shared by guests and the Cump family, and the guest rooms are large enough to provide a comfortable upstairs escape if you need some privacy. The bedrooms may not be elegant, but are comfortably furnished and include such special touches as a bedspread crocheted by Dorothy's grandmother and several patchwork quilts that are family heirlooms.

An old-fashioned porch runs across the front of the house and is a great place to watch the sun rise or unwind at the end of the day. Guests are free to walk around the property and pick cherries from the orchard during the summer or look for morel mushrooms in the spring.

Address: *2856 Hammond Rd. E, Traverse City, MI 49684, tel. 616/947-9806.*
Accommodations: *3 double rooms share 2 baths.*
Amenities: *Air-conditioning, restricted-diet breakfasts prepared on request.*
Rates: *$47-$60; full breakfast. MC, V.*
Restrictions: *No smoking indoors, no pets.*

Lee Point Inn

Nestled in the woods at the tip of Lee Point, on the picturesque Leelanau Peninsula, is the home that Fred and Patty Kilbourn built in 1979 and opened as a bed-and-breakfast three years ago. They manage to blend their family life (they have two school-age children) and their business quite well. Guest rooms, one of which has a king-size water bed (great for a bad back), are upstairs with the family bedrooms. To provide privacy, some areas of the house are designated for guests only, but Patty reports that many a visitor ends up curled up on the couch in the Kilbourns's family room off the kitchen, and that's fine with them. The living room, on the south side, has a wood stove and classic country decor.

The dining room leads out onto a multilevel deck, which runs across the back of this large, contemporary home and offers a wonderful view of West Bay. Steps lead down to the private beach, which guests are welcome to use. Cross-country trails start outside the front door, making the inn a great place for beach lovers and ski enthusiasts alike.

Address: *2885 S. Lee Point La. (Rte. 2, Box 374B), Suttons Bay, MI 49682, tel. 616/271–6770.*
Accommodations: *1 double room with bath, 2 doubles share 1 bath.*
Amenities: *Ceiling fans in guest rooms; picnic table, canoe.*
Rates: *$55–$95; full breakfast. MC, V.*
Restrictions: *No smoking indoors, no pets.*

Leelanau Country Inn

John and Linda Sisson opened the Leelanau Country Inn in the spring of 1984, placing more of an emphasis on cuisine than on accommodations. The excellent restaurant features a varying menu, drawn from at least 20 appetizers and nearly 50 entrées, ranging from fresh seafood flown in from both coasts to homemade linguine. There's a Continental breakfast, but guests may want to pay a little extra for the elaborate daily brunch, voted "best in the region" by a local magazine.

The inn is across the street from Little Traverse Lake, in the heart of the Leelanau County countryside. The spacious, two-story clapboard house was built in 1891, and an addition was put on four years later. The

guest rooms are small but nicely decorated in country style with fresh flowers, plants, quilts, and pine furniture. Request any of the four rooms that are a bit larger than the rest. This is not always the quietest bed-and-breakfast, since you can often hear the restaurant and bar well into the night, but memories of your meals may well make up for it.

Address: *149 E. Harbor Hwy., Maple City, MI 49664, tel. 616/228–5060.*
Accommodations: *10 double rooms share 2 baths.*
Amenities: *Off-street parking.*
Rates: *$35–$50; Continental breakfast. AE, MC, V.*
Restrictions: *Smoking in restaurant only, no pets.*

Neahtawanta Inn

In the early 1980s the Neahtawanta Inn started to establish itself as a center for peace research and now houses the nonprofit Neahtawanta Research and Education Center, focusing on "peace, community, sustainable use of resources, and personal-growth issues." Innkeepers Sally Van Vleck and Bob Russell maintain a healthy and quiet environment for the inn's guests. Sally leads a weekly yoga class, where guests are welcome.

The three-story inn was built around the turn of the century as a summer hotel called the Sunrise Inn. Antique beds and dressers from the hotel's early days are still used to furnish the guest rooms, and original washbasins with marble counters are found in two of the rooms. The common area on the first floor is open and airy but almost cluttered with books, newspapers, magazines, and tapes. The room's centerpiece is a sunken fieldstone fireplace.

The inn sits on a bluff overlooking Bowers Harbor on Old Mission Peninsula, about 12 miles north of Traverse City. Lush woods add to its natural, peaceful appeal.

Address: *1308 Neahtawanta Rd., Traverse City, MI 49684, tel. 616/223-7315.*
Accommodations: *4 double rooms share 1 bath, 1 double suite.*
Amenities: *Sauna; private beach.*
Rates: *$55-$65, double suite $110; Continental breakfast. MC, V.*
Restrictions: *No smoking, inquire about pets.*

Old Mill Pond Inn

Michigander David Chrobak has spent his winters running a florist business in the Virgin Islands for more than 20 years, but in the summers he heads back north to live in and operate the Old Mill Pond Inn. Built in 1895, the three-story wood house is tucked away in a beautiful setting and accented by gardens galore, all of them designed by David. The biggest is the side garden, which displays several larger-than-life statues. There is also a thriving rose garden.

A delightful eclectic collection of David's treasures makes up the interior decor. In one room you might find Marilyn Monroe memorabilia mingled with fine crystal; in another, South American tapestries hang next to original 20th-century masterpieces. Even the guest rooms have a relaxed personality all their own. Since David believes that most guests seldom use dressers, he has replaced them with comfortable chairs to give each room a cozy sitting area.

David, an excellent cook, serves a wide variety of food: vegetable quiche, eggs with herbs and mushrooms, crêpes, and fresh fruit.

Address: *202 W. 3rd St., Northport, MI 49670, tel. 616/386-7341.*
Accommodations: *5 double rooms share 2½ baths.*
Amenities: *Bicycles.*
Rates: *$60-$75; full breakfast. MC, V.*
Restrictions: *No pets; closed Nov.-May.*

Little Traverse Bay Region

About five hours north of Detroit and seven hours from Chicago lies the small but lively area around Little Traverse Bay. The two-lane highway running through the region (U.S. 31) winds along the rugged Lake Michigan shoreline, providing constant glimpses of the water. The towns of Charlevoix, Petoskey, and Harbor Springs dominate the area, largely made up of rolling terrain, picturesque farms and orchards, numerous inland lakes, and sleepy summer-resort towns with names like Walloon Lake and Boyne City.

The region has had a varied history. Since the late 1800s, it has served as a lumbering mecca, as an escape from law and order for the likes of Al Capone, and as a playground for elite families from Chicago and Detroit. Ernest Hemingway spent most of his childhood summers at a family home on Walloon Lake and in the small town of Horton Bay, which provided the background for some of his early short stories, most notably the Nick Adams stories and "Up in Michigan."

Today the region has evolved into one of northern Michigan's finest resort areas. Visitors enjoy beaches, golf, and culture galore during the summer months, and crackling fireplaces, magical winter landscapes, and some of the Midwest's best Alpine and Nordic skiing in the winter. Nearby ski areas include Boyne Highlands, Schuss Mountain–Shanty Creek Resort, Nubs Nob, and Boyne Mountain. A variety of annual festivals and art fairs are held throughout the year as well.

The summer season, from Memorial Day weekend through Labor Day, is crowded with tourists from all over the country and around the world. Art galleries and exclusive shops mix comfortably with the delights of small-town Americana: Petoskey's concerts in the park; Charlevoix's colorful Petunia Mile, a stretch of Main Street lined with flowers planted by residents each spring; and evening strolls in town parks and along beaches. Harbor Springs, often referred to as the "Newport of the Midwest," boasts a deep natural harbor and attracts a world-class boating community as well as a growing colony of artists.

Places to Go, Sights to See

The **Bay View Association,** founded by the Methodist Church in 1875, is a well-preserved summer community occupying 400 acres just north of Petoskey. Beautiful turn-of-the-century cottages are part of this historical landmark, where resort life is still enjoyed. Excellent cultural and musical programs abound during the summer months and are open to the public; a full schedule is available at the Petoskey Chamber of Commerce (tel. 616/347–4150).

Beaver Island, settled by descendants of Irish fishermen, is a rustic island with 400 year-round residents. Its claim to fame is that it was once a kingdom. Mormon leader King James Jesse Strang broke away from the church in the 1850s and took some 2,000 followers with him to the island. He was later assassinated by one of his own dissatisfied followers. For information on the two-hour ferry ride from Charlevoix, contact Beaver Island Boat Company (tel. 616/547–2311).

The **Earl Young Houses** were designed and built by a Charlevoix real-estate agent and self-taught architect. These eccentric homes, made of natural stone and cedar shakes, have an almost magical look. Their mushroom cap–shape roofs, low ceilings, and tiny doorways belie conventional construction methods and make them look like houses for gnomes. Most are now privately owned, but you can obtain a map showing their location from the Chamber of Commerce (tel. 616/547–2101).

The **Gaslight District,** named after the gaslights that line the streets of Petoskey's renovated downtown, has more than 75 distinctive shops and art galleries, most of them open year-round.

Little Traverse Historical Museum (100 Depot Ct., Petoskey, tel. 616/347–2620) occupies the now-defunct 1892 Chicago and West Michigan Railroad depot. Converted into a delightful museum, it features 100-year-old handcrafted Ottawa quill boxes, a passenger-pigeon display, and information on Ernest Hemingway's ties to the region. It is open from May to December.

Petoskey Stones are pieces of fossilized coral from millions of years ago, now in the form of greenish gray stones. Their distinctive designs can be seen only when held underwater. You can buy these popular stones in stores or search for them along the beach, which can be the most satisfying way to obtain this souvenir unique to northern Michigan.

Thorn Swift Nature Preserve and Beach (Rte. M–119, just north of Harbor Springs, tel. 616/526–6401) is 30 acres of beach, dunes, and fragrant cedar swamp offering hiking trails and panoramic views of Little Traverse Bay. Naturalist-rangers give guided tours from Memorial Day through October, but you can call ahead for permission to enter during the rest of the year.

Beaches

Visitors will discover many beautiful beaches along this stretch of Lake Michigan and Little Traverse Bay. Two state parks, **Petoskey State Park** (U.S. 119, 1½ mi. north of U.S. 31, tel. 616/347–2311) and **Fisherman Island State Park** (U.S. 31, outside Charlevoix), offer larger beaches and rugged shoreline. Smaller downtown beaches include **Michigan Avenue** and **Lake Michigan beaches** (off Grant St., Charlevoix); **Pennsylvania Park** (off U.S. 31, Petoskey), complete with an old-fashioned band shell used throughout the summer for free concerts; and **Zorn** and **Ford parks** (1 block east of Main St., Harbor Springs). These town beaches offer calmer water in protected bays and may provide picnic areas and playgrounds. A drive through neighboring Antrim County will reveal the small public beaches and boat launches of northern Michigan's pristine **Chain of Lakes** (including Torch Lake). It encompasses 163 miles of shoreline and includes a 65-mile inland waterway.

Restaurants

Found in the town of Ellsworth, about 10 miles southeast of Charlevoix, are two of Michigan's finest restaurants: the **Rowe Inn** (603 E. Jordan Rd., tel. 616/588–7351) and **Tapawingo** (9502 Lake St., tel. 616/588–7971; open Wed.–Sat.). They are recognized nationally for their gourmet regional cuisine and use of such local delectables as whitefish and morel mushrooms. At the **Arboretum** (7075 S. Lakeside Dr., tel. 616/526–6291), in Petoskey, you can enjoy good steaks, chops, and seafood, and get your car washed at the same time. In Harbor Springs, **Juillerett's** (131 8th St., tel. 616/526–2821) is known for its whitefish dinners, and **Stafford's Pier** (102 Bay St., tel. 616/526–6201), overlooking the bay, offers elegant Continental cuisine. Charlevoix's **Great Lakes Whitefish Company** (415 Bridge St., tel. 616/547–4374) serves Michigan's most popular catch in classic fish-and-chips style, while **Willie's Up North** (1273 S. Advance Rd., tel. 616/536–2666), in East Jordan, may have the best barbecued ribs in the region.

Tourist Information

Boyne Country Convention and Visitor Bureau (Box 694, Petoskey, MI 49770, tel. 800/845–2828); **Charlevoix Area Chamber of Commerce** (408 Bridge St., Charlevoix, MI 49720, tel. 616/547–2101); **Michigan Travel Bureau** (333 S. Capitol, Lansing, MI 48933, tel. 800/543–2937); **Petoskey Regional Chamber of Commerce** (Main St., Petoskey, MI 49770, tel. 616/347–4150).

The Benson House

As a former Chamber of Commerce executive transplanted from downstate, Rod Benson knows how to make people comfortable, and, with his charming wife, Carol, they make an unbeatable team when it comes to hosting a bed-and-breakfast. The Bensons go out of their way to help you enjoy your stay by providing area restaurant menus, a travel planner, and chocolates in each guest room.

Set in a quiet, tree-filled neighborhood in Petoskey, the Benson House has an enviable location. As the locals tell it, when it opened in 1879 as the Ozark Hotel, people were aghast that anyone would put such an establishment so far from downtown. Nowadays, however, guests are only a few blocks' walk from the shopping and entertainment of the Gaslight District and minutes by car from first-class golf and skiing, but they still feel miles away.

The two-story wood-frame house has been thoroughly renovated to provide modern amenities while still retaining elements of its Victorian history: high ceilings, wood moldings, pocket doors, old gas fixtures, floral prints, hardwood floors, and area rugs. The spacious guest rooms have individual themes, from the cathedral ceiling, dark wood, and fruitwood four-poster bed of the Grand Master Suite to the white wicker and original wooden water closet in the bathroom of the Wicker Room.

Adjacent to the large living room is a game room, complete with an elegant parquet floor, entertainment center, backgammon and cribbage boards, puzzles, books, and a cozy couch, where the Bensons say they often discover guests relaxing with a short nap.

The most popular gathering spot is the 80-foot veranda, which wraps around two sides of the house and overlooks Little Traverse Bay. Furnished with white wicker and ablaze with colorful hanging plants, it is the perfect place to enjoy Carol's hearty breakfasts during the warmer months. Her menu varies and includes a shrimp quiche she calls Neptune's Delight, Irish Cream bread, and sticky-bun French toast. And, after a long day of shopping or recreating, you can return to the veranda, where the Bensons' afternoon hors d'oeuvres quell those hunger pangs and make you feel at home once again.

Address: *618 E. Lake St., Petoskey, MI 49770, tel. 616/347-1338.*
Accommodations: *4 double rooms with baths.*
Amenities: *Fireplace in living room, turn-down service with chocolates.*
Rates: *$78–$98; full breakfast. MC, V.*
Restrictions: *No smoking indoors, no pets; 2-night minimum on weekends, 3-night minimum on holidays.*

The House on the Hill

As part of their early retirement plan, lifelong Texans Buster and Julie Arnim considered opening an art gallery in the Southwest, but after a tour of New England bed-and-breakfasts, they decided to open their own. Selling their Houston suitcase business in 1984, the Arnims moved north to see the turn-of-the-century farmhouse they had purchased, sight unseen, after an eight-state hunt for the perfect rural setting. A real-estate ad stated it was "near a gourmet restaurant"; Julie was convinced their B&B would be a success if good food was near at hand. Indeed, two of northern Michigan's finest restaurants, Tapawingo and the Rowe Inn, are within two blocks.

After some hard work during the renovation process, the Arnims have made the House on the Hill a successful and elegant B&B. The carefully restored gray and white Victorian (including an addition used as their private quarters) sits on a hill near the little village of Ellsworth, overlooking 53 acres of countryside and the St. Clair Lake. Guests are free to hike or ski cross-country around the property and even borrow the boat docked at the lake. A spacious, veranda wraps the house and is filled with white wicker furniture and rocking chairs.

Inside, a curved staircase leads to the guest rooms upstairs. They are all spacious, immaculate, and pleasantly decorated. Each has its own thermostat, fresh flowers, candy, ice water, and lights on either side of the beds. A favorite is the Pine Room, with its cathedral ceiling, custom-built four-poster bed draped in white lace, and peaceful view of the woods behind the house. Antiques and such touches as a 200-year-old ebony hand-carved Oriental desk, Julie's rose-colored glass collection, and Oriental porcelain could make you nervous about kicking back and really relaxing, but the Arnims make you feel at home with a perfect blend of friendliness and reserve.

Julie and Buster serve a marvelous hearty breakfast on their large oak table, complete with fine china and silver. A culinary whiz, Julie rotates 65 different breakfast menus. For early risers, Julie puts out a basket filled with home-baked muffins, juice, and coffee. The delicious breakfasts prove Julie right: A B&B is a success when good food is near at hand.

Address: *Lake St. (Box 206), Ellsworth, MI 49729, tel. 616/588–6304.*
Accommodations: *5 double rooms with baths.*
Amenities: *Ceiling fans in rooms, cable TV in parlor.*
Rates: *$95–$125; full breakfast. MC, V.*
Restrictions: *Smoking on porch only, no pets.*

Kimberly Country Estate

The colonial-plantation-structure and hospitality of the Kimberly Country Estate recall the genteel era of the Old South, but the interior is an elegant, gracious recreation of an English country estate. Either impression is a treat to discover at this 8,000-square-foot house in the heart of northern Michigan.

Owners Billie and Ronn Kimberly spent more than a year carefully remodeling this 30-year-old home in an effort to enhance its architecture while adding some modern conveniences. They put in new fireplaces, an updated kitchen, recessed lighting, and traditional mullion-style windows to take the place of the modern casements. In the living room, they replaced the sliding glass doors leading to the terrace with more graceful French doors. This attention to detail is evident throughout the house.

The Kimberlys moved from the Detroit area to Harbor Springs in the early 1980s, after owning a flower shop as well as restoring and decorating three homes together. Once in Harbor Springs, they first opened the shop Kimberly's Nest; the bed-and-breakfast followed in 1989. Throughout their 38-year marriage, they have been avid antiques collectors, adding such treasures as a Dutch pin armoire, a cast-iron chandelier, four-poster beds, and numerous chairs and accessories.

Floral chintz mixed with stripes and plaids creates a warm, romantic look, as do the fresh flowers, overstuffed sofas and chairs, Oriental rugs, and Battenburg lace spreads in the guest rooms. The B&B has become a very popular place for weddings; the entire house is often rented out on these occasions (or for the occasional executive retreat).

All the guest rooms are very spacious. The two larger rooms are the Lexington, with a fireplace, sitting area, and separate study, and the Verandah, which opens to a private terrace and has a fireplace and whirlpool bath. Guests are free to use the main-floor library, which, with its North Carolina black walnut paneling, fireplace, English-style armchairs, and paisley fabric–covered ceiling, has the feel of an old club—an old club nestled in a stately southern plantation.

Address: *2287 Bester Rd., Harbor Springs, MI 49740, tel. 616/526–7646.*
Accommodations: *6 double rooms with baths, 1 suite.*
Amenities: *Baby-grand piano in living room, swimming pool.*
Rates: *$100–$250; Continental breakfast, afternoon tea. MC, V.*
Restrictions: *No smoking, no pets; 2-night minimum weekends, 3-night minimum holidays.*

La Bergerie

The name, loosely translated, means "Shepherd's Inn," or, as innkeeper Deborah Taylor describes it, "a place of warmth, comfort, and personal attention." Having spent nearly 20 years living in the south of France, Deborah has brought a bit of that country back to the region where she spent her childhood summers. Experience managing a British-owned bed-and-breakfast in Key West has given her the know-how to run one.

This stately Victorian house, built in 1887, was a "cottage" in Charlevoix's elite summer colony, the Belvedere Club, and the broad tree-lined streets surrounding the structure are as peaceful and elegant as they were in their heyday. It was operated as the Cabana Hotel around the turn of the century and was later converted to a boardinghouse. Recently restored, it opened three years ago as La Bergerie.

Lovers of art and literature will have trouble just getting past the large and inviting living room. The overstuffed couch and easy chairs, upholstered in a French country motif, are perfect for enjoying the hundreds of books spilling out of the floor-to-ceiling bookcases. Monet prints, museum and gallery posters, and photographs adorn the walls upstairs and down. In one corner, a backgammon table awaits the next players, and puzzles are also available. The whole house is filled with Deborah's belongings, but it doesn't feel cluttered. Just perusing these treasures is a nice way to pass the time.

Similarly, the guest rooms are clean and decorated with a comfortable elegance, each with its own interesting character. A queen-size wicker bed stands out in one room, which can be connected to a room with twin beds for extra space.

Stating that she likes as few rules as possible, Deborah is a flexible innkeeper who takes into account each guest's needs. She serves a Continental breakfast buffet that varies from day to day; she is also happy to bring coffee to your room if you ask her. Don't be surprised if, in the late afternoon or early evening, Deborah invites you onto the porch to enjoy some hors d'oeuvres and her favorite Burgundy wine or apple brandy. You will soon find that the sun has set, that you are in delightful company, and that you can't remember feeling this relaxed.

Address: *306 Belvedere Ave., Charlevoix, MI 49720, tel. 616/547-2251.*
Accommodations: *5 double rooms with baths, 2 doubles share 1½ baths.*
Amenities: *Turn-down service with chocolates, bathrobes, fireplace and cable TV in living room.*
Rates: *$85–$100; Continental breakfast. MC, V.*
Restriction: *No smoking in bedrooms.*

Stafford's Bay View Inn

I t's hard to miss Stafford's Bay View Inn, set just off the main road running through Petoskey's historic Bay View district. A popular dining spot for both tourists and residents as well as a bustling inn, the imposing three-story Victorian was built in 1886; it served as lodging for summer visitors coming north via the now-defunct railroad to enjoy Bay View's cultural programs.

Owners Stafford and Janice Smith met and fell in love while working at the inn for the previous owner. They purchased it during the early 1960s and have now been joined in running the inn by their son and daughter-in-law, Reg and Lori, who are the day-to-day innkeepers. Over time, they have redecorated, and added onto the inn—including five new suites—while retaining its comfortable charm. Furnishings in the second- and third-floor guest rooms include canopy and four-poster beds, richly colored wallpapers, antique dressers, wicker furniture, and such details as handmade eyelet and ribbon pillows.

The third floor was renovated in 1987, and the Smiths, keeping in mind that the house should remain a place for young families to visit, added a third-floor sitting room so parents could enjoy stepping out without venturing too far away from sleeping children. Children can often be seen happily romping in the first-floor common areas while parents finish their meal at a leisurely pace.

Open and airy, the main dining room is decorated with chandeliers, draped tables with fan-backed chairs, fresh flowers and plants, and white lattice dividers between booths. Sometimes it may feel as though the restaurant crowd has taken over the inn, but a trip to the third floor or a stroll down to the water offers a good escape for overnight guests. The menus include such specialties as steaming bread pudding with raisins and cream. A splendid buffet awaits guests for Sunday brunch; selections may include ham, turkey, whitefish, chicken, biscuits, and scrumptious desserts. Although the inn does not serve alcoholic beverages, guests are invited to bring their own wine to dinner.

What the Bay View Inn may sometimes lack in quiet, it makes up for in its delicious food and the unending hospitality of its hosts.

Address: *613 Woodland Ave., U.S. 31, Petoskey, MI 49770, tel. 616/347–2771.*
Accommodations: *27 double rooms with baths, 7 suites.*
Amenities: *Air-conditioning, gas fireplaces and whirlpool baths in 5 suites, cable TV in sun room.*
Rates: *$60–$120; full breakfast. MC, V.*
Restriction: *No pets.*

Bear River Valley

Russ and Sandra Barkman, avid bicyclists and cross-country skiers, moved north a few years ago and created a marvelous, year-round, rustic retreat. Sandra used to manage the VIP Guest House at the University of Michigan, and her experience contributes to the private, relaxed aura at Bear River Valley. Sitting on 2 acres of natural woodlands south of Petoskey, the contemporary cedar-sided home is nestled among birches, maples, and pines. Skiing and boating are just minutes away, and the country roads are perfect for cycling.

Porches and decks surround three sides of the home. The open living room has vaulted ceilings, lots of windows, and a fireplace, ideal for the Barkmans' cozy après-ski refreshments. Guest rooms are not large, but they are clean and comfortably decorated in a Scandinavian/country motif. A wood-fired Finnish sauna will relax you instantly.

Freshly squeezed juices and whole-grain cereals are standard breakfast fare, but Sandra's signature recipe is wild blackberry oatmeal muffins.

Address: *03636 Bear River Rd., Petoskey, MI 49770, tel. 616/348–2046.*
Accommodations: *1 double room with bath, 2 doubles share 1 bath.*
Amenities: *Terry-cloth robes, TV and VCR in common room.*
Rates: *$48–$60; Continental breakfast. No credit cards.*
Restrictions: *No smoking, no pets, 2-night minimum on weekends.*

The Bridge Street Inn

Although just a block from downtown on Charlevoix's busy main street, this three-story, 1895 Colonial revival house, with a tulip-lined walkway and wraparound porch, has a cozy, calm air. John and Vera McKown moved from California three years ago to run the inn. John has been in the hotel business for 25 years.

Maple floors and artistic touches— a Renoir reproduction over the living-room fireplace and stained glass in the front window—lend an elegance to the inn. Guest rooms vary, however. Some look worn and in need of refurbishing, while others like the Bridal Suite and Garden View offer a pleasant Victorian getaway, complete with four-poster beds, lace curtains, washstands, floral carpets, and, in the case of Evening Glow, a beautiful view of the sunset. Belgian waffles, homemade strawberry bread, and raspberries from his garden are a few of John's breakfast specialties.

Address: *113 Michigan Ave., Charlevoix, MI 49720, tel. 616/547–6606.*
Accommodations: *3 double rooms with baths, 6 doubles share 3 baths.*
Amenities: *Ceiling fans in some rooms, baby-grand piano in common area.*
Rates: *$74–$105; full breakfast, afternoon and evening refreshments. MC, V.*
Restrictions: *No smoking, no pets; 2-night minimum on weekends July–mid-Oct., closed Nov.–Apr.*

The Gingerbread House

Sisters Mary Gruler and Margaret Perry have avoided making this pink-and-white, turn-of-the-century Victorian home too cute despite what the name implies. Surrounded by hedge roses, morning glories, and a new English garden, the cottage is right in Bay View, enabling guests to take advantage of all its activities.

Inside are spacious rooms, like Country Blues, with a handpainted iron bed and white wicker; Classic Rose, whose rosebud ruffled window seat has a view of Little Traverse Bay; and the Victoria, decorated in the style of an English rose garden, which has a sitting area, day bed, and French doors leading to a private balcony. The large dining and sitting area downstairs provides a welcome place for guests to gather, peruse its bookshelves, or enjoy their breakfast.

Mary and Margaret are delightful hostesses who share a marvelous sense of humor and sincere interest in their guests' well-being but operate with a nice respect for privacy.

Address: *205 Bluff St. (Box 1273), Bay View, MI 49770, tel. 616/347–3538.*
Accommodations: *3 double rooms with baths, 1 housekeeping double with bath, 1 housekeeping suite.*
Amenities: *Private outside entrances to guest rooms.*
Rates: *$50–$95; Continental breakfast. MC, V.*
Restrictions: *No smoking, no pets; closed Nov.–Apr.*

Main Street Bed & Breakfast

Donna and Jerry Karson's restored, two-story, wood-frame home is indeed located on Harbor Springs's Main Street, but it is a far cry from the big city of Detroit, which they left four years ago.

The most popular gathering spot is an enclosed wraparound porch in a blue-and-white country motif: white-wicker flower baskets and blue-patterned cushions on wicker furniture. The Karsons' tasteful decorations are found throughout the home, including a blue-and-white Delft collection in the kitchen. Guest rooms are large, immaculate, and quiet.

Donna is a marvelous cook, who, with Jerry's friendly assistance, serves a delicious assortment of her own creations, including cinnamon-bread French toast, cornmeal pancakes, and lemon-poppyseed waffles. Breakfast can be enjoyed on cooler days in the dining room or, in summer, on the porch, with a view of Main Street and Little Traverse Bay.

Address: *403 E. Main St., Harbor Springs, MI 49740, tel. 616/526–7782.*
Accommodations: *4 double rooms with baths.*
Amenities: *Ceiling fans in rooms, TV in common room, complimentary wine on anniversaries and honeymoons.*
Rates: *$70–$90; full breakfast. MC, V.*
Restrictions: *No smoking, no pets; 2-night minimum on weekends May–Oct.*

Torch Lake Bed & Breakfast

Situated with a full view of and only a short walk from Torch Lake (once named one of the world's most beautiful lakes by *National Geographic*), this turn-of-the-century clapboard house has been lovingly restored by its owners, Patti and Jack Findlay.

An oak staircase, handcrafted by a local carpenter, leads to the second-floor guest rooms. The Violet Room has a private bath and overlooks the lake; crisp white linens of lace and eyelet on the brass-and-iron bed make it clean and fresh. Stained-glass windows and Australian-sheepskin rugs add to the room's distinct personality.

The parlor, which has lace curtains and bright prints, has a country feel;

and the front porch, which of course has a view of the lake, is outfitted with rocking chairs for friendly, Alden-style relaxation. Patti is an excellent cook; her breakfast specialties include sausage-filled crepes, raisin scones, French toast with pecan-praline syrup, and locally made fruit preserves.

Address: *10601 Coy St., Alden, MI 49612, tel. 616/331-6424.*
Accommodations: *1 double room with bath, 2 doubles share 1 bath.*
Amenities: *Ceiling fans in guest rooms.*
Rates: *$65–$80; full breakfast. No credit cards.*
Restrictions: *No smoking inside, no pets, closed mid-Sept.–Memorial Day weekend.*

Walloon Lake Inn

Some inns are recognized for their ambience or their hosts, and, while Walloon Lake Inn is up to snuff in both areas, it is the food that's first-rate here.

Innkeeper David Beier is an accomplished chef, and, even though a delicious Continental breakfast is included with a guest room, dinner is the most popular meal. Regional specialties include fillet of brook trout smoked on the premises; venison covered with a sauce of prosciutto, Madeira, and thyme; morel sauce over breast of chicken; strawberry-almond duck; and daily veal specials; not to mention the desserts, which include homemade ice cream and pastries. A special children's menu makes for perfect family dining.

The two-story, cottage-style home was built nearly 100 years ago, and the guest rooms were completely renovated in 1986. They are clean and comfortable, although at times noise from the restaurant can be disruptive. No worry, just head to the common area that overlooks Walloon Lake or down to the dock to dangle your feet in the water.

Address: *4178 West Rd. (Box 85), Walloon Lake Village, MI 49796, tel. 616/535-2999.*
Accommodations: *5 double rooms with baths.*
Amenities: *Beach and dock access on lake, restaurant.*
Rates: *$50–$60; Continental breakfast. MC, V.*
Restrictions: *No pets; closed partial weeks in Apr.*

Minnesota

1990 Dupont, **35**

Oakhurst Inn, **31**

Park Row
Bed & Breakfast, **60**

Park Street Inn, **3**

Peace Cliff, **4**

Peters' Sunset
Beach, **28**

Pincushion Mountain
Bed & Breakfast, **17**

Prairie House on
Round Lake, **59**

Prairie View
Estate, **20**

Pratt-Taber Inn, **52**

Quill & Quilt, **49**

Red Gables Inn, **54**

Rivertown Inn, **48**

Robards House, **26**

Rose Bed &
Breakfast, **33**

Schumacher's New
Prague Hotel, **62**

Snuggle Inn
Bed & Breakfast, **18**

Sod House on the
Prairie, **58**

Spicer Castle, **29**

St. James Hotel, **53**

Stone Hearth Inn
Bed & Breakfast, **12**

Stonehouse
Bed & Breakfast, **23**

Superior Overlook
B & B, **19**

Thorwood Historic
Inns, **42**

Tianna Farms, **5**

Victorian Bed &
Breakfast, **55**

Walden Woods, **25**

William Sauntry
Mansion, **48**

Twin Cities Area

Hollywood certainly knew what it was doing when it placed Mary Tyler Moore's fictional television character, Mary Richards, here. Like Mary, the twin cities of Minneapolis and St. Paul can be cosmopolitan while still wearing sensible shoes. A good example of this blend of style and practicality is the area's clean and efficient mass-transit system, which includes an extensive network of climate-controlled glass skyways that allows citizens to spend an entire day downtown without once setting their galoshes outdoors.

Minneapolis was formed in 1872 when the lumbering village of St. Anthony, which sat on the east bank of the Mississippi, joined hands with a hamlet on the west bank. Its name derives from the Indian word for water ("minne") and the Greek suffix for city ("polis"). St. Paul, on the other hand, had an uproarious past. The original settlement was called Pig's Eye, a tribute to a French trader named Pierre "Pig's Eye" Parrant, an evil-eyed villain who sold whiskey to the Native Americans. Presumably as an act of repentance, the name was changed in 1841 to honor a log chapel dedicated to St. Paul. Over time, railroad and steamboat traffic transformed St. Paul into a booming transportation center. Meanwhile, flour mills in Minneapolis grew into giant international corporations, such as General Mills, Pillsbury, and Cargill. As a result, hundreds of thousands of immigrants settled hereabouts in the 19th and early 20th centuries.

Like a long-married couple, these geographical partners are beginning to look more and more alike, although St. Paul is still considered the more conservative of the two, perhaps because Prince, the flamboyant rock star, hails from Minneapolis. He is one of the reasons the metro area has a rich and varied popular music scene and has envolved into the cultural center of the Upper Great Lakes.

*There are more than 90 theaters, including the Guthrie
Theater; the country's first and only full-time chamber
orchestra, the St. Paul Chamber Orchestra; the Walker Art
Center; a large art gallery district in Minneapolis; and
many thriving music and dance groups.*

*Both communities have masterfully blended the old with
the new. State-of-the-art research facilities and glass-walled
skyscrapers tastefully co-exist with turn-of-the-century
neighborhoods and historic commercial districts. Summit
Street in St. Paul, for instance, has a 5-mile stretch of
Victorian homes, including the house where F. Scott
Fitzgerald wrote* This Side of Paradise.

*For a metropolitan area of some 2 million people, the
cities remain delightfully small-town in character, due in
no small part to the Minneapolis park system, thoughtfully
designed by farsighted urban planners of an earlier era
and unusual in its proximity to the city. You can stroll or
bicycle along the river or a lake just blocks from the center
of downtown. Minneapolis alone has 22 lakes and 153
parks, giving it a lush appearance in summer and
a romantic* Dr. Zhivago *setting when the snow falls. And
the winters here are not nearly as severe as legend and the
popular St. Paul Winter Carnival might have you believe.
The average daily temperature in February is 26 degrees,
certainly comfortable enough to enjoy the cross-country
skiing and ice-skating available right in the cities.*

*While it's easy to get around the Twin Cities, it's also easy
to get* turned *around. To the frustration of outsiders, the
interlocking grid of highways and streets often appears to
have the organization of a spilled bag of pretzels. Blame it
on the mighty Mississippi, which doesn't simply divide the
cities but also cuts through sections of each, including the
center of St. Paul. The Big Muddy actually takes several
turns, forcing streets to run on a diagonal and baffling
tourists hoping to use the river as a north–south compass.
Make sure you carry a good street map. Inconvenience*

aside, generations of locals, from Pig's Eye Parrant to Mary Richards, would undoubtedly attest that there is hardly a more pleasant place to get lost.

Places to Go, Sights to See

Mall of America (U.S. 494 and U.S. 77, Bloomington, tel. 612/851–3500), dubbed the Mega Mall, is the nation's largest shopping and entertainment complex. Twenty minutes south of downtown Minneapolis, it features 400 stores, Knott's Camp Snoopy indoor amusement park, Underwater World, restaurants, and nightclubs.

Minneapolis's Parks and Lakes. Minneapolis has an extensive park system with bike and walking paths that meander past and along Minnehaha Creek, the Mississippi River, and six lakes (Cedar Lake, Lake of the Isles, Lake Calhoun, Lake Harriet, Lake Hiawatha, and Lake Nokomis). At *Lake Harriet* (W. Lake Harriet Pkwy., tel. 612/348–2243), be sure to catch a free summer concert at the bandshell, visit the rose garden, take a boat ride, or ride the old streetcar line between Lake Harriet and Lake Calhoun.

Minnesota State Capitol (Cedar and Aurora Sts., St. Paul, tel. 612/296–2881), built on a hill overlooking downtown, was designed by renowned St. Paul architect Cass Gilbert in 1905 and contains more than 25 varieties of marble, sandstone, limestone, and granite. Near the south entry are cases displaying Minnesota's two constitutions and artifacts from early statehood years. Take time to walk around the exceptionally beautiful grounds. Free 45-minute tours are given daily.

A half-hour south of the Twin Cities, the **Minnesota Zoo** (13000 Zoo Blvd., Apple Valley, tel. 612/431–9200) was built to resemble the natural habitat of the wild animals that reside there. The zoo contains some 1,700 animals and more than 2,000 plant varieties. Other features include a zoo lab, children's zoo, bird and animal shows, camel rides in summer, and daily film and slide shows. Among the amenities are eating facilities, picnic areas, rest areas, and stroller rentals.

Mississippi River Cruises (Padelford Packet Boat Co., tel. 612/227–1100). Daily sightseeing tours, Sunday brunch, and weekday and weekend dinner tours of the Mississippi between downtown St. Paul and Fort Snelling are offered aboard the *Anson and Betsey Northrop, Josiah Snelling,* and *Jonathan Padelford,* modern stern-wheelers modeled after 19th-century Mississippi riverboats. Excursions last 1¾ hours and leave from Harriet Island, St. Paul, or Boom Island Park, Minneapolis.

Riverplace (25 Main St. SE, tel. 612/378–1969) and **St. Anthony Main** (210 Main St. SE, tel. 612/378–1226), neighbors on the historic east bank of the Mississippi, are complexes with horse-drawn carriage rides, stores, and waterfront restaurants. Riverplace's new Mississippi Live entertainment pavilion has seven nightclubs with live and recorded music and four restaurants for one cover charge. There are river walkways and a bridge linking the area to Nicollet Island, which has outdoor concerts in its park. This area is especially popular in the summer months.

Summit Avenue, long one of St. Paul's most prestigious addresses, runs 4½ miles from the Cathedral of St. Paul, built in 1915, to the Mississippi, and is the nation's longest row of intact residential Victorian architecture. F. Scott Fitzgerald lived at number 599 in 1918 while writing *This Side of Paradise. Mount Zion Temple*, home of the oldest Jewish congregation in Minnesota (founded in 1856), is at number 1300. Number 240 is the *James J. Hill House* (tel. 612/297-2555), the 19th-century mansion home of the famous railroad baron; tours include a skylit art gallery with changing exhibits.

Walker Art Center (725 Vineland Pl., Minneapolis, tel. 612/375-7600) was founded in 1879 by Thomas Barlow Walker and was established at its current location in 1927. It has been described by *The New York Times* as "one of the best contemporary art exhibition facilities in the world." The permanent collections are strong on 20th-century American and European art, especially paintings, sculpture, prints, and photography from the past two decades. The center offers regular programs of dance, theater, music, and films. In autumn 1988, the Walker opened the *Minneapolis Sculpture Garden*, the largest urban sculpture garden in the nation. The garden is currently being expanded from 40 works to almost twice that many. The adjoining *Guthrie Theater* (tel. 612/347-1111), known for its balance of classics and more avant-garde productions, offers tours that include dressing rooms, prop rooms, backstage, and other areas. Reservations are not necessary; meet the tour guide at the ticket office in the lobby on Saturday mornings at 10.

Warehouse District (call the New North Artscape, tel. 612/337-5198, for dates and gallery guides). More than a dozen art galleries, cafés, eclectic shops, and avant-garde theater companies are clustered in Minneapolis's 3-block Warehouse District, just north of downtown.

Restaurants

Thanks to an influx of immigrants, restaurants in Minneapolis and St. Paul offer a diverse range of cuisines—including Thai, Vietnamese, and Sri Lankan—that belie the stereotype of bland Midwestern cooking.

In Minneapolis, the bohemian **Loring Cafe** (1624 Harmon Pl., tel. 612/332-1617), which overlooks Loring Park, is near the Guthrie Theater and Walker Art Center on the edge of downtown Minneapolis. It features pastas and fish with creative sauces, and salads; in the summer, you can relax and dine on an unusual alley patio accompanied by the sounds of a saxophone player. **The Nicollet Island Inn** (95 Marriam St., tel. 612/331-1800), with large windows that overlook the Mississippi River, specializes in regional cuisine that uses such local produce as walleyed pike and wild rice. The more elegant **Yvette** (65 Main St. SE, tel. 612/379-1111) is a French restaurant on the river at Riverplace.

If you're looking for elegant dining in St. Paul, try the **St. Paul Grill** (350 Market St., tel. 612/224–7455) in the newly restored St. Paul Hotel. For a more casual meal, check out **W. A. Frost & Co.** (374 Selby Ave., tel. 612/224–5715), a restored turn-of-the-century landmark. American-style food is served by the fireplaces or out on a large patio. The newer **Café Latté** (850 Grand Ave., tel. 612/224–5687) is a modern restaurant serving sandwiches, salads, and coffee cafeteria-style in the heart of the popular Grand Avenue shopping area.

Tourist Information

Greater Minneapolis Convention and Visitors Association (1219 Marquette Ave., Minneapolis, MN 55403, tel. 612/348–7000); **Minneapolis Park and Recreation Board** (310 Fourth Ave. S, Minneapolis, MN 55415, tel. 612/348–2226 or 612/348–2142); **Minnesota Office of Tourism** (375 Jackson St., 250 Skyway Level, St. Paul, MN 55101–1848, tel. 612/296–5029 or 800/657–3700); **St. Paul Convention and Visitors Bureau** (101 Norwest Center, 55 E. Fifth St., St. Paul, MN 55101, tel. 612/297–6985).

The Ann Bean House

The Ann Bean House was an eight-unit apartment building when proprietors Victoria and Bruce Brillhart bought it. Converting it to a country inn was a challenge, but they had a lot to work with. Their 1880 Victorian Stick-style house is a graceful one, with many bay windows and towers and turrets of varying heights. The interior of the house is filled with woodwork that reflects Minnesota's lumbering past, including a beautiful carved oak banister and cherry, oak, and walnut parquet flooring in the vestibule. The abundance of large windows makes the house light and airy.

Two of the five bedrooms, the Guest Room and Ann and Albert's Room, measure a luxurious 20 feet square. The Guest Room has a brass sleigh bed, an enormous bay window, and a working fireplace with a carved oak mantel. The private bathroom has maple floors and 1930s fixtures. Ann and Albert's Room has an east-facing bay window and maple floors, as well as a new bath with a tempting whirlpool that fits into the shorter of the building's towers.

Even more impressive, perhaps, is the whimsical pink Tower Room with a slanted ceiling and a white cast-iron bed. A few stairs up, you'll find a delightful white wicker table for two, perfect for morning coffee or wine in the evening. Up another flight of stairs at the top of the tower is the star attraction—a 7-foot-square aerie with windows on four sides, offering spectacular views of hilly Stillwater and the St. Croix River.

The house's charm is accentuated by the Brillharts' hospitality, especially Victoria's cooking. When you check in here you're offered homemade herb bread, cheeses, and hot artichoke dip, with a glass of wine. Breakfast is a mélange of four or five of Victoria's fruit-and-yeast breads, fresh fruit, sausage rolls, and hot dishes such as eggs Florentine. After breakfast, your hosts can tell you about paddleboat trips, hot-air ballooning, and antiques hunting in the area.

Address: *319 W. Pine St., Stillwater, MN 55082, tel. 612/430–0355.*
Accommodations: *5 double rooms with baths.*
Amenities: *Fireplace in 1 room, whirlpool tubs in 2 rooms.*
Rates: *$95–$140; full breakfast, afternoon refreshments. AE, MC, V.*
Restrictions: *No smoking, no pets.*

Asa Parker House

On a rainy day, the Asa Parker House, in the tiny historic village of Marine on St. Croix, looks like something out of a British miniseries. Extensive grounds, elaborate flower gardens, a tennis court, and a gazebo make the setting of this Greek Revival one of the finest of any Minnesota B&B. The house, built in 1856 by lumber-industry pioneer Asa Parker, was distinctive enough to tempt owner and innkeeper Marjorie Bush not to retire; she had previously owned two other Minnesota B&Bs.

The public and guest rooms are all airy and bright if almost oppressively feminine. The parlors, painted pink, have white wicker, chintz, and lots of doilies and dried-flower wreaths.

If you can get past the frills, the guest rooms can be lovely. The rose and dusty green Isabella Parker Room, with white wicker furniture and claw-foot tub, offers spectacular river valley views from its corner spot. The Alice O'Brien Suite, tucked under the eaves, has gabled windows, a large bath with whirlpool tub, and a private deck with white Adirondack chairs and views of the flowering lawns. A screened porch downstairs overlooks Marjorie's attractive herb garden.

Marjorie uses Minnesota products to make her delicious and very caloric breakfasts, such as wild rice and bacon-and-egg casserole. She'll also pack picnic baskets for guests to take to the screened gazebo or on a hike in William O'Brien State Park, just down the road. The park has miles of hiking, biking, and cross-country ski paths. There's also a marina a couple of blocks away where you can rent canoes. But the sweeping views of the St. Croix River are so beautiful—particularly in fall and winter—that guests may just want to relax on the lawn.

Address: *17500 St. Croix Trail N, Marine on St. Croix, MN 55047, tel. 612/433-5248.*
Accommodations: *4 double rooms with baths, 1 suite.*
Amenities: *Air-conditioning, down comforters, whirlpool bath in suite, stove in 1 room; tennis court, screened gazebo.*
Rates: *$99–$135; full breakfast, afternoon refreshments. MC, V.*
Restrictions: *No smoking, no pets; 2-night minimum on holiday weekends.*

Le Blanc House

L e Blanc House is an elegant piece of the 19th century tucked into a modest and modern Minneapolis neighborhood. The 1869 Queen Anne is a striking structure with a delicate lavender exterior. In summer, its banks of petunias and walls of morning glories and nasturtiums are famous in the neighborhood. Add sparkling stained-glass windows and inviting front and back porches—the latter with the traditional swing—and you could be back in the days when the original owner, William Le Blanc, returned home each evening from the grain mills of the Mississippi.

Current owners Barb Zahasky and Bob Schulstad, a retired salesman who now runs the inn full time, have kept the decor faithful to the inn's period, and named the three guest rooms after the daughters of its former owners. Both Zofie's and Amelia's rooms have great views of the city skyline. Zofie's Room, a corner room with a bay window and a private bath—perfect for weekday business travelers—is furnished with a 19th-century high-topped walnut bed and matching marble-top dresser. Marissa's Room, the smallest of the three, is invitingly cozy. It has an antique brass bed, oak furnishings, handmade quilts and linens, and an unusual porthole window. All rooms have colorfully patterned Victorian reproduction wallpaper.

You'll awaken to the aroma of Bob's homemade breakfasts wafting from the dining room. Dishes include "heavenly" Belgian waffles, spinach-pistachio quiche, French toast stuffed with jelly and cream cheese, and filled crêpes. Barb's sister owns a St. Paul bakery, and many mornings she brings over fresh muffins and pastries. Each evening, Bob and Barb serve coffee and cheesecake or Barb's chocolate-banana ice-cream treats.

Le Blanc House is just blocks away from the many attractions of the Minneapolis riverfront, where you'll find Mississippi Live, a new bar and restaurant complex; Boom Island Park, offering paddleboat cruises and a riverfront walk; and the exclusive shops of St. Anthony Main and Riverplace. A wide variety of restaurants are within walking distance.

Address: *302 University Ave. NE, Minneapolis, MN 55413, tel. 612/457-1434 or 612/379-2570.*
Accommodations: *1 double room with bath, 2 doubles share 1 bath.*
Amenities: *Air-conditioning, TV, phone in rooms; off-street parking.*
Rates: *$65–$95; full breakfast, evening dessert and coffee tray. AE, MC, V.*
Restrictions: *Smoking on front porch only, no pets.*

The William Sauntry Mansion

The William Sauntry Mansion is a meticulous restoration of an enormous 1890 Queen Anne home. The work done in the parlor, which was re-created down to wall beading and corner ornaments, was so accurate that a former resident who came to visit remarked to owners Duane and Martha Hubbs on how well the wallpaper had held up. Some things are original: the parquet flooring laid in four woods and the parlor's oil-on-canvas ceiling, as well as light fixtures, fireplaces, and special stained-glass windows.

The Hubbses have restored houses in both Chicago and St. Louis. When they moved to Stillwater in 1988, they found the 25-room mansion converted to apartments and deteriorating. They opened as a bed-and-breakfast in 1990, after a two-year restoration in which the second floor was stripped down to the studs.

The rooms, which have large windows and fireplaces, are done in Victorian style, with Oriental and floral motifs and the rich-hued paints favored by 19th-century builders.

Bertram's Room, with its south-facing tower bay window overlooking the gardens, green-tiled fireplace, spoon-carved cherry bedroom set and private bath, is especially pleasant. For a Japanese ambience, try William's Room, in exotic gold, blue, and rust wallpaper and crown dentil molding.

Eunice's Room, in rose and blue, has an antique headboard, parquet floor, and a delicate oak fireplace ringed by the original rose and cream ceramic tiles. Its private bath, down the hall, has a galvanized tin tub dating from the 1860s.

Sauntry, an Irish immigrant turned lumber baron, had maverick ideas about home construction: He sent his architects as far as the Alhambra Palace in Spain to gather details. Behind his home he built a recreation facility complete with ballroom, bowling alley, and swimming pool, and connected it to the house with Minnesota's first skywalk. The skywalk is gone, and the building is owned by another family, but Sauntry's spirit lives on in his enormous house.

Address: *626 N. Fourth St., Stillwater, MN 55082, tel. 612/430-2653.*
Accommodations: *6 double rooms with baths (2 nonadjoining).*
Amenities: *Bathrobes, fireplaces in 4 rooms.*
Rates: *$89–$119; full breakfast, early morning coffee, afternoon refreshments. AE, MC, V.*
Restrictions: *No smoking, no pets.*

The Afton House Inn

T his 1867 hotel, just a few miles south of Interstate 94 in the old town of Afton, stands on the edge of the St. Croix River.

The hotel's guest rooms, all rather dark, have a reproduction country look, with print wallpaper, carpeting, pine furniture, bedspreads patterned to look like patchwork quilts, and lots of ducks. Rooms 44, 45, and 46 on the first floor, recently added, are the nicest, with pine four-poster beds, whirlpool baths, gas fireplaces, tiny skylights over the beds, and sliding glass doors leading to small patios.

Hotel owners Gordy and Kathy Jarvis offer dinners and Sunday brunches in the Wheel Room, which is accented by wood carvings from local artists and has a view of the river. The bar, which serves more casual lunches and dinners, specializes in catfish caught just out the back door in the St. Croix.

Address: *3291 St. Croix Trail S (Box 326), St. Croix Trail, MN 55001, tel. 612/436–8883.*
Accommodations: *15 double rooms with baths, 1 guest cottage with 2 bedrooms.*
Amenities: *Air-conditioning, TV, phone in rooms, gas fireplaces in 8 rooms, double whirlpool baths in 10 rooms, private balconies in 4 rooms, restaurant, bar.*
Rates: *$60–$135; Continental breakfast. AE, D, MC, V.*
Restrictions: *No smoking in some bedrooms, no pets.*

Battle Hollow Bed and Breakfast

B attle Hollow, on a 2-acre hilltop with a St. Croix River view, was built in 1890 by Stillwater's founder for his daughter. Beth and Jeff Griffith, B&B devotees for 18 years, opened the Queen Anne as an inn in 1991, following three years of remodeling.

An imposing oak staircase makes a dramatic entryway on the first floor. Original pale pink stained- and leaded-glass windows and pocket doors, as well as an unusual Art Nouveau–style morning-glory frieze in the sitting room, are the attention getters. There's also a baby grand piano in the music parlor. Guests can relax on a wraparound front porch furnished in white wicker.

From the balcony off George's Room, decorated in teal and rose, guests can enjoy the St. Croix river valley views. Ella's Room, in mauve and pink, doesn't have the same view but does have a huge bay window, gas fireplace, and pale pink fainting couch.

Address: *903 N. Fourth St., Stillwater, MN 55082, tel. 612/439–0449.*
Accommodations: *2 double rooms with baths.*
Amenities: *Imported herbal soap, fresh flowers, TV/VCR in library.*
Rates: *$85–$105; full breakfast, afternoon refreshments. No credit cards.*
Restrictions: *No smoking, no pets; open weekends only in winter.*

Brasie House

Last year, Mari Griffin bought a 1913 Craftsman-style house in south Minneapolis and turned it into a bed-and-breakfast. By Mari's own admission, Brasie House is eclectic. Her guests comment most frequently on how comfortable the house is. Indeed, it does seem designed for a "make yourself at home," fuss-free stay, with its deep sofas, extensive library, and large second-floor deck overlooking a lovely urban garden.

The guest rooms, with their maple floors, chenille bedspreads, ceiling fans, and corner windows, are comfortable, if not luxurious. Guests planning a long stay will like the unusually large closets (complete with built-in dressers, windows, hooks, and hangers).

Mari caters particularly to business clients, who are grateful for the shared bathroom's magic drawer. Labeled "forgotten necessities," it is stocked with scissors, hair dryer, bath pillow, clothes steamer, and other helpful items, altogether a metaphor for the thoughtfulness of this urban innkeeper.

Address: *2321 Colfax Ave. S, Minneapolis, MN 55405, tel. 612/377–5946.*
Accommodations: *3 double rooms share 1 bath.*
Amenities: *Air-conditioning, small refrigerator in kitchen for guests; off-street parking.*
Rates: *$60; Continental breakfast, afternoon snacks. AE, MC, V.*
Restrictions: *No smoking, no pets.*

The Brunswick Inn

Owners Duane and Martha Hubbs had so many requests for fireplaces and whirlpool baths at the William Sauntry Mansion that they immediately had them installed in the three guest rooms of their latest venture, The Brunswick Inn.

At the Brunswick, a simple 1848 Greek Revival House in the middle of downtown Stillwater, everything is geared toward cozy romance; guests may lounge in bed or the whirlpool bath as breakfast arrives in a basket at the door.

Despite these conveniences, much of the charm of the Brunswick is rather superficial. Rooms without intrinsic character are overlaid with a confection of Victorian furniture,

although this may matter less, perhaps, to the honeymoon set. Avoid Annie's Room, however—Annie's view is of the wall of the next-door building.

Space that would otherwise be devoted to street-level public rooms is taken by a restaurant, where high tea and fixed-price seven-course dinners are served.

Address: *114 E. Chestnut St., Stillwater, MN 55082, tel. 612/430–2653.*
Accommodations: *3 double rooms with baths.*
Amenities: *Double whirlpools and fireplaces.*
Rates: *$129–$139; full breakfast. AE, MC, V.*
Restrictions: *No smoking, no pets.*

Chatsworth B&B

This may be the only bed-and-breakfast in the world with a yoga studio in the basement: Owner Donna Gustafson is an enthusiast. She runs the B&B with her husband, Earl, in the 1902 Victorian home where they raised eight children.

The first floor has leaded-glass windows and glowing birch woodwork with an especially lovely birch buffet in the dining room, though the overall effect is badly marred by the lime green shag carpeting.

Each of the five guest rooms has a theme. The African-Asian Room—with African knickknacks, beaded curtains, and modern black and rust whirlpool bath—is somewhat out of place, but has the advantage of a private deck. The Victorian has antique carved walnut dresser and bed and large bay windows with table and chairs; the corner Scandinavian is done in soothing rose and blues with pine furniture.

Address: *984 Ashland Ave., St. Paul, MN 55104, tel. 612/227–4288.*
Accommodations: *3 double rooms with baths, 2 doubles share 1 bath.*
Amenities: *Air-conditioning in 1 room, whirlpool tubs in 2 rooms, private deck in 1 room, personalized soaps, phone for guests in foyer; off-street parking.*
Rates: *$60–$100; Continental breakfast. No credit cards.*
Restrictions: *No smoking, no pets.*

Evelo's Bed & Breakfast

Opening their inn in 1979 made David and Sheryl Evelo Twin Cities bed-and-breakfast pioneers. They picked a convenient location and managed to keep the prices reasonable. "We try to be the affordable alternative," says David.

Even with a front screened porch with white wicker furniture, their 1897 neoclassical Victorian house looks fairly modest. Inside, it's a different story: The first-floor parlor and dining-sun room are full of distinguished ball-and-stick woodwork, walnut and oak parquet floors, a cozy fireplace, and gorgeous Art Nouveau glassware and lamps.

The three third-floor guest rooms, accessible by a separate back stairway, are under the eaves in the former servants quarters. The cozy rooms have slanted ceilings and painted wood floors with rag rugs.

As testimony to the Evelo's comfortable atmosphere, many visitors are repeat or long-term guests.

Address: *2301 Bryant Ave. S, Minneapolis, MN 55405, tel. 612/374–9656.*
Accommodations: *3 double rooms share 1 bath.*
Amenities: *Clock radios in rooms, refrigerator, coffeemaker, and phone on third floor landing, additional single bed in 2 rooms.*
Rates: *$50; Continental breakfast. AE, MC, V.*
Restrictions: *Smoking on porch only, no pets.*

The Garden Gate Bed and Breakfast

"**Y**ou can take lots of good walks around here, or I'll read Irish poetry aloud, if you'd like," offers charming host Miles Conway, who along with his wife, Mary, run the Garden Gate Bed and Breakfast. If you prefer solitude, the Conways will also leave you alone, which is easy to do in this unusual duplex-style Victorian house built in 1906. Mary and Miles live in one half, while in the other guests share their own dining room, first-floor half bath, and living room with television. Lots of white woodwork, refinished oak and maple floors, and a wide inviting front porch make the Garden Gate bright and comfortable.

Upstairs, the vividly painted guest rooms are named after appropriate flowers: The Delphinium is a purp-lish blue, the Gladiola a rich yellow, and the Rose a deep pink. The Delphinium has floral bedspreads, twin beds, table and chairs, and two large, south-facing windows.

On a quiet block just south of St. Paul's historic district and busiest shopping area, the inn is quite convenient.

Address: *925 Goodrich Ave., St. Paul, MN 55105, tel. 612/227-8430.*
Accommodations: *3 double rooms share 1 bath.*
Amenities: New York Times *delivered daily, fresh flowers; off-street parking.*
Rates: *$45–$60; Continental breakfast. No credit cards.*
Restrictions: *Smoking on porch only.*

The Heirloom Inn

"**H**ere, small is beautiful. Stillwater's Heirloom Inn, a simple 1860s Italianate house built by Swedish craftsmen, has seen few alterations in its century-plus lifespan.

Owners Sandy and Mark Brown have made their inn reasonably priced and quite comfortable for guests. Even with its fireplace, oak parquet floors, baby grand piano, and big bay window, this is not a luxurious place to stay, but it is a restful one.

The three upstairs guest rooms are light and airy, especially Annie's Room (so named because "Annie" was seen penciled on plaster uncovered during some restoration work), a blue and white corner room with pine floors, four windows, and lots of southwest sun.

Guests will appreciate the antique quilts on display, the large perennial garden, and the inn's proximity to both downtown Stillwater and the bluff overlooking the St. Croix River. The three- or four-course breakfast is served in the dining room or on the screened porch.

Address: *1103 S. Third St., Stillwater, MN 55082, tel. 612/430-2289.*
Accommodations: *1 double room with bath, 2 doubles share 1 bath.*
Amenities: *Air-conditioning, fresh flowers and candy.*
Rates: *$65–$75; full breakfast, afternoon refreshments. No credit cards.*
Restrictions: *Smoking on porch only, no pets; closed Dec. 24–25.*

James A. Mulvey Residence Inn

When avid collectors of pottery Truett and Jill Lawson entered the Mulvey Inn and saw a magnificent Grueby tile fireplace in the living room, they knew they had to buy the beautiful little 1878 Italianate house. In 1905, owner and prosperous lumberman James A. Mulvey bought the fireplace (one of only two in Minnesota) from the Grueby Tile Co. of Boston, and then added the dining room's heavy oak beams and wainscoting, and the gold and green tulip-design stained-glass windows bordering the front door. Indicative of the Italianate style, huge windows make the house light, airy, and seemingly larger than it is.

The Lawsons' pottery collection is spread throughout the house, and each guest room, named after a pottery style, includes a book describing the specific technique. The nicest guest room is the Rookwood Room, in gold, black, and maroon with Renaissance Revival furniture, inlaid oak and walnut floors, cranberry glass lamps, and huge corner windows.

Address: *622 W. Churchill St., Stillwater, MN 55082, tel. 612/430–8008.*
Accommodations: *4 double rooms with baths.*
Amenities: *Air-conditioning, fireplaces in 2 rooms; mountain bikes, outdoor spa.*
Rates: *$85–$95; full breakfast, afternoon refreshments, picnic lunches available. MC, V.*
Restrictions: *No smoking, no pets.*

Linné Bed and Breakfast

The inn is named after Swedish naturalist Carl von Linné, the first scientist to classify plants and animals according to class, genus, and species. *Linnaea borealis,* a small pink-and-white Swedish wildflower named for the naturalist, was happily adopted by Robert Eriksson as the inn's logo.

Linné was built in 1896 for a former seaman, so it's not surprising that the dining room, with high casement windows and original gas wall sconces, looks like a ship's cabin. Beyond the dining room, the decor is more Scandinavian than nautical. The woodwork is by Swedish immigrants, and the furniture and artwork are by co-owner Robert Eriksson, whose background is Swedish.

The Swedish influence continues in the clean and uncluttered bedrooms. Room 1 is typical, a large corner room in traditional Scandinavian blue and white with an oak and mahogany floor, white wicker furniture, and white lace curtains. Room 3 has a four-poster bed and access to a three-season porch.

Address: *2645 Fremont Ave. S, Minneapolis, MN 55408, tel. 612/377–4418.*
Accommodations: *3 double rooms share 1 bath.*
Amenities: *Ceiling fans in room.*
Rates: *$50–$60; Continental breakfast, evening snack. AE.*
Restrictions: *No smoking, no pets.*

Nicollet Island Inn

This 1893 limestone building, on a small island in the middle of the Mississippi River, was formerly the Island Sash and Door Company. In the mid-1980s, the building was gutted, leaving only maple floors and a few exposed-brick and limestone walls, and converted into the Nicollet Island Inn.

The first floor is occupied by a restaurant where you can dine on regional cuisine at tables overlooking the river. There's also a pleasant, sunny bar with equally good views, and a lounge with a fireplace and baby grand piano.

Guest rooms, on the second and third floors, have Early American and country-style reproduction furniture. The rooms aren't large, but they are quite comfortable, and half have river views. The best rooms are corner rooms 209 and 309, which overlook the river and the park, where free concerts are held on summer evenings.

Address: *95 Merriam St., Minneapolis, MN 55401, tel. 612/331-1800, fax 612/331-6528.*
Accommodations: *24 double rooms with baths.*
Amenities: *Cable TV, VCRs, phones, hair dryers, mineral water, cookies, newspapers; whirlpool tubs in 2 rooms; restaurant and bar, 3 meeting rooms, movies for rent; off-street parking.*
Rates: *$110–$145; breakfast extra. AE, D, MC, V.*
Restrictions: *No smoking in some rooms.*

1900 Dupont

This B&B has the best location of the Minneapolis bed-and-breakfasts in the tree-lined, prosperous Kenwood/Lowry Hill neighborhood, just blocks from downtown, the Guthrie Theater, Walker Art Center, and Lake of the Isles. Its location is only the beginning of what this 5,000-square-foot 1896 Colonial Revival House has to offer. Enter the unusual library on the landing between the first and second floors through leaded-glass doors into a wonderful mahogany-lined retreat full of leather sofas, built-in bookcases, and a huge fireplace. In contrast to the masculine library is a lovely small solarium with a glass table and chairs. Because of owner Chris Viken's background in house restoration, there are well-kept antiques throughout.

All three guest quarters are corner rooms with bay windows. Joseph's Room, the largest, shares a bath with Elliott's Room. Leslie's Room, the nicest of the three rooms, has a bay window, queen-size bed, sunny exposure, and private blue-and-white tiled bath. Breakfast is served in the dining room or in guest rooms.

Address: *1900 Dupont Ave. S, Minneapolis, MN 55403, tel. 612/374-1973.*
Accommodations: *1 double room with bath, 2 doubles share 1 bath.*
Amenities: *Air-conditioning, TV in den.*
Rates: *$59–$85; Continental breakfast. No credit cards.*
Restrictions: *No smoking, no pets.*

The Rose Bed and Breakfast

The Rose Bed and Breakfast is a charming 1926 English Tudor brick house set on 1.6 acres. Owners Carol Kindschi and Larry Greenberg's tastes are quite eclectic: There's a built-in buffet in the dining room, Oriental rugs, leather furniture, lots of ethnic wall hangings, and some very modern purple barrel chairs. Even more unusual are the Welsh Deacon's bench from the 19th century and the turn-of-the-century dental cabinet (complete with tools) in the living room.

Both suites overlook the University of Minnesota's golf course and the house's tennis court. The third-floor Rosepointe Suite has the best views of the grounds and the most privacy. Its large, carpeted bedroom has Scandinavian furniture, a sitting area has a wicker chaise longue, a new black and white bathroom centers around a large deep bathtub, and sliding glass doors lead to a private deck. The less private second-floor suite, with bedroom, bath, and a corner study, opens onto the same hallway as the master bedroom.

Address: *2129 Larpenteur Ave. W, Falcon Heights, MN 55113, tel. 612/642-9417 or 800/966-2728.*
Accommodations: *2 suites.*
Amenities: *Air-conditioning, TVs, clock radios, in rooms, down comforters, fresh flowers, bedtime snacks, phone in 3rd-floor suite; tennis court.*
Rates: *$65–$75; full breakfast. MC, V.*
Restrictions: *No smoking, no pets.*

Schumacher's New Prague Hotel

Schumacher's New Prague Hotel was originally the Broz Hotel, established in 1898 and designed by Cass Gilbert, the architect who also designed the Minnesota State Capitol and the Library of Congress. Although the exterior, which is listed in the National Register of Historic Places, was restored in 1974, the interior was essentially gutted by owner John Schumacher. Now managed by John and his wife, Kathleen, the hotel is well run, albeit overdecorated. The guest rooms, each with a German feather bed, are a comfortable if rather incongruous mixture of modern amenities alongside European antiques and handmade Bavarian-style furniture.

John, a former chef for the Marriott Hotel Corporation, has brought his talent to the hotel's well-respected Central European Restaurant. Especially popular are the baked goods, such as the home-baked *kolaches* (sweet rolls).

Address: *212 W. Main St., New Prague, MN 56071, tel. 612/758-2133.*
Accommodations: *11 double rooms with baths.*
Amenities: *Air-conditioning, half-bottle of wine, chocolates, phones, sound systems, and whirlpool tubs, gas fireplaces in 7 rooms, restaurant.*
Rates: *$104–$150; breakfast extra. AE, D, MC, V.*
Restrictions: *No pets.*

Mississippi River Valley and Historic Bluff Country

The glaciers that steamrollered Minnesota eons ago somehow missed shearing off the high points in the southeastern part of the state. The result is a sawtooth collection of bluffs and valleys known as Bluff Country.

Bluff Country is farm country, but it's also heavily wooded with oaks and maples. Here you'll find soaring hills and plunging valleys marbled with gently flowing streams and top-notch bike and Nordic ski trails. Scattered about are drowsy little towns, some that bear few signs of modern times. One is the almost impossibly picturesque town of Lanesboro, nestled in the bluffs just east of the intersection of Routes 16 and 52. This isolated community of 900 or so souls is so unspoiled that its entire downtown district has been placed on the National Register of Historic Places.

The Mississippi River is the headline act in this region, of course. There's no better way to view it than from U.S. 61 between Red Wing and Winona. This is a dramatic drive. The road unravels past towers of limestone that at times stretch 500 feet into the sky. According to legend, a despondent Native American maiden named We-No-Nah jumped to her death from these bluffs, giving Winona its name. Today, falcons and eagles can occasionally be spotted circling in the sky where We-No-Nah made her fatal plunge.

The river towns that populate the banks of the Mississippi vacillate between maintaining their independent character as onetime lumber and shipping centers and giving in totally to the tourist trade.

Popular as destinations for folks from Rochester and the Twin Cities, places like Wabasha, Frontenac, and Lake City are still largely uncrowded and pleasant. Unlike in Red Wing, which is particularly frenzied on autumn Saturdays, it's still possible to quietly enjoy river scenes in these communities.

Places to Go, Sights to See

Cannon Valley Trail (306 W. Mill St., Cannon Falls, tel. 507/263–3954). Bike, hike, or ski along the 19.7-mile asphalt and crushed-limestone Cannon Valley Trail, which follows the Cannon River from Cannon Falls to Red Wing along the Cannon Valley Line's abandoned railbed. The trains ran from 1883 until 1976; bicyclists and skiers can be found there almost year-round now.

Frontenac State Park (Rte. 2, Box 134, Lake City, tel. 612/345–3401), 10 miles southeast of Red Wing along the Mississippi River's Lake Pepin, is comprised of more than 1,700 acres, including 13.4 miles of hiking trails, 6 miles of cross-country ski trails, rustic and semimodern campsites, and picnic grounds. It's also a premier site for watching the migration of birds, including warblers, bald and golden eagles, and peregrine falcons.

Northfield, home to both St. Olaf and Carleton colleges, is just 45 minutes south of the Twin Cities. On September 7, 1876, eight members of the infamous James-Younger band of outlaws rode into this community with the intent of robbing the First National Bank. The gang, thwarted midway through their crime by alarmed townspeople, didn't get a dime. Only Frank and Jesse James escaped. Northfield holds a "Defeat of Jesse James Celebration," reenacting the seven-minute bank raid and shoot-out, on the weekend after Labor Day. The bank is now the *Northfield Historical Society Museum* (408 Division St., Northfield, tel. 507/645–9268).

Red Wing. A historic limestone-bluffed river port and former grain-milling and -shipping town, Red Wing is just an hour south of the Twin Cities. Partake of three self-guided walking tours of the town's historic districts by picking up maps at the *Red Wing Heritage Preservation Commission* (City Hall, 315 W. 4th St., Red Wing, tel. 612/388–6734). On your tour check out what's playing at the recently restored *T. B. Sheldon Auditorium Theatre* (Third St. at East Ave., tel. 612/388–2806), which hosts everything from dramas to country-western concerts. Golfers will love the 27-hole course at the new world-class *Mississippi National Golf Links* (409 Golf Links Dr., tel. 612/388–1874). Observe pottery being made at the *Red Wing Stoneware Company* (U.S. 61, 4 mi west of Red Wing, tel. 612/388–4610), or watch how the famous *Red Wing Shoes* (U.S. 61 and Cannon River Ave., tel. 612/388–8211) are put together from the factory's observation deck. Red Wing has many lovely and historic homes and buildings, and from May through October you can enjoy a narrated ride through these historic sections of town aboard *Red Wing Trolley's* "Spirit of Red Wing" (604 Bush St., tel. 612/388–3300).

Winona. The *River City Carriage Company* (673 Olmstead St., tel. 507/457–3239) offers horse-drawn carriage tours of this historic river town, as well as package rides that include a picnic, dinner, and lodging. History buffs will also enjoy the *Juluis C. Wilkie Steamboat Center* (in Levee Park on Main St. at the river, tel. 507/454–6880), a full-scale replica of an old-time steamboat. The first deck contains a museum of the river's history, steamboat artifacts, and a slide presentation prepared by Winona State University. For a real river ride, the *Jollie Ollie Paddlewheeler* (75 Kansas St., tel. 507/454–6027) travels south on the Mississippi River from Winona, with brunch, dinner, and sightseeing cruises during warm-weather months. The *Polish Cultural Institute of Winona* (102 Liberty St., tel. 507/454–3431) houses Kashubian artifacts, family heirlooms, religious articles, and folk art. *Garvin Heights Park* (straight south on Huff St. past U.S. 14 and U.S. 61) offers hiking trails, a scenic drive, and a 500-foot overlook, all with splendid views of the city, the Mississippi, and Wisconsin on the opposite shore.

Restaurants

In Lanesboro there are two pricey places and an alternative noted for its traditional home-cooked meals. The **Victorian House** (709 Parkway Ave. S, Lanesboro, tel. 507/467–3457), a French restaurant in a house setting, offers lamb Provençal and filet mignon. **Mrs. B's** (101 Parkway Ave., Lanesboro, tel. 507/467–2154) serves multiple-course meals table d'hôte style using such Minnesota products as wild rice and berries. The lower-priced **Chat and Chew Cafe** (701 Parkway Ave. S, Lanesboro, tel. 507/467–3444) stands out for home-baked rolls and homemade soups. The American-style dining is good at the St. James Hotel's **Port of Red Wing** (406 Main St., Red Wing, tel. 612/388–2846 or 800/252–1875). In Wabasha stop in at **The Anderson House** (333 W. Main St., Wabasha, tel. 612/565–4524 or 800/862–9702), where the country-style cooking is hearty and the breads and pastries home-baked. Many people staying in Wabasha, Lake City, and even Winona cross Lake Pepin to Pepin, Wisconsin, to have dinner at the justifiably famous **Harbor View Cafe** (First and Main Sts., Pepin, tel. 715/442–3893), to savor its superb breads, creative cookery, and equally creative wine list.

Tourist Information

Minnesota Office of Tourism, Southern Regional Office (Box 286, Mankato, MN 56001, tel. 507/389–2683 or 800/657–3700); **Red Wing Area Chamber of Commerce** (Box 133–B, Red Wing, MN 55066, tel. 612/388–4719 or 800/762–9516); **Winona Convention and Visitors Bureau** (67 Main St., Winona, MN 55987, tel. 507/452–2272); **Northfield Area Chamber of Commerce** (Box 198, Northfield, MN 55057, tel. 507/645–5604 or 800/658–2548).

JailHouse Inn

At any other time in the past century, law-abiding citizens would have hurried past this 1869 Italianate redbrick building, which served as the Fillmore County Jail for more than 100 years. Now they linger. After sitting empty for 15 more years, the jail, and the adjacent sheriff's quarters and offices, were turned into a 12-room inn, having been so extensively remodeled in 1985 that it is almost impossible to guess the structure's original use. Almost. One room provides an unforgettable reminder: The Cell Block Room still has its bars. Otherwise it is much more comfortable than any inmate could have dreamed. Two queen-size beds with tufted bedspreads occupy separate cells and are fitted with rag rugs, a whirlpool bath big enough for two, a sitting area, and the original toilet and basin.

Rest assured that you won't feel the least bit incarcerated in the other bedrooms, all of which have beautiful pine or oak floors, and many of which are decorated with Eastlake furniture. The blue and rose Master Bedroom has a crocheted bedspread, large windows, and a huge old 1,000-pound china tub. The Oriental Room has a large, comfortable bathroom with claw-foot tub and a purple-and-black marble fireplace. The pine-floored, maroon and rust Detention Room has access to the south-facing second-floor porch. Even some of the JailHouse's smaller rooms—such as

the bright yellow and white Sun Room or the blue and white Amish Room—are just as light and clean as the larger rooms.

There are plenty of public spaces, including the front parlor, which has a pine floor, marble fireplace, and grandfather clock; the larger and brighter oak-floored kitchen; and the first- and second-floor porches. Breakfast is served in a sunny, spacious basement dining area.

Owners Jeanne and Marc Sather, former restaurant designers from San Francisco, are accomplished cooks and veteran hosts, happy to lend their premises and their talents to special events or even impromptu trout dinners if you should find yourself lucky enough to catch one in the nearby Root River.

Address: *109 Houston 3 NW (Box 422), Preston, MN 55965, tel. 507/765-2181.*
Accommodations: *11 double rooms with baths, 1 2-bedroom suite.*
Amenities: *Air-conditioning, fireplaces in 4 rooms, breakfast room and parlor, whirlpool baths in 3 rooms, 1 meeting room, audiovisual equipment.*
Rates: *$40–$140; Continental breakfast weekdays, full breakfast weekends, afternoon refreshments. D, MC, V.*
Restrictions: *No smoking, no pets.*

Mrs. B's Historic Lanesboro Inn

This inn spent part of its 120-year history as a combination retail furniture company—funeral home, but no vestige of its former use can be found today. A cheery, four-story 1870 limestone structure on the Root River in downtown Lanesboro, Mrs. B's is bright, light, and bursting with the energy of the outdoors people who make up much of its clientele.

Lanesboro is a picturesque small town in the heart of bluff country. The 35-mile asphalt recreation trail for hiking, biking, and cross-country skiing that follows the Root River runs right by Mrs. B's. You can rent bikes and canoes just down the street, or enjoy the view of the river from the two side decks or the backyard garden patio that faces it.

Inside, Mrs. B's is cozy if not historically significant. Before its opening as an inn in 1984, it was essentially gutted—and rooms and baths added. The bathrooms are jarringly modern. The guest rooms however, are much more creatively decorated, with most of the furniture (including sleigh and cupboard-style beds) locally made, some of it reflecting the Scandinavian heritage of the town's residents. The nicest rooms are the two back corner ones, which have river views. Also desirable are the three rooms with direct access to the inn's wooden side decks, furnished with large, comfortable, wood rocking chairs.

The inn's only common area is a rather small but comfortable lobby, equipped with a piano, warmed by a fireplace, and brightened by huge arched windows facing the street. In summer, guests can use the two-story side porch and the riverfront patio.

"Our goal is to make guests comfortable," says owner Bill Sermeus and his wife, Mimi Abell, who bought the inn in early 1991. "We don't have antiques but we do have good beds, soft chairs, and good food."

Indeed, Mrs. B's is well known for its dinners, which are five-course table d'hôte affairs that take advantage of local products. Dinners are available by reservation only and include such specialties as wildflower salad, corn and wild-rice chowder, and wild-berry sorbet.

Address: *101 Parkway Ave. (Box 411), Lanesboro, MN 55949, tel. 507/467-2154.*
Accommodations: *10 double rooms with baths.*
Amenities: *Air-conditioning, 2 rooms with gas fireplaces; restaurant.*
Rates: *$53–$63 weekdays, $85–$95 Fri. and Sat.; full breakfast, afternoon tea served on Fri. and Sat. No credit cards.*
Restrictions: *Smoking in bedrooms only, no pets.*

Pratt-Taber Inn

If you're still a little sleepy at breakfast and you see a woman in Victorian clothes serving the fruit salad, don't be alarmed. Owner Jane Molander likes to serve breakfast wearing antique hats and dresses from her large collection. Her cleaning staff also dresses in period garb.

Jane and her husband, Dick, are innkeepers of a white-trimmed brick Italianate Victorian house in Red Wing, a historic Mississippi River town. Jane, who was born and grew up in Red Wing, named the inn after banker A. W. Pratt, who built it for his family, and for Robert Taber, his son-in-law, who bought it in 1905.

The house, which is listed in the National Register of Historic Places, was restored in 1984. Old photographs guided much of the exterior work, including replacement of the porches; one of them is embellished by an interesting detailed star pattern that honors the Centennial year, 1867, when the house was built. Inside there are parquet floors, butternut and walnut woodwork, glass chandeliers, feather-painted slate fireplaces, and in the dining room, a large bay window. Throughout the house you'll find antique furniture that dates from 1860 to 1880, including a 110-year-old Murphy bed housed in a Victorian buffet.

Three of the four upstairs rooms are corner rooms, and all are large and full of antiques. Polly's Room is par-

ticularly nice, with its queen-size brass bed, soft blue-and-ecru decor, and black marble fireplace. Jane proudly tells guests that radio personality and author Garrison Keillor stayed in antique-filled Mary Lu's Room, which has views of Barns Bluff, while he was in Red Wing to perform at the T. B. Sheldon Theatre.

Breakfast is served in the dining room, on the porches, or in the guest bedrooms, all of which contain tables for two. Jane usually uses her collection of original 1932 Orleans patterned Red Wing pottery.

Being a native and a bit of a town booster, she's also glad to provide guests with information on local activities, especially the summer trolley tours that stop right at the inn's front door.

Address: *706 W. Fourth St., Red Wing, MN 55066, tel. 612/388–5945.* **Accommodations:** *2 double rooms with baths, 4 doubles share 2 baths; the 2 downstairs rooms, library, and bath can be rented as a suite.* **Amenities:** *Air-conditioning, clock radios, fireplace in 1 room; pickup service at airport, dock, or train station; bicycles.* **Rates:** *$59–$89; full breakfast, afternoon refreshments. MC, V.*

Thorwood Historic Inns

If you want a luxurious bed-and-breakfast visit, as so many of the repeat guests do, the Thorwood Historic Inns—the 1880 Queen Anne Rosewood and the 1880 Second Empire–style Thorwood—are for you.

Pam and Dick Thorsen, a down-to-earth and friendly couple, fell in love with the river town of Hastings, 20 miles south of St. Paul, and opened Thorwood in 1983. The 6,600-square-foot house was built by a local lumber baron, William Thompson, and his wife, Sara, as their family home. Then, in 1989, the Thorsens opened the 10,000-square-foot Rosewood, six blocks away.

Interestingly, both inns were hospitals at one time, and occasionally people who were born in the buildings come back as guests to celebrate their birthdays.

Thorwood and Rosewood are not cozy, family-style bed-and-breakfasts. Thorwood has retained more of its original rooms and fixtures, and because the Thorsens live there, is the homier of the two inns. It has a bay window and a fireplace in its main parlor, an interesting square bay in the front parlor, and maple floors throughout.

Rosewood has a grand piano, a large fireplace, large ornate public rooms, and several bay windows big enough to park a Volkswagen in. Dark green wallpaper and carpet, and white and oak woodwork, along with the building's great size, make Rosewood almost overwhelmingly formal.

Remodeling has given fireplaces and whirlpool baths to both inns' guest rooms. The largest and most ornate is a 1,200-foot suite called Mississippi Under the Stars, which has a baby grand piano, a fireplace, a double whirlpool tub under a skylight, a round shower, a copper soaking tub, and a queen-size bed.

Thorwood's most elaborate rooms are Sara's Suite, a purple and white three-level arrangement with a skylight over the bed, a double whirlpool tub, and the best view; and the Steeple Room, with a built-in whirlpool bath set right into the steeple and a glass-domed fireplace dividing the bath area from the bedroom.

The Thorsens have taken to offering breakfast either in the public rooms or in baskets at your door.

Address: *315 Pine St., Hastings, MN 55033, tel. 612/437-3297.*
Accommodations: *12 double rooms with bath, 3 suites.*
Amenities: *Air-conditioning, fireplaces in 8 rooms, whirlpool baths in 10 rooms, gift shop.*
Rates: *$75–$225; full breakfast, afternoon refreshments, dinners available. AE, MC, V.*
Restrictions: *No smoking, no pets.*

The Victorian Bed & Breakfast

Wonderful views of Lake Pepin from each guest room make Lake City's Victorian Bed & Breakfast special. The lake, which many people claim is the most beautiful spot on the Mississippi, dominates the downstairs public rooms, whose large windows face it.

Owners Sandy and Joel Grettenberg are teachers in Rochester, Minnesota, some 35 miles to the west of Lake City. They came to town one fall Saturday to buy apples and ended up buying the inn.

The building, although an 1896 Stick-style Victorian, has a refreshing simplicity inside. Butternut wood on the staircase banisters and elsewhere is carved but not elaborately so; small and simple stained-glass windows, in rose, amber, and blue, are set atop larger plain-glass windows.

Decorated in antiques, modern sofas, and German and Japanese furniture acquired by Sandy's military family, the Victorian B&B is eclectic and comfortable, but not overstuffed. The most interesting items are the 19th-century German music boxes, one of which plays a variety of tunes including, strangely enough, "The Marseillaise."

Juliette's Room (named after the wife of Thomas Morrow, the local bank director for whom the house was built) is the best one, with sweeping lake views from the huge bay window and a private bath with wide-plank pine floor and rare antique pillbox toilet.

Teresa's and Kari's rooms (named after the Grettenbergs' grown daughters) share a full bath downstairs, but each has its own private half-bath. Teresa's Room is a large corner room at the front of the house with wonderful lake views, a sitting area with white wicker furniture, and a king-size bed that can be divided into two twin beds.

An elaborate Continental breakfast of fresh fruit compote and home-baked breads and muffins is served either in the sunny dining room, which also overlooks the lake, or in guest rooms.

Address: *620 S. High St., Lake City, MN 55041, tel. 612/345-2167.*
Accommodations: *1 double room with bath, 2 doubles with half-baths share downstairs bath.*
Amenities: *Air-conditioning, TV in sitting room.*
Rates: *$55–$70; Continental breakfast, afternoon refreshments. No credit cards.*
Restrictions: *Smoking on porch only, no pets; closed Christmas and Thanksgiving.*

The Anderson House

Minnesota's oldest operating hotel, The Anderson House was built in 1856, two years before Minnesota became a state, and was purchased in the early 1900s by the Anderson family. Except for 12 years in the late 1960s to early '70s, it's been run by Andersons and their heirs ever since.

Owner John Hall, who has been remodeling the hotel in stages since 1976, has taken care to leave some of the things that give character to an old lodging. Thus, although the baths are modern, the floors slant, the halls are crooked, and the doors occasionally stick.

Guest rooms are furnished with a mixture of antiques, reproductions, and new pieces.

The Anderson House is justly famous for two things: the 15 resident cats that guests can "check out" for the night (complete with food and litter box), and the Pennsylvania Dutch–style food served in its first-floor restaurant, where all baking is done from scratch.

Address: *333 W. Main St., Wabasha, MN 55981, tel. 612/565-4524.*
Accommodations: *22 double rooms with baths, 8 doubles share 2 baths, 5 suites.*
Amenities: *Air-conditioning, whirlpool baths in 2 suites, 17 rooms have river views, 1 banquet/ conference room, restaurant, bar.*
Rates: *$35–$105; breakfast extra. MC, V.*
Restrictions: *Closed Nov. 2–Mar. 31.*

The Archer House

Owner Dallas Haas and his wife are constantly adding to or renovating the 1877 Second Empire–style hotel and the block of adjacent buildings he bought in 1981. The Haases have figured out what appeals to the historic hotel aficionado and, with the constant college trade in Northfield, they have a busy establishment on their hands.

The hallways and guest rooms, heavy on dried flowers, crocheted bedspreads, and wallpaper, are mostly small and dark, for this was originally a modest tradesman's hotel. Hence, the smaller rooms seem right but the larger ones with whirlpool baths seem a bit out of place.

The lobby is cluttered with bric-a-brac, but there's a nice restaurant

on the riverfront level that's especially cozy on a winter's day. In summer, have dinner outdoors on a patio overlooking the river.

Address: *212 Division St., Northfield, MN 55057, tel. 507/645-5661, fax 507/645-4295.*
Accommodations: *35 double rooms with baths, 3 suites.*
Amenities: *Air-conditioning, TV, phones in rooms, whirlpool baths in 19 rooms (these rooms also get complimentary champagne), children's game and toy area on third floor, ice and soft-drink machines, restaurants, shops, 4 conference rooms.*
Rates: *$40–$145; breakfast extra. D, MC, V.*
Restrictions: *No pets.*

The Candle Light Inn

John Falter and Ruth Lane traveled around Mississippi River towns searching for a large home to make into a bed-and-breakfast. In Red Wing, they found the one for them—a Queen Anne, built in 1877 by Horace Rich, who once managed the Red Wing Stoneware Company. Much of the woodwork, including the grand staircase, is of walnut, although oak, cherry, and butternut accent the cabinetry, parquet floors, and trim. There are five fireplaces, including a feather-painted one in the parlor and another in the cherry cabinet–lined library. Unusual rose, blue, and orange beveled stained-glass windows mark the entryway.

Ruth had previously owned a bed, bath, and drapery shop in Wisconsin, so the beautiful decor in the four guest rooms is not surprising. The second-floor Rose Garden Room, done in green, rose, and white, is especially charming with its sunny corner location, white woodwork, fireplace, whirlpool bath, and large bay window.

Address: *818 W. Third St., Red Wing, MN 55066, tel. 612/388–8034.* **Accommodations:** *3 double rooms with bath, 1 suite.* **Amenities:** *Air-conditioning, fireplaces in 2 rooms, whirlpool baths in 3 rooms.* **Rates:** *$75–$135; full breakfast, afternoon refreshments. MC, V.* **Restrictions:** *No smoking, no pets.*

Carriage House Bed & Breakfast

This 1870 carriage house is the largest remaining in a river city that once had many such buildings. The three-story structure, white with green shutters, lies behind a matching Italianate house, the home of bed-and-breakfast proprietors Debi and Don Salyards. Both houses are directly across the street from the Winona State University campus, where Don works as an economics professor.

All four guest rooms are on the second floor of the carriage house. Two are expanded versions of the former stable boys' quarters, which retain their original windows and woodwork; the other two are somewhat larger with high ceilings and windows. The best guest room is the Village Loft, which has a small table and chairs and a large bathroom with a skylight over the miniature claw-foot tub.

Guests can have tea and coffee on the first floor in a sunny, four-season porch. Breakfast is delivered to the porch at a time arranged by guests. Debi can direct guests to bike trails, golf courses, and other local activities.

Address: *420 Main St., Winona, MN 55987, tel. 507/452–8256.* **Accommodations:** *2 double rooms with baths, 2 doubles share 1 bath.* **Amenities:** *Air-conditioning; bicycles, shuttle service from boat docks or train station.* **Rates:** *$60–$85; Continental breakfast. MC, V.* **Restrictions:** *No smoking, no pets.*

Carrolton Country Inn

Half the fun of staying at this 100-year-old farmhouse is getting to it. From Lanesboro follow an old oxcart trail for 3 miles, crossing the Root River and the historic Scanlon-Ford Bridge, as the trail winds along a narrow valley. At the end, you'll reach the Carrolton Country Inn, a nine-room farmhouse built by a Norwegian immigrant family in 1880. Owners Gloria and Charles Ruen opened it as a bed-and-breakfast in 1987 when they moved to a nearby farm (guests pick up the keys there).

The charm of the modest and rather inexpensively decorated house lies in its bucolic pastoral setting.

Guests prepare their own breakfast each morning, helping themselves to the things in the well-stocked refrigerator.

The guest rooms are on the dark side, with modern wallpaper and furniture. The best one by far is the Carrolton Room, a large corner room facing north and east with a small private balcony and views of the beautiful little farm and dramatic bluffs beyond.

Address: *RR 2 (Box 139), Lanesboro, MN 55949, tel. 507/467-2257.*
Accommodations: *2 double rooms with baths, 2 doubles share 1 bath.*
Amenities: *Air-conditioning, clock radios, piano, TV in parlor, phone in 1 room; picnic table.*
Rates: *$55–$85; full breakfast. MC, V.*
Restrictions: *No smoking, no pets.*

Cottonwood Inn

The Cottonwood Inn was moved when the new interstate bridge over the Mississippi River was built. A handsome 1872 Italianate house, built as the Congregational Church's parsonage, the inn is across U.S. 61 from Wabasha and the river and set among the bluffs that line the Mississippi here.

The decor is modern with just a few antiques, although the oak and maple floors and walnut and mahogany banister are original. The best bedrooms are the three upstairs, which are light, with views of the surrounding bluffs and countryside. The Paisley Room, which has a private bath with a claw-foot tub, is especially nice. The other two, which share a bath, also have their own half-baths; the Rose Room, decorated, of course, in pinks and reds, has a particularly beautiful view. The two downstairs rooms in the recently remodeled contemporary basement are rather dark. Alice Bach-Johnson, who bought the inn in 1991, serves a full breakfast in the dining room or in the new three-season garden room, which has plenty of light and country air.

Address: *100 Coulee Way, Wabasha, MN 55981, tel. 612/565-2466.*
Accommodations: *3 double rooms with baths, 2 doubles share 1 bath.*
Amenities: *Air-conditioning in 1 room, VCR/TV in library and family room, fireplace in back parlor.*
Rates: *$50–$70; full breakfast, picnic lunches available upon request. No credit cards.*
Restrictions: *No smoking, no pets.*

Dr. Joseph Moses House

This 1930s Cape Cod house is the first, and as yet the only, bed-and-breakfast in busy, charming Northfield, the home of two well-respected liberal-arts colleges, St. Olaf and Carleton. On a pleasant, tree-lined street four blocks from downtown, the Moses House is a cozy, quiet alternative to the much larger Archer House Hotel or the city's several motels.

Although it's not an ornate house, owners Ron Halversen and Kathleen Murphy have made it quite a pleasant one; they've often served as hosts to parents of students and will even rent out the entire house for graduations, weddings, recitals, and other events.

Maple floors, slanted ceilings, gabled windows, and distinctive 1930s tiled bathrooms make the upstairs far more charming than the carpeted, rather sparsely furnished first floor.

Address: *1100 S. Division St., Northfield, MN 55057, tel. 507/663–1563.*
Accommodations: *3 double rooms and 1 single share 2 baths.*
Amenities: *Air-conditioning, clock radios, fireplace in 1 room, cedar-lined closets; cable TV, stereo, and VCR on 4-season porch.*
Rates: *$32–$85; full breakfast. No credit cards.*
Restrictions: *No smoking, no pets.*

Historic Scanlan House

All of downtown Lanesboro is on the National Register of Historic Places. At the quiet end of the main street, the Scanlan House is an architectural gem, with its whimsically painted 1889 Queen Anne exterior and balconied, onion-dome turret. It's also just a few blocks from the Root River and the popular 35-mile-long bike-ski trail.

The public areas and bedrooms of the Scanlan House are a bit crowded with Victoriana, but most of the guest rooms are sunny and several (including the Masquerade and Grandma Bell's rooms) are spacious corner rooms. The Masquerade Room also has the best view of the neighboring bluffs from its second-floor balcony.

The dining room and parlor are rather dark, and less than romantic in the evenings, when owners Kristen, Mary, and Gene Mensing watch TV in the adjoining living room. Outdoors, however, the tiny front porch provides a nice summer spot for two.

Address: *708 Parkway Ave. S, Lanesboro, MN 55949, tel. 507/467–2158 or 800/944–2158.*
Accommodations: *3 double rooms with baths, 2 doubles share 1 bath.*
Amenities: *Air-conditioning, chocolates, minibottle of champagne, TV in rooms, whirlpool baths in 2 rooms; bicycles, off-street parking.*
Rates: *$55–$125; full breakfast, coffee and baked goods all day. AE, MC, V.*
Restrictions: *No smoking, no pets.*

Hungry Point Inn

As you drive up the road to the Hungry Point Inn you may feel you've been transported to the 18th century. The inn is part of an unusual 1960 development where all the houses' exteriors where made to look as if they had been built before 1820—in other words, before Minnesota was even settled. The Revolutionary War–era atmosphere continues inside Merriam Carroll Last's inn, with its wide-plank pine floors, beamed ceilings, and giant fireplace. Rooms are also in a 1770s style with quilts, rag rugs, and antique beds and chests.

The most popular room in the inn is actually a separate little house—an authentic 1870s log cabin restored to hold a kitchen, two bedrooms (with two beds in each), a small parlor with a Vermont casting fireplace, and a room with a whirlpool tub. It's a bit on the claustrophobic side, with its small size and tiny windows, so it's a better cozy hideaway than a summer retreat, but its palpable history and romantic seclusion (breakfast is delivered to the door) keep it booked year-round.

Address: *1 Old Deerfield Rd., Welch, MN 55089, tel. 612/437–3660 or 612/388–7857.*
Accommodations: *4 double rooms share 1½ baths, 1 2-bedroom log cabin with bath.*
Amenities: *Air-conditioning, fireplaces in 2 rooms and cabin, whirlpool bath in cabin.*
Rates: *$69–$135; full breakfast, afternoon wine and cheese. D, MC, V.*
Restrictions: *No smoking, no pets.*

Martin Oaks

Martin Oaks stands out not for opulence but for its lovely simplicity, quiet setting, and the great charm of its proprietors, Frank and Marie Gery, who opened their 1869 Victorian Italianate bed-and-breakfast a year ago in tiny Dundas, where Frank teaches economics at St. Olaf College. Marie works as a professional storyteller and is an accomplished cook. Lovely multiple-course breakfasts of fresh fruit, homemade breads, herbed French toast, or Belgian waffles are served in the dining room or on the screened porch.

Guest rooms overlook the trees and gardens, and all three, including the smallest, called The Hideaway, have original wide-board pine floors. The largest, the Martin Suite, has an extra single bed and a sitting area. Sara Etta's Room, which may be the most attractive, has a hand-stenciled ivy pattern along the tops of the walls. Marie changes the rooms' decor seasonally, with cozy handmade quilts and warm draperies in winter and white chenille spreads and airy sheer curtains in summer.

Address: *107 First St., Box 207, Dundas, MN 55019, tel. 507/645–4644.*
Accommodations: *3 double rooms share 1 bath.*
Amenities: *Air-conditioning, grand piano in living room.*
Rates: *$45–$65; full breakfast, late-afternoon tea, bedtime snacks in room. MC, V.*
Restrictions: *No smoking, no pets.*

Quill & Quilt

The unusual name of this bed-and-breakfast, a Colonial Revival house built in 1897, makes perfect sense once you've met the proprietors. "Quill" alludes to owner David Karpinski's part-time freelance writing; "quilt" to the occupation of his wife, Denise Anderson—quiltmaking. It's this occupation that truly distinguishes their inn, for Denise's handiwork decorates each of the five bedrooms, and she offers occasional two-day quilting seminars during the inn's slow season in late winter—although, the slow season is very short.

The Colvill Suite is probably the nicest room: It has a bedroom, sitting room, a great airy bathroom with a double whirlpool bath, and a private deck overlooking the busy town baseball diamond. Avoid the Quilters' Room unless you don't mind a downstairs room right by the front door, and a bath adjacent to the dining room.

Address: *615 W. Hoffman St., Cannon Falls, MN 55009, tel. 507/263-5507 or 800/488-3849.*
Accommodations: *4 double rooms with baths (2 nonadjoining), 1 suite.*
Amenities: *Air-conditioning, coffee-makers, clock radios, basement recreation room with TV, VCR, and gift shop.*
Rates: *$45–$105; full breakfast, evening dessert and coffee. MC, V.*
Restrictions: *Smoking in recreation room and on porches only, no pets; closed Thanksgiving weekend, Dec. 24 and 25.*

Red Gables Inn

Douglas DeRoos, a lifetime military man, traveled with his wife, Mary, throughout Europe, staying in bed-and-breakfasts. The DeRoos decided to buy the already operating 1865 Italianate Red Gables Inn as their "retirement project."

On a summer afternoon, the most pleasant place to sit at the Red Gables is on the screened porch, where Mary serves appetizers and beverages. The home, built from the trees found on the site, is unusual in that it doesn't have hardwood floors, but rather painted fir floors, which Mary has overlaid with Oriental rugs.

The best room is the large, bright Cotton Blossom, a white, rose, and blue corner guest room that faces east and south but stays cool even on the hottest summer days. Its large, sunny bathroom, shared with one other room, has a huge comfortable claw-foot tub provided with plenty of bubble bath, a pedestal sink, cheerful pink wainscoting, pink and yellow wallpaper, and a large west-facing window.

Address: *403 N. High St., Lake City, MN 55041, tel. 612/345-2605.*
Accommodations: *2 double rooms with baths, 2 doubles share 1 bath.*
Amenities: *Sherry and candies in room; bicycles, antiques store.*
Rates: *$58–$75; full breakfast, afternoon refreshments, picnic boxes, dinner if renting whole house. MC, V.*
Restrictions: *No smoking indoors, no pets.*

St. James Hotel

n 1875, when the St. James Hotel was built by 11 local businessmen, Red Wing was a bustling river town and the largest wheat market in the world. Today what remains (besides the facade) are the black walnut–paneled library and the lobby with its grand staircase, tin ceiling, and 104-year-old Steinway. The guest rooms, about half of which have river views, are new with mostly reproduction Victorian furniture and modern baths, although there's one antique in every room and a handmade quilt on every bed. Stay in the hotel's original section; a newer wing built in 1979 has lower ceilings, narrower corridors, and generally less charm.

The St. James is a hotel, restaurant, shopping area, and meeting complex of a size that belies its Main Street facade. If you're looking for a quiet spot, try the library on the main floor; in the afternoons stop in at Jimmy's, the elegant top-floor English-style pub.

Address: *406 Main St., Red Wing, MN 55066, tel. 612/388-2846 or 800/252-1875.*
Accommodations: *60 double rooms with baths.*
Amenities: *Air-conditioning, newspapers, phones, cable TV, and clock radio, whirlpool baths in 6 rooms, 9 meeting and banquet rooms, 2 restaurants, 2 bars, 11 shops; shuttle service from airport and dock.*
Rates: *$70–$135; breakfast extra, complimentary champagne, coffee. AE, MC, V.*
Restrictions: *No pets.*

Superior, the road winds past waterfalls, streams, secluded

Railroad, which offers three-hour round-trip excursions
between downtown Duluth and the state's first iron port,
Two Harbors.

The north shore was only spottily settled until the highway
was built in the 1920s, and the towns between Duluth and
Thunder Bay, Ontario, are still little more than flyspecks.
Duluth, however, is the state's fourth-largest city. Along

*with its sister city, Superior, Wisconsin, it remains
a major seaport. More than 300 years old, Duluth has
several museums and neighborhoods that call to mind the
glory days of the late 19th century, when the iron and steel
industries made it a harbor city of great wealth.*

*Lake breezes have a moderating influence on temperatures
in the region. Winters are surprisingly mild, while
summer temperatures rarely top 80°. This accounts for the
wild beauty visitors enjoy year-round. Yellow marsh
marigold, hawkweed, and stands of purple and pink lupine
share space with wild strawberries, gooseberries, and
blueberries during the summer. In autumn the hardwood
forests are ablaze with red, gold, and orange, while in the
winter the pines poke holes in the lumpy gray clouds,
releasing snowflakes as fat and lazy as feathers. Despite
the growing number of Nordic ski trails, tourists are rare
this time of year. On a weekday in the middle of January
you can stop in the woods, break open a bag of trail mix,
and feel as if you have the entire world to yourself. It's
a bit of selfishness that's understood by anyone who has
ever been here.*

Places to Go, Sights to See

Canal Park Marine Museum (First Ave. at the foot of Main St., Duluth, tel.
218/727–2497). This museum, adjoining Duluth's famous *Aerial Lift Bridge
and Lighthouse*, exhibits shipwreck relics, reconstructed ships' cabins, and
other artifacts relating to Lake Superior and its history.

Glensheen (3300 London Rd., Duluth, tel. 218/724–8864). The restored 39-
room Jacobean-style mansion of attorney, mining entrepreneur, and state
legislator Chester Congdon, Glensheen is furnished with period pieces and
antiques, some original furnishings. Seven and a half acres of lawns and
formal gardens overlook Lake Superior. For Minnesotans, the mansion holds
dark allure as the site of the 1977 double murder of Chester's daughter,
Elizabeth Congdon, and her nurse; you won't hear much about the murder on
the tour, however.

Gooseberry Falls State Park (17 mi north of Two Harbors on U.S. 61, tel.
218/834–3855). This 1,600-acre park 40 miles north of Duluth has picnic
tables and 12 miles of trails for hiking and cross-country skiing. There is also
a nature trail. The Gooseberry River enters the park at a height of 240 feet,

creating five waterfalls, two of which are 30 feet high. Interesting igneous volcanic rock outcroppings are common, in the second-growth forest of birch, poplar, alder, and black spruce.

Grand Marais is a village of 1,300 located at a natural harbor. It's a bustling little town, and one of the jumping-off places for trips to the *Superior National Forest and Boundary Waters Canoe Area* (U.S. 61, Grand Marais, tel. 218/387-2451). The Gunflint Trail, a 57-mile hiking and cross-country ski trail that runs northwest to Saganaga Lake on the Canadian border, begins in the forest. Many outdoor lovers consider this area to be the greatest canoe country in the world.

Judge C. R. Magney State Park (15 mi north of Grand Marais on U.S. 61, tel. 218/387-2929). In this state park waterfalls and turbulent rapids of the Arrowhead River have carved unusual designs into the hardened lava. There are picnic areas, hiking trails, and fishing spots. It's directly across the highway from Naniboujou Lodge.

The Kayak and Canoe Institute (University of Minnesota, Duluth, tel. 218/726-6258), part of University of Minnesota-Duluth Outdoors Program, offers weekend and day kayak trips as well as longer excursions. The package includes three days of instruction and kayaking along the north shore of Lake Superior, meals, and three nights of lodging at local resorts and bed-and-breakfasts.

Lutsen Mountains Resort (90 mi northeast of Duluth on U.S. 61, tel. 218/663-7281) is the area's largest downhill ski resort, with 27 runs and an average annual snowfall of 9½ feet. Mountain gondola and chair-lift rides operate year-round, and are especially popular during the fall foliage season. *Lutsen Resort* (tel. 218/663-7212) offers lodging on the lake, while *Lutsen Village Inn and Resort* (tel. 218/663-7241) offers lodging on the mountain. Area activities include horseback riding, cross-country skiing, tennis, stream fishing, hiking, and an 18-hole championship golf course that stretches along the lake and the Poplar River.

Split Rock Lighthouse State Park (18 mi northwest of Two Harbors on U.S. 61, tel. 218/226-3065). Perched on a cliff that juts out 170 feet over the water, this 54-foot octagonal lighthouse was built in 1910 to help prevent iron-ore ships from wrecking on the rocky reefs because of fog. The lighthouse is no longer in use and is now open to tourists, as is the lighthouse keeper's home. A new interpretive center is on the sight. Also in the park are 6 miles of foot trails and 5 miles of cross-country ski trails.

The **St. Louis County Heritage and Arts Center,** better known as the **Depot** (506 W. Michigan St., Duluth, tel. 218/727-8025), is in the restored 1892 Duluth Union Depot and houses a wide array of cultural organizations, as well as a historical museum and art gallery.

Vista Fleet (610 Missabe Bldg., Duluth, tel. 218/722-6218) has narrated sightseeing boat tours of Duluth-Superior Harbor. Lunch, dinner, or moonlight cruises are offered from May through October.

Wolf Ridge Environmental Learning Center (230 Cranberry Rd., Finland, tel. 218/353–7414). A few miles west of Little Marais, the center offers classes on astronomy, birds, nature photography, cross-country skiing, rock climbing, and more for adults, kids, and family groups.

Restaurants

Duluth, a sizable city, has many fine restaurants. Try the **Chinese Lantern** (402 First St., Duluth, tel. 218/722–7486) for Cantonese cuisine; if you crave something spicier, go down to the tiny **Hacienda Del Sol** (319 E. Superior St., Duluth, tel. 218/722–7296), which some consider to be the best Mexican food in the state. All-American steak-and-seafood meals are offered at the **Pickwick Restaurant** (508 E. Superior St., Duluth, tel. 218/727–8901). Sandwiches and salads are offered at **Grandma's** (522 Lase Ave. S, Duluth, tel. 218/727–4192), a waterfront landmark.

Restaurants are harder to find as you make your way up the north shore so don't miss **Betty's Pies** (on U.S. 61, 4 mi north of Two Harbors, tel. 218/834–3367). If you get as far north as Grand Marais, try the **Birch Terrace** (W. Sixth Ave. and Wisconsin St., Grand Marais, tel. 218/387–2215), a log cabin with a view of the lake and a menu of great steaks and fish. Right on the water is the smaller and more casual **Angry Trout Cafe** (U.S. 61, Grand Marais, tel. 218/387–1265), whose specialty is coal-grilled lake trout. A further 14 miles north along the lake, the **Naniboujou Lodge and Restaurant** (U.S. 61, 15 mi east of Grand Marais, tel. 218/387–2688) serves a Sunday brunch that is a favorite with the locals.

Tourist Information

Minnesota Office of Tourism (375 Jackson St., 250 Skyway Level, St. Paul, MN 55101–1848, tel. 612/296–5029 or 800/657–3700); **Minnesota Office of Tourism's Northeastern Minnesota Regional Office** (320 W. 2nd St., Suite 707, Duluth, MN 55802, tel. 218/723–4692); **Duluth Convention and Visitors Bureau** (100 Lake Place Dr., Duluth, MN 55802, tel. 218/772–4011); **Grand Marais Chamber of Commerce** (Box 1048, Grand Marais, MN 55604, tel. 218/387–2524 or 800/622–4014).

Barnum House Bed & Breakfast

Dick and Dorothy Humes brought up their nine children in this 1910 brick Arts and Crafts–style home. Last year, after some of their children had moved out, they opened it as a B&B with their daughter Susan Watt, and named it after the original builder, George G. Barnum, who ran the Duluth Grain Exchange. But it has retained the warmth of a well-lived-in, much-loved family home.

Quarter-sawn oak, a reminder of the city's past as a center of the lumber industry, panels the main-floor hall, the staircase, the dining room, and the upstairs hallway. The staircase has a lovely carved-oak newel post.

The Mission-style influence makes itself felt on the first floor in the huge oak beams, light fixtures (all original to the house), and the spare design of the leaded glass window at the landing. The staircase hall has a seating area with an arched fireplace.

Guest quarters are upstairs. The Barnum Suite, a large, masculine corner room, is decorated in browns and tans, with heavy, dark furniture. It shares a deck that overlooks the ravine and creek (and in winter the lake) with the large Humes Suite, perhaps the best room of the four. It is done in peach, muted gray-greens, and cream, and has a huge bay window, gas fireplace, and marvelous fainting couch. The only incongruous

note is the 1970s-style brown ceramic bathroom vanity.

Fresh-ground coffee makes a fine beginning for the elegant and filling breakfast of fruit and entreés such as hash brown–crusted quiche or caraway-seed French toast. It's served on Sue's delicate antique plates and crystal with whimsical animal-design pewter napkin rings.

Because the Barnum House is at the end of a dead-end street, it has a quiet, relaxed feel as well as peaceful views.

Address: *2211 E. Third St., Duluth, MN 55812, tel. 218/724–5434 or 800/879–5437.*
Accommodations: *3 double rooms with baths, 1 double with private nonadjoining bath.*
Amenities: *Clock radios, gas fireplaces in 2 rooms; off-street parking.*
Rates: *$95–$115; full breakfast, afternoon refreshments. MC, V.*
Restrictions: *No smoking, no pets.*

Bearskin Lodge

Dave Tuttle had worked at Bearskin Lodge Resort when it was just an old lodge and several cabins 25 miles down the Gunflint Trail from Grand Marais and Lake Superior. Then, in 1973, while he was still a senior in college, he bought it.

Today it remains low-key and woodsy, but a bit more ambitious. You'll find hiking and cross-country ski trails; boat, ski, and mountain-bike rentals; a naturalist program; even a masseuse. The lodge, built in 1980, has four large town houses; there are also 10 new or spruced-up log or log-frame cabins. The multi-level town houses, though within a wing of the lodge, feel secluded and each has a private deck. Some of the seven older cabins, built in the '20s, '30s, and '50s, have been remodeled to include room-brightening skylights above the beds. All are pleasant and have two or three bedrooms, wood stoves, and large, well-stocked kitchens. In addition, several have screened porches—critical during the buggy Northwoods summers.

The rooms in both the town houses and cabins are simple and comfortable, with chenille bedspreads and pine furniture. Each of the five two- or three-bedroom log cabins is charming, though cabins 9 and 10, built in 1990 of Engelmann spruce, are especially lovely. These cabins have birch hardwood floors, braided rugs, brand-new kitchens as well out-

fitted as any home's, and big screened porches, although they're a bit far from the lake.

One of the resort's most popular spots is the Hot Tub Hus, which guests sign up for ahead of time to use privately. Its walls, benches, and ceiling are pine, and it has a large deck and separate men's and women's changing rooms and showers.

Originally a summer-only resort, Bearskin now draws kudos from winter-sports lovers for its ice rink, sleigh rides, and 30 miles of cross-country ski trails (1 mile lighted). Lodge-to-lodge skiing packages are available.

Address: *275 Gunflint Trail, Grand Marais, MN 55604, tel. 218/388-2292 or 800/338-4170, fax 218/388-4410.*
Accommodations: *10 2- to 3-bedroom cabins and 4 1- to 3-bedroom lodge town houses.*
Amenities: *Wood stoves, grills in cabins; spa house, sauna, masseuse, full meal service available in lodge dining room, 30 miles of hiking/cross-country ski trails, ski school, ski rental, boat and mountain-bike rental, horse-drawn sleigh rides, baby-sitting, children's program, naturalist program, ice-skating rink, wine and beer for sale.*
Rates: *$110-$231; breakfast extra. AE, MC, V.*
Restrictions: *No smoking in public areas of lodge, no pets.*

The Ellery House

If it's a comfortable family place you're looking for, Jim and Joan Halquist's beautiful 1890 Queen Anne is the place to stay. The house is on a fairly busy street, yet feels rather removed because of its ¾-acre lot, hilltop location, and backyard ravine with creek.

The style inside is more arts-and-crafts than Victorian, and rooms are large, light, and sunny. The large bay window in the living room has a lake view that's best in the winter (shade trees partially obscure the view in summer).

Breakfast is served in the dining room or in three of the four guest rooms. All of these are delightful. The Ellery Suite, at the front of the house, has a small private balcony and 1920s-style bathroom. The Sunporch, a three-room suite, is made up of a cozy floral-wallpapered bedroom with a brass bed, a large bath with oversized claw-foot tub, and a sunny, plant-filled porch with wood-burning stove and treetop views. The Thomas Wahl Room is particularly nice with a tiny table for two tucked into a large lakeview bay window, the 1890s gas fireplace in the corner, the double marble shower, maple floors, and the cabbage rose hooked rug.

Joan, a violinist with the Duluth-Superior Symphony orchestra, encourages duets on the parlor's baby grand piano. Jim, whose background is in hotels, makes a point of offering comfort and relaxation to tired and stressed-out guests. In addition, with two small children themselves, the Halquists don't mind accommodating the families of others. Their congeniality make the Ellery House very homey indeed.

Address: *28 S. 21st Ave. E, Duluth, MN 55812, tel. 218/724-7639.*
Accommodations: *2 double rooms with baths, 2 suites.*
Amenities: *Fireplace in 2 rooms, 1 room with balcony, ceiling fans, fresh flowers; off-street parking.*
Rates: *$65–$98 winter, $75–$115 summer; full breakfast. AE, MC, V.*
Restrictions: *Smoking on porches only, no pets.*

The Mansion Bed
& Breakfast Inn

Though imposing from the front, this 1928 rubblestone and half-timbered Tudor mansion is really oriented toward its backyard. And what a backyard: Five hundred feet of Lake Superior shore provides the house with incredible views from almost every room.

Built for mining executive Harry C. Dudley and his wife, Marjorie Congdon Dudley, daughter of Duluth lumber baron Chester Congdon, The Mansion is an inviting combination of grandeur and comfort. The main floor has a sunny dining room with a terrazzo floor, a wood-paneled library, a large gallery with four window seats and three sets of French doors leading to a lakefront stone terrace, and a huge living room that opens onto a screened porch, a favorite of guests.

Sunny, lined with bear- and wolf-skins and mooseheads, and fitted with a huge lake-view window seat, the third-floor Trophy Room is the inn's designated quiet room. Guests use it for reading and dreaming, and "fall asleep here all the time," says proprietor Sue Monson, who, along with her husband, Warren, bought the building in 1983. Warren is a busy physician, so Sue, who likes to cater to the guests, runs The Mansion herself with some help from her three grown children and a small part-time staff.

The bedrooms that belonged to members of the Dudley family, such as the Anniversary Suite and the Master Suite, are the largest, but the coziest are the former maids' quarters, now called the Peach and Beige rooms. All the bedrooms, large and small, are carpeted and rather unimaginatively decorated with a hodge-podge of mostly reproduction furniture. They seem too scantly furnished, impersonal, and motel-like for such a grand setting.

The 7-acre grounds are given over to lawns, gardens, and a forest of northern hardwoods, pine, and cedar; there's a private beach, where guests often build bonfires in summer.

Address: *3600 London Rd., Duluth, MN 55804, tel. 218/724-0739.*
Accommodations: *6 double rooms with baths, 4 doubles share 2 baths, 1 3-bedroom, 2-bath housekeeping carriage house.*
Amenities: *Large screen TV and VCR in Master Suite, kitchenette in carriage house; private beach, off-street parking.*
Rates: *$85–$195; carriage house is $325 or $155 rented as 1-bedroom suite; full breakfast. MC, V.*
Restrictions: *Smoking in library and on screened porch only, no pets; open weekends only in winter, closed Wed. mid-May–mid-Oct.*

Pincushion Mountain Bed & Breakfast

After four winters with no snow in Flagstaff, Arizona, Scott Beattie, a longtime cross-country skier and instructor, moved to a place where snow was guaranteed. He and his wife, Mary, checked out locations around the country and came to a spot 3 miles up the Gunflint Trail from Grand Marais. They built the Pincushion Mountain Bed & Breakfast in 1986. The almost unreal quiet here is broken only by the occasional birdcall.

The modern pine building sits on the Sawtooth Mountain ridgeline, a thousand feet above Lake Superior. The woodsy inn has fir beams, pine and aspen paneled walls, and country-style furnishings and knick-knacks.

Downstairs is a living room equipped with a wood stove and a dining room where a hearty breakfast is served. There are spectacular views of Lake Superior and the surrounding pine, aspen, and birch forest. This is the true northwoods; don't be surprised if you see a deer, a moose, or even a bear passing by.

The four guest rooms upstairs are somewhat small but comfortable. The largest and probably the most desirable is the corner Pine Room, which has an extra single bed, comfortably sized bath, and a great view of Lake Superior. The Birch and Aspen rooms have tiny but adequate built-in baths with showers only; the latter has no lake view. The Maple Room has a private but nonadjoining bath across the hall.

Scott gives skiing lessons, rents and repairs skis, and grooms Pincushion's own 15½ miles of trails. Although Pincushion accommodates skiers in particular, its 44 acres are equally attractive in summer and fall when its ski trails are used for hiking. Because the inn's trails adjoin the 130-mile Superior Hiking Trail, Pincushion takes part in the north shore lodge-to-lodge hiking program and ski programs. There's also a 15½-mile, seven-loop mountain-bike trail system here, and an additional 200 miles in the woods nearby.

Address: *220 Gunflint Trail, Grand Marais, MN 55604–9701, tel. 218/387–1276 or 800/542–1226.*
Accommodations: *4 double rooms with baths.*
Amenities: *Fans, clock radios; sauna, mountain bikes and cross-country skis for rent, 15½ miles of cross-country ski and hiking trails from the lodge door, 1 mile of lighted trails on winter Saturday nights, cross-country ski instruction, trail bag lunches available.*
Rates: *$70–$90; full breakfast, afternoon refreshments. MC, V.*
Restrictions: *No smoking, no pets; 2-night minimum stay on winter, late summer, and fall weekends; closed Apr.*

The Stone Hearth Inn Bed & Breakfast

In 1989, when Charlie Michels came to Little Marais, he wanted to buy some land on Lake Superior. Two years later he had a five-bedroom, 70-year-old inn, and a wife, Susan, who'd been one of his first guests.

The Stone Hearth Inn was the original homestead of the Benjamin Fenstad family. Benjamin built a log cabin on the site in 1893 and, in 1924, built the home that Charlie owns today. An accomplished Twin Cities carpenter and contractor, Charlie did most of the renovation work himself. He made 10 rooms into six, stripped the narrow-plank maple floors, added beams and molding downstairs, and collected stones from the shores of Lake Superior to build the large living-room fireplace.

Just 80 feet from the lake, the house has a wonderful, long porch furnished with Adirondack chairs, perfect for relaxing in these serene surroundings. French doors open from the simple dining room with a large handmade pine table in the center, and from the living room, where soft chairs and sofas flank the giant hearth and guests take turns playing the piano.

In all five guest rooms you can fall asleep to the comforting sounds of the lake, but you'll get the best views from Rooms 2, 3, and 4. Room 2, a corner room in blue and white with a four-poster canopy bed, has a lake view even from its pink and white ceramic-tiled bathroom.

An old boathouse just 30 feet from the lake was torn down in 1992 and rebuilt as a two-unit cottage. One unit is a suite with a bedroom, bathroom, living room, and kitchenette. Both are upstairs and have fireplaces, whirlpool baths, and especially dramatic views from their picture windows.

Blueberry wild-rice pancakes, Austrian apple pancakes, lake trout sausage, and vanilla poached pears are perfect examples of Susan and Charlie's innovative cooking. On most clear nights there is a bonfire down by the lake, with marshmallow s'mores provided by the Michels and, if you're lucky, northern lights provided by Mother Nature.

Address: *1118 Hwy. 61 E, Little Marais, MN 55614, tel. 218/226–3020.*
Accommodations: *6 double rooms with baths, 1 suite with kitchenette.*
Amenities: *Wine glasses and chocolates in rooms, fireplace, coffeemaker, and whirlpool bath in 1 room and suite, kitchenette in suite, special dinners and trail lunches available; canoe and mountain bikes for rent, bonfire, lodge-to-lodge hiking program.*
Rates: *$75–$124; full breakfast in inn, Continental breakfast in boathouse. MC, V.*
Restrictions: *No smoking, no pets.*

Caribou Lake B&B

I t's hard to find a bed-and-breakfast with a more spectacular setting than this one overlooking the clear water and surrounding forest of Caribou Lake. In 1989, when Jeanne and Carter Wells purchased this red cedar log house and guest cabin, built just over 10 years ago, they got all they wanted and more: They're right on a lake with lots of hiking and cross-country ski trails, swimming, boating, fishing, and wildlife-watching.

The lower-level suite doesn't have the same great views of the lake as the main-floor dining and living rooms. In addition, the low ceilings make it feel rather claustrophobic, despite the relatively spacious room with two double beds and large sliding-glass door. But it has a private sit-ting room with TV, a bathroom, and a fairly large sauna. The two-bedroom cabin has a kitchen and offers more privacy but feels cramped. Nevermind, since most guests visit this area for the outdoors, few will find a better place to enjoy it than this hilltop retreat.

Address: *Box 156, Lutsen, MN 55612, tel. 218/663-7489.*
Accommodations: *1 suite, 1 cabin.*
Amenities: *TV, VCR, and sauna in suite; kitchenette, wood-burning stove and gas grill in cabin; tape players in both; 2 docks, boat and canoe rental.*
Rates: *$82-$98; full breakfast, dinners and trail lunches available. MC, V.*
Restrictions: *No smoking, no pets.*

Fitger's Inn

O nly the stone walls in a few of the guest rooms and the lovely leaded-glass skylight and 19th-century iron registration cage in the high-ceilinged lobby reveal the origins of this inn on Lake Superior, near downtown Duluth: In the 1850s, it was a brewery. Now extensively renovated, it is on the National Register of Historic Places.

Although the guest rooms are furnished in reproduction antiques, they seem more like upscale hotel rooms than those of a historic inn. But all are spacious and have big beds, desks, wing chairs, and modern baths. Thirty-one rooms have lake views.

Fitger's is centrally located, convenient for exploring the town. It's also on Duluth's new Lake Walk, which goes past the Aerial Lift Bridge and ends in Canal Park. In summer, outdoor concerts are held nearby.

Address: *600 E. Superior St., Duluth, MN 55802, tel. 218/722-8826 or 800/726-2982.*
Accommodations: *42 double rooms with bath, 6 suites.*
Amenities: *Air-conditioning, phone, cable TV, clock radio in bedrooms, room service; conference facilities, including 160-seat theater; off-street parking, adjoining shopping and restaurant complex.*
Rates: *$79-$95, suites $135-$260; breakfast extra. D, DC, MC, V.*
Restrictions: *No pets.*

The Inn at Palisade Bed & Breakfast

This little five-unit motel, built in 1955 and now a unique B&B, lies in one of the prettiest little coves on Lake Superior's north shore. Owners Mary and Bob Barnett were driving in the area in 1988 when the property caught their eye; it was in good shape, and the location was a winner.

The units' doors open out onto the parking lot, but the Barnetts have converted the central common room into a breakfast room with fireplace. Each guest room has a view of Lake Superior and of the property's small crescent-shaped rock beach. Four of the regular-size rooms are on the main level, with 1950s-pink ceramic-tiled showers. On the building's lower level is one large room, which contains a queen-size bed, sitting area with a foldout sofa, table and chairs, kitchenette, fireplace, and two large picture windows. Also on this floor are a flagstone patio with a campfire circle and stairs leading down to the beach. Adjoining the inn's property on the northeast side is Tettegouche State Park, with hiking paths and waterfalls.

Address: *384 U.S. 61, Silver Bay, MN 55614, tel. 218/226-3505.*
Accommodations: *4 double rooms with baths, 1 large room with bath and kitchen.*
Amenities: *TV, clock radio, kitchen and fireplace in 1 room; campfire.*
Rates: *$65–$80; full breakfast, afternoon snack, coffee available all day. MC, V.*
Restrictions: *No smoking, no pets; closed mid-Oct.–May.*

Lindgren's Bed & Breakfast

When this log house on Lake Superior was Robert and Shirley Lindgren's vacation home and the couple owned a landscaping business, they loaded the property with flowers, trees, shrubs, and vegetable gardens. Since 1987, it has been their year-round home and B&B. Inside, it's clear that the Lindgrens are also avid hunters and anglers. There are stuffed and mounted animals and skins everywhere in the house—the large living room displays a bear, moose, wolf, fox, and beaver.

The living-dining area has a huge stone fireplace and a table overlooking the lake. Three of the four guest rooms are also on the main level, perhaps a bit too close to the public rooms for some guests. Bobby's Room, the best, has a double whirlpool bath and two walls of windows, one overlooking the lake. The downstairs guest room, despite its fireplace and large glass doors with lake access, remains essentially a recreation room with beds enough for a dozen people. The classic basement bath is very dark with no windows.

Address: *Box 56, Lutsen, MN 55612-0056, tel. 218/663-7450.*
Accommodations: *4 double rooms with baths.*
Amenities: *TV, phone in 2 rooms, whirlpool in 1 room, fireplace in 1 room; bonfire pit, Finnish sauna, horseshoe pit, volleyball area.*
Rates: *$80–$110; full breakfast. MC, V.*
Restrictions: *No smoking in public areas, no pets.*

Mathew S. Burrows 1890 Inn

Tired of the 9-to-5 life in Washington, DC, David and Pam Wolff went back to Duluth, Pam's hometown, to open a bed-and-breakfast. They chose an imaginative red and green Queen Anne with an unusual gazebo-style front porch.

The public rooms—a music room with an upright piano and a parlor with a carved mahogany fireplace—are Victorian: comfortable if overstuffed. But the house's standout feature is its white oak-paneled dining room, which has a carved built-in white oak mirrored buffet; a maple, walnut, oak, mahogany, and birch parquet floor; and the most magnificent blue and gold stained-glass window ever seen outside a church.

The best guest room is probably the Lakeview Suite, with its lace-draped four-poster canopy bed and twin French doors joining the bedroom to a private sitting room with corner windows and beautiful views.

Address: *1632 E. First St., Duluth, MN 55812, tel. 218/724-4991.*
Accommodations: *2 double rooms with baths, 2 suites.*
Amenities: *Alarm clock, radio-tape player, fireplace and unique full-body marble shower in 1 suite; off-street parking.*
Rates: *$95–$125; full breakfast. MC, V.*
Restrictions: *No smoking, no pets; 2-night minimum on summer weekends, closed Thanksgiving, Dec. 24–25.*

Naniboujou Lodge

Conceived in the 1920s as the cornerstone of an exclusive sportsmen's club, the Naniboujou Lodge, 15 miles northeast of Grand Marais, never grew beyond the hotel and its restaurant—but what a hotel and restaurant they are.

The lodge's focal point is the Great Hall, which has a huge 200-ton native rock fireplace. This room, now used for dining, is emblazoned with Cree motifs. The guest rooms are small but pleasant, remodeled and furnished with pine furniture and modern baths. Owners Tim and Nancy Ramey have kept the prices reasonable.

There is an abundance of recreational opportunities, but the lodge is def-

initely a place to lounge in the Adirondack chairs and enjoy the views of Lake Superior.

Address: *U.S. 61 (HC 1, Box 505), Grand Marais, MN 55604, tel. 218/387-2688.*
Accommodations: *25 double rooms with baths, 2 doubles share 1 bath.*
Amenities: *Fireplaces in 4 rooms, lake views from 21 rooms, restaurant; basketball and volleyball courts.*
Rates: *$39–$75; breakfast extra. D, MC, V.*
Restrictions: *Smoking in nondining part of Great Hall only, no alcohol in restaurant, no pets; closed mid-Oct.–Mother's Day and weekdays Dec. 26–mid-Mar.*

Snuggle Inn

Before Maribeth Nelson and Bill Doucette moved into this early 1900s house just off U.S. 61 near Grand Marais, renters had parked snowmobiles in the living room and otherwise abused the place. So there was plenty of cleaning and redecorating to do before they opened their B&B in 1990.

The most charming thing about the inn are the four guest rooms. They're simply decorated with floral comforters, pine paneling, and maple floors. Three have views of Lake Superior.

Downstairs, the small living room has a painted maple floor. Despite the new French doors overlooking the lake, the downstairs rooms are rather dark and feel close.

Maribeth and Bill own a small motel and restaurant, so they're busy, unobtrusive hosts.

Address: *8 Seventh Ave. W (Box 248), Grand Marais, MN 55604, tel. 218/387-2281.*
Accommodations: *4 double rooms with baths.*
Amenities: *Cable TV, VCR, and tape player in living room; lodge-to-lodge hiking packages.*
Rates: *$72–$80; full breakfast, afternoon snacks, restaurant packages. D, MC, V.*
Restrictions: *No smoking, no pets; 2-day minimum on winter weekends, 3-day minimum on holiday weekends.*

The Superior Overlook B&B

Perched on a hill overlooking Lake Superior, 2 miles north of Grand Marais, this bed-and-breakfast truly lives up to its name.

Jack and Viola Kerber built their house in 1985 when they retired here from California. A few years later they converted the first floor to a three-bedroom B&B. It's a good spot for those who prefer to minimize their interaction with innkeepers since there's a separate entrance, deck, living room with wood stove, and kitchenette with toaster oven, microwave, coffeemaker, and fridge.

It's quite a modern house—the living-room walls are light blue cinder block and the ceiling is acoustic tile—but then the real view is outside, anyway. The living room and

two of the guest rooms, the twin-bedded Deck Room and the Lake Room, have wonderful views. The Lake Room, which has a queen-size bed, pink walls, a floral spread, and a separate entrance leading down a lake path, is a particularly nice spot.

Address: *U.S. 61, Milepost 112 (Box 963) Grand Marais, MN 55604–0963, tel. 218/387-1571.*
Accommodations: *3 double rooms share 2 baths.*
Amenities: *TV, VCR, phone, and wood-burning stove in living room, kitchenette, sauna.*
Rates: *$70–$75; full breakfast. AE, MC, V.*
Restrictions: *No smoking, no pets.*

Dakota Country

*Southwestern Minnesota, along with St. Louis or Texas, is
a gateway to the American West. The West that begins here
is the northern prairie, a vast sea of grass that sustained
herds of buffalo along with one of the greatest of all Native
American nations, the Dakota (otherwise known as the
Sioux, although that's actually an insulting term that
roughly means "snake"). The Dakota considered the region
near the South Dakota border sacred, and they quarried its
soft red stone to make peace pipes (hence the town name
Pipestone). They believed that their tribe originated here,
and that the color of the stone came from the blood of their
ancestors.*

*The white people who settled here were predominantly
German and Scandinavian immigrants who brought with
them cherished relics of their homelands—the German
influence in New Ulm, for example, is still very strong. For
all the prairie's beauty, what the newer settlers valued even
more was its rich soil. Families like the Ingallses, whose
daughter Laura grew up to immortalize her Walnut Grove
home in such books as* The Little House on the Prairie, *were
called sodbusters because they had to plow up dense mats
of roots to plant their corn. It took a lot of pioneer grit,
but once the land was plowed, it yielded good crops.*

*In Dakota Country, the pleasures of life are generally on
a small-town scale. Its lesser communities, although
pleasant, are practical rather than beautiful. (Many
communities lost a good deal of their historic charm
during the 1960s, when the main streets were modernized.)
The towns are often lively, proudly celebrating their
heritage with summer events such as Pipestone's annual
Civil War Festival and Walnut Grove's yearly Little House
pageant. St. Peter, a trim college town in the bucolic
Minnesota River Valley, was originally planned as
Minnesota's capital (until St. Paul's wheeler-dealers stole*

that plum for themselves), and it still has the original wide streets, along which parade many gracious homes. Other county seats, such as Blue Earth and Pipestone, are equally prosperous and charming, with typically handsome country courthouses (often constructed from the same local quartzite that you can occasionally see cropping out even in the farm fields). Their small county historical museums provide fodder for an hour's low-key browsing, nothing more.

When it comes to outdoor activities, the offerings are quietly unspectacular. There's fishing and swimming in many fine small lakes here, especially around New Ulm and Mankato, but they are not the pine-ringed sky-blue waters of the North. The prairie terrain makes for pleasant, if unchallenging, cycling; a 68-mile loop has been mapped around the Pipestone countryside.

The mid-19th-century white settlers called the land "plains" because it is relatively flat and treeless. The prairie, however, is in fact anything but plain: It is one of the richest and most subtly beautiful ecosystems on earth. These days, farming has made untouched prairie as hard to find as full-blooded Dakota people, but both are there if you know where to look. Good places to start are in several of the state parks: Blue Mound State Park (near Luverne) has some attractive grasslands as well as a small buffalo herd; you'll also find grasslands in Kilen Woods (near Worthington) and the Jeffers Petroglyphs Historic Site (see below). Make your base camp in a town, then go out and explore the world of the Dakota. Like fine wine, it is better appreciated the more you learn about it.

Places to Go, Sights to See

August Schell Brewery (Box 128, New Ulm, tel. 507/354–5528). One of the prettiest little breweries in the United States, Schell's is set on the founder's estate, where there is also a mansion and a deer park. It's not only the source of some fine beer (its Pils and Weiss beers have won national awards), it's rich in regional history, for beer has been brewed here for more than 125 years. Schell's survived the Dakota conflict of 1862, local historians claim, because the Schell family maintained good relations with the local Dakota. Tours (including beer tastings) are available.

Jeffers Petroglyphs Historic Site (County Rd. 2, Jeffers, tel. 507/877–3647 or 507/697–6321). There are two notable things to see here: several acres of unplowed prairie, rich with wildflowers and tall grass; and the petroglyphs themselves, historic records carved in quartzite by native Dakotas as far back as 3,000 BC. The site is open from May through Labor Day.

Katherine Ordway Prairie (near Sunburg, 7 mi. southwest of Brooten, tel. 612/331–0750). Managed by the Minnesota Chapter of the Nature Conservancy, the Ordway Prairie comprises 582 acres of sharply rolling hills with numerous moist lowlands. It was once cultivated, and has not been completely taken over again by prairie plants, but it is still one of the best places in the state to see what Minnesota looked like before the coming of the *wasicu* (Dakota for "white man").

Laura Ingalls Wilder Museum (330 Eighth St., Walnut Grove, tel. 507/859–2358). Exhibits depict the life of the *Little House on the Prairie* author and her family, as well as the early history of the tiny town of Walnut Grove. Memorabilia include Laura's hand-stitched quilt, family photos, and a bench from the Congregational Church attended by the Ingalls family. Open May–October, daily; June–September, by appointment only.

Lower Sioux Agency (Box 308, Morton, tel. 507/697–6185). The Interpretive Center at this Mdwakantan Dakota community, set in the Minnesota River Valley south of Willmar, is key to understanding Dakota life and culture. Also on the grounds are Tipi Maka Duta, the Lower Sioux pottery shop, and St. Cornelia's Episcopal Church (listed on the National Register of Historic Sites). A powwow, open to the public, is held the second weekend in June.

New Ulm Glockenspiel (Schonlau Park Plaza, Fifth and Minnesota Sts., New Ulm). New Ulm, settled by German immigrants in 1854, was nearly destroyed in the Dakota Conflict of 1862. Animated figures in this 45-foot-high musical clock tower depict the town's history daily at noon, 3, and 5 PM while the 37 bells in the carillon ring in the hour.

Pipestone Historic District (stop by Pipestone County Museum, 1 Hiawatha Ave., tel. 507/825–2563). Guided tours (on request) or self-guided tours (outlined in a free brochure) explore the historic center of the town of Pipestone, where 20 buildings are listed on the National Register of Historic Places. Nearly all were built, before the turn of the century, of local quartzite in a heavy Romanesque style, full of quirky details.

Pipestone National Monument (1 mi north of Pipestone, then ½ mi west, tel. 507/825–5464). These quarries were legendary throughout Native America for the soft red stone used for making the sacred calumets (peace pipes) smoked not only by the Dakota but by other tribes as well. Native craftspeople still quarry and make pipes here. The 283-acre monument also features an Indian Culture Center and walking trail.

Sod House on the Prairie (Rte. 2, Sanborn, tel. 507/723–5138). This authentic reconstruction of two pioneer sod houses—a poor man's dugout and a richer man's "soddy"—is open as a small museum of early settlers' life; it is also available for overnight guests as a bed-and-breakfast (*see below*).

Restaurants

Minnesota's special restaurants are nearly all in the eastern part of the state, but the **Calumet Inn** (104 W. Main St., Pipestone, tel. 507/825–5871) has a restaurant that's highly regarded for its creative touch with beef and pork. In New Ulm, the **Glockenspiel Haus** (400 N. Minnesota St., tel. 507/354–5593) serves good German food and the locally brewed Schell's beer. Though it's not the colorful joint it once was, the **Magnolia Steak House** (U.S. 75 exit off I–94, Luverne, tel. 507/283–9161) still has custom-aged beef, and its onion rings are legendary.

Tourist Information

Mankato Area Convention and Visitors Bureau (120 S. Front St., Suite 200, Mankato, MN 56002, tel. 507/345–4519); **Minnesota Office of Tourism, Southern Regional Office** (Box 286, Mankato, MN 56001, tel. 507/389–2683); **New Ulm Chamber of Commerce** (220 N. Minnesota St., New Ulm, MN 56073, tel. 507/354–4217); **Pipestone Chamber of Commerce** (117 S.E. Eighth Ave., Pipestone, MN 56164, tel. 507/825–3316).

Park Row
Bed and Breakfast

L ike many of the older large houses in rural Minnesota, Ann Burckhardt's bed-and-breakfast, a few blocks from St. Peter's Main Street, is two houses fused together. The larger of the two, a Carpenter Gothic, was built in 1874 with wooden gingerbread trim on porch railings and eaves. In 1903, the house was purchased by a probate-court judge, who added what was tantamount to another building, a Queen Anne–style wing with an apron porch and a turreted circular staircase. After the judge's death in the 1930s, his home suffered the fate of many such big houses: It was turned into a duplex. A local professor bought it in 1971, bringing it back to its eclectic late-Victorian grace.

It's this combination of styles that Ann, who bought the house in 1989, has maintained in her decor. The interior is as eclectic as the exterior, but it has a homey Victorian look, as opposed to the dark, heavy version of Victorian. The downstairs is light and spacious. In the dining room, where a huge bay window draws in daylight from three directions, late-Victorian antiques blend with modern reproductions. Small-scale furnishings, wicker chairs, and lace curtains reinforce the sense of sunshine and fresh air.

Each of the four guest rooms is furnished with period antiques and has its own ethnic theme. But Ann is not heavy-handed about it, and is simply out to create a *feeling* of Englishness (or Frenchness, or Germanness). There's a Norwegian-style painted floor in the Scandinavian Room. In other rooms, bright colors and fabrics project the same decorative frilliness as the exterior gingerbread. It never gets cute, however.

"I want my guests to feel as if they're stepping back into 1910," Burckhardt says. Granted, it's a modernized 1910—there's wall-to-wall carpeting, though done in a Victorian pattern, but the shower you take will be in a claw-foot tub with its original oak rim, and there'll be no TV in your bedroom.

Expect an exceptional breakfast. The indefatigable Burckhardt still commutes 66 miles to Minneapolis three days a week to work as a food journalist, so food is a passion with her. And, since she is a writer, reading is another passion: Books and magazines, mostly of local and regional interest, are plentiful throughout the house. Pleasures here are quiet ones—that's why people come to Park Row.

Address: *525 W. Park Row, St. Peter, MN 56082, tel. 507/931-2495.*
Accommodations: *3 double rooms share 2 baths.*
Amenities: *Air-conditioning, cable TV in living room.*
Rates: *$45–$65; full breakfast. D.*
Restrictions: *No smoking, no pets.*

Sod House on the Prairie

When Stan McCone was growing up, older relatives told him tales of his fore-bears—sod-busting white settlers of the Great Plains, just like those Willa Cather and Laura Ingalls Wilder wrote about. Since few trees sprouted on the grasslands, pioneers literally built their houses out of the earth. These sod houses, made of blocks of cut turf, were held together by the dense root systems of the prairie grass.

McCone dreamed of re-creating this lost type of architecture. After working several years as a cattle buyer, he got a chance to make his dream come true when he learned that one of his neighbors in rural Sanborn had a patch of virgin prairie on his land. Soon Stan set to work, with the same kind of grit and sweat as his pioneer ancestors, cutting massive blocks of sod (he describes the sound as "the ripping of a giant canvas"). The result is two buildings set amid acres of (reseeded) prairie grass: a rudimentary "poor man's dugout" and a larger "rich man's soddy," both open to the public as a museum. For those who want a full dose of pioneer experience, the larger also does service as a snug, rustic bed-and-breakfast.

The house's furnishings—antique bedsteads and buffets, kitchen and farm implements hanging on the walls and beams—are practical and sturdily beautiful. The only piece that could be considered at all fancy is the leather fainting couch that doubles as a bed, across which is spread a heavy, shaggy buffalo-hide blanket.

Authenticity is the watchword here. There are no wires or pipes running through the soddy's turf walls—heating comes from a pot-bellied stove, air-conditioning from open windows, light from oil lamps. The bathroom is a two-seat outhouse steps away; to wash, guests must pour water from a jug into the 100-year-old pitcher and bowl.

The McCones provide a simple, hearty country breakfast, incorporating quality meats, which is Stan's other line of business. If you want to cook your other meals, throw some logs into the mighty Monarch stove. One family spent a prairie Christmas here, cooking up a feast on the Monarch, with the soddy so snug that the kids padded about in shorts. Though few of us today could survive the rigors of pioneer life, we still can savor a sample of it, thanks to Stan McCone.

Address: *Rte. 2 (Box 75), Sanborn, MN 56083, tel. 507/723–5138.*
Accommodations: *1 house with 2 double beds and outhouse.*
Amenities: *Wood-burning stoves.*
Rates: *$39–$99; full breakfast. No credit cards.*
Restrictions: *No smoking, pets only by prior consent.*

Fering's Guest House

harles and Phyllis Fering freely admit that Blue Earth, while attractive, isn't a tourist hot spot, despite its many antiques shops, attractive courthouse, and lovely woods. Neither is this large frame Victorian house, built in 1889, where the Ferings have lived for more than 20 years. Instead it looks like the ideal small-town home, all porch and tall windows with a shady yard. Original oak woodwork exists alongside more recent birch paneling and country-style wallpaper; family knickknacks are scattered about. When the Ferings opened their bed-and-breakfast in 1990, after most of their kids had grown and gone, they expected to attract folks who were just looking for a good night's lodging.

Still, the Ferings' guests often send them Christmas cards, bottles of wine, invitations to visit. Why? "We're like family," says Charles. They're affable, open-minded, and flexible—for example, although they usually serve only Continental breakfasts, once when guests were stranded by a sudden snowstorm, they whipped up three square meals a day until the snow cleared. That's small-town America for you.

Address: *708 N. Main St., Blue Earth, MN 56013, tel. 507/526–5054.*
Accommodations: *1 double room with bath, 2 doubles share 1 bath.*
Amenities: *Air-conditioning, cable TV and phones in rooms.*
Rates: *$40; Continental breakfast. No credit cards.*
Restrictions: *No smoking, no pets.*

Prairie House on Round Lake

n 1879, Chicago commodity trader Owen Roche built this grand American Bracket-style house, nicknamed "Roche's Roost" and surrounded by a 2,500-acre estate on Round Lake. It's smaller than it used to be, having been truncated to save money during the Depression (in an odd twist, the bottom floor rather than the top was removed); the estate has shrunk to 44 acres, but it still remains a good place to escape urban stress.

Now owned by horse-breeders Ralph and Virginia Schenk, the house is set amid horse barns and wildlife preserves. Inside, there are some antiques (claw-foot tubs, some fine old tables) and beamed ceilings, but the wall-to-wall carpets and other fixtures suggest the interior of a well-

scrubbed and recently built suburban house. Fresh flowers from the Schenks' greenhouse and the whinnying of their American paint horses help to remind you of your rural surroundings. Canada geese, white pelicans, and other waterfowl thrive in peace here. Outside of outdoor recreation, there isn't much to do here—but that's enough.

Address: *R.R. 1 (Box 105), Round Lake, MN 56167, tel. 507/945–8934.*
Accommodations: *1 double room with bath, 1 double with half-bath, 2 doubles share 1 bath.*
Amenities: *Air-conditioning, TV in 1 room.*
Rates: *$45–$55; full breakfast. No credit cards.*
Restrictions: *No smoking, pets only by prior consent.*

The Northwest and
the Cuyana Iron Range
Including Brainerd and Detroit Lakes

When Twin Cities people talk about "going up north," they usually mean up to Arrowhead, along the Lake Superior shore from Duluth to the Gunflint Trail. But to people in the more rural western parts of the state, "up north" means the Northwest and the Cuyana Iron Range, around Alexandria, Detroit Lakes, Brainerd, and Walker.

Studded with wooded lakes and state forests, threaded through with hiking trails and streams teaming with fish, the region seems ideal for outdoor vacations. Here you'll find crystal-clear Lake Itasca, source of the Mississippi River, surrounded by the virgin pine forest preserved in Itasca State Park. Leech Lake, much lovelier than its name implies, is surrounded by the Chippewa National Forest; the town of Walker, on Leech Lake's southwestern corner, is a fishing favorite. Mille Lacs Lake, just east of Brainerd, is another popular body of water, and the towns of Detroit Lakes and Alexandria, to the west, have long attracted tourists for their proximity to a number of small, beautiful lakes. Farther north, in a much more rugged and thinly settled part of Minnesota, Lake of the Woods stretches its many fingers up into neighboring Ontario and Manitoba.

Besides lake swimming, sailing, and fishing, there are plenty of opportunities in these parts to enjoy the outdoors. The Heartland Trail, a blacktop bicycle path created from an old rail bed, runs 27 miles from Walker to Park Rapids. The North Country National Scenic Trail, 68 miles long, winds through the Chippewa National Forest between Walker and Romer. Among the many rivers designated as canoe trails are the Crow Wing River, Red Lake River, Pine River, and the Mississippi River, from Lake Itasca down to Anoka, just north of Minneapolis.

Tying into the region's logging past, several towns (notably Brainerd and Bemidji) are touted as "Paul Bunyan's Hometown." An even more exotic bit of history is represented in Alexandria: A runestone there is said to be evidence that Viking explorers visited here in the 14th century.

Although Alexandria and Detroit lakes have long been tourist-oriented, traditionally the region was supported by logging and taconite mining. (The Cuyana is one of three iron ranges in the United States; the Mesabi and Vermilion ranges to the east are more familiar to Minnesotans.) Once the old-growth trees were felled and the mines were worked out, the region fell upon hard economic times, but it's making a modest comeback now, thanks in large part to tourism. Accommodations, however, tend to be smaller and less fancy than those in Arrowhead or the St. Croix Valley, but consequently, prices are still refreshingly low.

Places to Go, Sights to See

Bunyan House Information Center (301 Paul Bunyan Dr. (U.S. 197), Bemidji, tel. 218/751–3540). A so-called collection of the mythical lumberjack's tools and memorabilia is the main attraction here; there's also a small wildlife and historical museum, and the requisite giant statues of Paul and his blue ox, Babe. Open Memorial Day–Labor Day, daily; weekdays the rest of the year.

Deer Town (U.S. 71, 1 mi north of Park Rapids, tel. 218/732–5135). Deer, goats, geese, and sheep roam around this re-created pioneer village, which also has a small museum, playground, and observation tower. Open Memorial Day–Labor Day, daily.

Lake Itasca State Park (U.S. 71 and Rte. 92, about 20 mi northeast of Bemidji, tel. 218/266–3656). Minnesota's oldest state park is still one of its best—a 32,000-acre sanctuary of pine forest known for its excellent birding (at least one pair of loons stays on the lake each summer), hiking, biking, and cross-country ski trails. The lake contains the headwaters of the Mississippi River. Up here, you can cross the river by walking on a few smooth stepping-stones; farther down, it is a gentle, honey-colored stream, nothing like the muddy colossus it becomes. Also highly recommended: **Zippel Bay State Park** (Lake of the Woods, Williams, tel. 218/783–6252), which gives you a taste of wild northern Minnesota.

Lumbertown USA (U.S. 371, 12 mi northwest of Brainerd, tel. 218/829–8872). More than 30 replicas and restorations of 19th-century buildings re-create a logging town of the 1870s, complete with a maple-sugar plant, general store, ice-cream parlor, pioneer home, wax museum, old-fashioned train, and riverboat. Open Memorial Day–Labor Day, daily.

Oliver H. Kelley Historic Farm (U.S. Hwy. 10, 2½ mi southeast of Elk River, tel. 612/441–6896). A living museum of 19th-century agricultural practices, this farm on the banks of the Mississippi River has guides, dressed in period costume, out with their horses and oxen, demonstrating farm chores of the day. The original owner, Oliver Kelley, founded the Patrons of Husbandry, also known as the Grange, a farmers' fraternal organization that grew to have significant political influence.

Paul Bunyan Amusement Center (junction of Rtes. 210 and 371, 2 mi west of Brainerd, tel. 218/829–6342). Offering the standard assortment of children's rides, minigolf, go-carts, and performing animals, this small park has one outstanding feature: a 26-foot animated statue of Paul Bunyan (with a 15-foot Babe, the blue ox, behind him) that spins tall tales to youngsters. Open Memorial Day–Labor Day, daily.

Sinclair Lewis Interpretive Center and Museum (junction of I–94 and U.S. 71, Sauk Centre, tel. 612/352–5201). There was no love lost between Sinclair Lewis and his hometown, Sauk Centre, when the Nobel-laureate-to-be depicted the town as "Gopher Prairie" in his novel *Main Street*. More than 70 years later, Sauk Centre folks have embraced their most famous native son, renaming the main street Sinclair Lewis Avenue. This museum is full of interesting artifacts related to Lewis and his hometown, which is a fairly typical Minnesota small town—neither gorgeous nor plain, but pleasant and practical. Here the **Sinclair Lewis Boyhood Home** (612 Sinclair Lewis Ave.) displays family memorabilia and 1900s furnishings.

Summerhill Farm (U.S. 71, 7 mi north of Park Rapids, tel. 218/732–3865). Several buildings of an old farmstead have been converted into this collection of gift shops selling country collectibles, artwork, and handcrafted gifts. There's also a restaurant on the premises.

Restaurants

The area's restaurants, such as Bemidji's **Union Station** (Union Sq., 1st St. and Beltrami Ave., tel. 218/751–9261), serve a lot of walleye pike and prime rib. If you're looking for something different, head for the **Brauhaus** (U.S. 34, Nevis, tel. 218/652–2478), a little German place in the middle of the country, or **Compadres** (U.S. 226, Dorset, tel. 218/732–7624), a big, colorful Mexican spot in a very small town.

Tourist Information

Bemidji Chamber of Commerce (300 Bemidji Ave., Bemidji, MN 56601, tel. 218/751–3541); **Brainerd Lakes Area Chamber of Commerce** (110 N. Sixth St., Brainerd, MN 56401, tel. 218/829–2838); **Detroit Lakes Regional Chamber of Commerce** (700 Washington Ave., Detroit Lakes, MN 56501, tel. 218/847–9202 or 800/542–3992); **Fergus Falls Chamber of Commerce** (202 S. Court St., Fergus Falls, MN 56537, tel. 218/736–6951); **Minnesota Office of Tourism, Northcentral/West regional office** (1901 S. Sixth St., Box 443, Brainerd, MN 56401, tel. 218/828–2334); **Sauk Centre Area Chamber of Commerce** (1220 S. Main St., Sauk Centre, MN 56378, tel. 612/352–5201).

Hallett House

As you drive out of Crosby and approach the grand front lawn of Hallett House, you may experience a sense of déjà vu. A driveway that curves beneath oaks and jack pines brings you to the front door of a pale Georgian Revival house with green trim and a small arched portico. Inside, painted Georgian paneling suggests grandeur, but the lush green wool carpeting somehow shrinks the large rooms to livable size. Sun streams through the windows of a porch that's been made into a wicker-furnished guest room. The library, with a fireplace and built-in bookshelves, has the air of an old-fashioned men's club room.

Upstairs, past blue 1950s-era wallpaper with Early American scenes, the guest rooms give off that same feeling of luxury: big, carpeted rooms; bay windows with venetian blinds; solid furniture. It will remind you of a rich uncle's house you've always wanted to visit. Here is the room of "the lady of the house," with its mirror-lined dressing area and vanity—you can almost smell the Chanel No. 5 and hear the faint tinkling of silver bracelets. Here is the master bedroom, with a baronial bed facing the bay window, or the maid's quarters, with her rather small bed and her own sitting room (and an up-to-date TV set). Down the hall, the eldest son's room seems to have been kept as it must have been before he left for college, all hardwood floors and big oak bedstead.

The house was built in 1920 by E. W. Hallett, a construction and real-estate magnate who was once one of the richest men in the country. Hallett was a conservative man—he didn't lose his shirt in the Depression—and his house, though large, is not ostentatious, wearing its wealth lightly. He died in 1983 (at the age of 101!), and six years later a local couple, Kathy and Wes Pernula, bought the well-preserved home, along with many of the Halletts' furnishings. In turning it into a bed-and-breakfast, they've had the sense to leave well enough alone, adding only a few frills and figurines, most of them downstairs. But there are some lovely antiques to see, and the delicious feeling of quiet privilege still prevails.

Address: *Hwy. 210 (Box 247), Crosby, MN 56441, tel. 218/546-5433.*
Accommodations: *5 double rooms with baths.*
Amenities: *Air-conditioning in 1 room, cable TV in 2 rooms, TV/ VCR in library.*
Rates: *$50–$65; full breakfast. AE, MC, V.*
Restrictions: *No smoking, no pets.*

Oakhurst Inn

It was perhaps the most prestigious house in the prosperous town of Princeton at one time, but when David and Suzie Spain bought Oakhurst in 1989, it was a garbage-filled near-ruin. It took two years of hard work to return the house to something close to its days of glory. Unlike the original owner, banker John Skahen, the Spains aren't rich, so Oakhurst today feels more like a family home than a mansion. Still, much of the mansion remains.

Built in 1906, the three-story house is one of those Victorians that borrowed from many styles, hence the Queen Anne wraparound porch and the magnificent Romanesque fireplace in the front parlor. The front door opens onto a grand vestibule, with ceilings nearly 10 feet high, oak floors and woodwork, and a long bench built into one wall. To the left are the front and back parlors (the Spains have added oak wainscoting to the back parlor and turned it into a library); to the right is the dining room, complete with plate rail. The Spains hope to make the decor more consistent with one period: At present, an Eastlake chair, a Mission rocker, and a reupholstered camelback couch sit incongruously near each other. An air of homey middle-class nostalgia is perpetuated by Norman Rockwell plates, small stuffed bears, and braided area rugs.

Upstairs, the tasteful, comfortable guest rooms do better at creating a period look. The largest bedroom, for instance, features a velvet fainting couch and a pencil-post four-poster queen-size bed, covered with reproduction quilted lace. The smaller Sterling Room has a bathroom with such 1906-ish features as a pedestal sink, claw-foot tub, and wainscoting. The sunny Lucy Room has a white iron bed with lace coverlet, and lace curtains at the windows: It may be too frilly for some tastes, too sparsely furnished for others.

The Spains and their children live on the third floor of this big house, and perhaps their presence has something to do with the down-to-earth family atmosphere of the place. Guests are welcome to visit Suzie in the kitchen. They will most likely be offered a chocolate-chip cookie or two while Suzie talks of the horrors of renovation. It was no doubt hard to live through, but the result is a cozy success.

Address: *212 S. Eighth Ave., Princeton, MN 55371, tel. 612/389-3553 or 800/443-2258.*
Accommodations: *3 double rooms with baths.*
Amenities: *Air-conditioning, TV/VCR in library.*
Rates: *$55-$65; full breakfast, evening refreshments. MC, V.*
Restrictions: *No smoking, no pets.*

Park Street Inn

This little jewel box sits on a little street in a little town you'd miss if you drove too fast. Nevis, once a prosperous logging town, now makes a bid for tourism with the nearby Heartland Bike Trail and Lake Belle Taine. The Park Street Inn represents this newer Nevis, although it is also rooted in the town's history.

Built in 1912 by Justin Halvorsen, a well-to-do banker and local land developer, the house is more of a bungalow than a mansion, but it was done up in style—all kinds of styles, in fact, for Halvorsen apparently was no purist. The compact oak stairway and bannister were constructed out of state and brought to town by train. Other Midwestern craftsmen contributed a beveled-glass window fan and exquisite entry arches—carved oak in a French Empire style, with acanthus-topped fluted columns and flower-basket bas-reliefs. In contrast, an oak mantel sports the clean simple lines of Mission-style design.

Halvorsen lost his money in the Depression and moved to California. Given that Nevis, too, was declining, it's surprising that so many of the original treasures in the house were still there by the time Kathy and Jerry Carney bought it in 1989. In converting it into a bed-and-breakfast, the Carneys have shown the utmost respect for the builder's idiosyncracies, while bringing their own good taste to bear.

In the living room and dining area, subdued wallpaper and matching valances drape over lace-curtained windows. The Carneys' Eastlake chairs and rockers work surprisingly well, as do the folk-art engravings on the wall. Jerry tactfully introduced a modern stereo system (there's no downstairs TV) by installing the components inside a mahogany Victrola cabinet.

The upstairs is a bit less restrained, but still interesting. The largest guest room, which has a wicker-furnished sleeping porch facing Lake Belle Taine, also features a built-in cupboard bed whose oak arch came from a Lutheran church altar. Each room has its own wallpaper pattern and quilt—a handmade double wedding-ring quilt in one bedroom, a bright star pattern in another. The clutter of stuffed toys and antique dolls upstairs may seem a bit overdone, but by no means does this prevent the jewels here from sparkling.

Address: *Rte. 1 (Box 254), Nevis, MN 56467, tel. 218/652–4500.*
Accommodations: *3 double rooms with baths.*
Amenities: *TV in sitting room.*
Rates: *$60–$75; full breakfast, evening refreshments. MC, V.*
Restrictions: *No smoking, no pets.*

Peters' Sunset Beach

One look inside the main lodge's dining room gives you the flavor of this classic lakeside resort: knotty pine paneling, fish trophies, paintings of scenes from a Hiawatha-like Native American legend, light fixtures done up like painted drums, and a broad porch overlooking Lake Minnewaska.

The lodge, a gorgeous example of Craftsman-style design, is one of the resort's three buildings on the National Register of Historic Places. The place has changed a bit since train conductor Henry Peters jumped off the Soo Line in Glenwood and opened his summer hotel in 1915. It has grown from a small hostelry to a resort, complete with its own golf course, accommodating up to 175 guests in a variety of up-to-date rooms, cottages, and luxury town houses. But it's still run by the Peters family, and they have restored the historic 1923 Annex to its old-fashioned appearance—making it, in the words of Henry's grandson Bill Peters, "our country inn."

From the outside the Annex looks a lot like the main lodge, almost like a wing that detached itself and settled several steps away. Inside, the Peterses have installed antique bedsteads, tables, and dressers, many of them wood pieces from the turn of the century, to fit in with the refinished original woodwork. Quilts, made by a local artisan, grace each bed; the wallpaper is quietly floral.

The whole building has an agreeable, unpretentious air about it, although there are some discordant touches left over from the Annex's prerestoration interim years. Built-in couches, covered in tweedy fabrics, don't quite fit in, nor do the wall-to-wall carpeting and fluorescent lighting in the bathrooms.

Still, the Annex has a certain charm, and there are other compensations. The restaurant serves some of the more interesting food in the area. The nearby town of Glenwood is pretty, the resort's grounds gracious, and Lake Minnewaska itself is lovely. You can certainly see why Henry Peters jumped off the train at this spot.

Address: *2500 S. Lakeshore Dr., Glenwood, MN 56334, tel. 612/634–4501 or 800/356–8654 in MN.*
Accommodations: *23 double rooms (12 in Court Bldg., 3 in Main Lodge, 8 in the Annex) with baths; 9 town houses sleep 4–6 people; two 1-bedroom cottages, five 2-bedroom cottages, three 3-bedroom cottages, one 4-bedroom cottage; one 7-bedroom housekeeping cottage.*
Amenities: *Air-conditioning, cable TV in rooms, restaurant, snack bar, 1 meeting room; beach, golf, tennis, racquetball, sailboats.*
Rates: *$62–$65, $82–$195 for town houses and cottages; breakfast and dinner. MC, V.*
Restrictions: *No pets; 2-night minimum, closed Oct.–Apr.*

The Robards House

Driving through Alexandria, with its wide, treeless Broadway, fast-food row, and numerous commercial tourist attractions, you might not believe a place like the Robards House could exist here. But go several blocks from the main drag and there it is, on a shady street, its graceful grounds stretching down to meet Lake Winona. With its shingled front gable, this quietly handsome brown-brick house looks something like a small-town creamery that sprouted a sloped roof, chocolate-colored shutters, and several extra rooms off the back. Built in 1889 by local hardware magnate John Robards, it's listed on the National Register of Historic Places.

The spacious interior boasts high ceilings and Greek Revival oak moldings and door frames—some painted, some thankfully untouched—exuding a sense of late-Victorian elegance, with some Federal touches. Throughout the living room, parlor, and dining room, rich reds and greens are echoed in the wallpaper, carpeting, and drapery. It is all quite attractive, but the real beauty lies in the details, such as the Egypto-Celtic designs wrought into the window pulls and door hinges. The living-room decor includes velvet-upholstered oak sofas and chairs, a working Victrola with original records, and mementos of old Germany, heirlooms of owner Bernice Hillgruber (who now lives in California, leaving the daily operation to manager Georgia Melander).

Upstairs, each room has been individually styled, though all have maple floors and antique furniture (or good reproductions). The Pederson Room, a likely honeymoon suite, features a broad bay window, a lake view, and a custom-built oak bedstead and armoire that don't look new at all. The Leroy Room, which also has a lake view, has Eastlake furnishings and its own little porch (marred somewhat by painted built-in cabinets that look like relics of a 1940s kitchen). The smaller rooms, the Kinkead Room (with twin beds) and the Cowling Room, are pleasant as well.

The Penthouse suite, which fills the whole third floor, has a smattering of antiques and a vintage stained-glass Palladian window. Its other amenities (a deck, a minilibrary, and a dining area off the sunken living room) make it more expensive, but it's bland and somehow sterile—something you certainly can't accuse the rest of the house of being.

Address: *518 Sixth Ave. W, Alexandria, MN 56308, tel. 612/763-4073.*
Accommodations: *4 double rooms with baths, 1 suite.*
Amenities: *Air-conditioning, ceiling fans, TV/VCR in living room.*
Rates: *$75–$185; Continental breakfast. MC, V.*
Restrictions: *No smoking, no pets.*

Spicer Castle

I f you somehow missed the opportunity of living in an old country mansion, circa 1913, here's your chance. This imposing house was built in 1893 by farm developer John Spicer, one of the founders of the Democratic-Farmer-Labor Party (Minnesota's own version of the Democrats). According to current owner Allen Latham, Spicer's grandson, the last renovations on the house were done in 1913, shortly after it was wired for electricity, and the building hasn't been changed since. Set on the wooded shores of Green Lake, the Tudor-style half-timbered house was originally called Medayto Cottage, but in the 1930s, fishermen on the lake started referring to it as "The Castle," perhaps because of its crenellated tower. Though it's otherwise not particularly castlelike, the name stuck.

However beautiful its exterior, it's the interior that makes the Castle distinctive. The furnishings, rugs, and china, the Craftsman-style lamps and clocks are all antiques, and have been in place since the 1913 redecoration. Walking across the gleaming maple floors, through the living and dining rooms, the well-stocked library, and the grand porch overlooking the lake, it's the visitor who feels out of place, like an interloper from the future.

The first floor, with dark furniture and burlap wall coverings (a typical period Craftsman touch), might seem dark, but it's not oppressive—rather, it encourages quiet reflection and talk. In winter, it becomes downright cozy, as the fireplaces throw their flickering light on the ceiling beams.

Upstairs, it's almost like a different house. White beaded paneling and large windows give the place the bright air of a Nantucket summer cottage. Some renovation has been done up here, primarily in the bathrooms, but Allen and his wife, Marti, have kept to the period, with pedestal sinks and claw-foot tubs (some in the rooms themselves). The bedsteads and dressers are in various styles, but all belonged to the Lathams' forebears. Two equally well-preserved cottages offer more privacy.

Breakfast is served in the dining room in cool months, out on the lakeside porch in summer. There are no TVs, telephones, or air-conditioning. This is pure 1913—they won't be missed.

Address: *11600 Indian Beach Rd. (Box 307), Spicer, MN 56288, tel. 612/796–5870 or 800/821–6675.*
Accommodations: *7 double rooms with baths, 2 cottages.*
Amenities: *Ceiling fans, whirlpool bath in 1 cottage.*
Rates: *$60–$110; full breakfast, afternoon tea. AE, D, MC, V.*
Restrictions: *No smoking, no pets; closed weekdays Sept.–Apr.*

Carrington House

Save for its antebellum roof railing, Carrington House's facade is plain, almost stark. It's the back that's really inviting—a long, enclosed porch with tall windows facing Lake Carlos, awnings shading the windows, stairs leading down to a waterside deck.

Built in 1911, this is a typical lakeshore "cottage" of its era. Throughout the house, hardwood floors, high ceilings, and textured-plaster walls create a calm, light-filled setting. The large living room, with its big fireplace and wicker furniture, mingles antiques and modern items.

Guest rooms are decorated with antique pieces from owner Joan Pease's family. The walls of each room are stenciled with different patterns. In back is a cottage, with pink furnishings and a whirlpool tub. Though some rooms are a little over-frilly, the overall feeling is of a comfortable summer house made for easy relaxation.

Address: *Rte. 5 (Box 18), Alexandria, MN 56308, tel. 612/846-7400.*
Accommodations: *4 double rooms with baths, one cottage.*
Amenities: *Air-conditioning, ceiling fans, cable TV in living room, whirlpool bath in cottage.*
Rates: *$65-$95; full breakfast. MC, V.*
Restrictions: *No smoking, no pets; 2-night minimum weekends July–Aug.*

Dorset Schoolhouse Bed and Breakfast

The village of Dorset—population 38—was once the smallest town in the world to have its own bank. The bank has since closed, and in 1970, so did its three-room, two-story schoolhouse. Still, it's a place that comes alive at night, thanks to four popular restaurants, and it also attracts cyclists on the Heartland Trail that runs between Walker and Park Rapids, so Denise and Tom Hafner didn't make a mistake in 1988 when they converted the school into this unusual B&B.

Surrounded on three sides by fields and woods, the plain white clapboard structure with its neat red roof still has a spare, wind-whipped look. The original three schoolrooms have been cleaned up and broken into six bright guest rooms, while the old cloak room was enlarged and turned into a common room for the guests. The refinished maple floors are cool and spotless, the walls plain white, and the sliding-glass doors factory-fresh. (Each room opens out onto a deck.) The Hafners fashioned old school desks into tables; the stairways still show the wear-and-tear of generations of young feet.

Address: *Box 210, Dorset, MN 56470, tel. 218/732-1377.*
Accommodations: *6 double rooms share 3 baths.*
Amenities: *Air-conditioning, ceiling fans.*
Rates: *$40-$60; Continental breakfast. MC, V.*
Restrictions: *No smoking, no pets.*

Grandma's Attic

Grandma's Attic, half a mile from downtown Detroit Lakes, and just across the street from the lake the town was named after, is not as old a place as the name makes it sound. It was built in 1937 as a large single-family house, though it was a decaying duplex when the Schultzes bought it in 1988. Bill, a former hotel executive, and his wife, Peggy, converted it into a bed-and-breakfast that feels light and modern, despite some of the requisite Victorian touches.

The first floor, where the common rooms are, feels like a weekend house, lived in and cluttered with family life. Two stairways (remnants of the duplex days) with refinished wood risers lead up to the five guest rooms. Though the bedrooms have new brass beds and dressers, the floors are the original oak, and Peggy's handiwork—twig wreaths and miniature wicker chairs—decorate walls and dresser tops and give an air of beachside comfort. The result is neither particularly grandmotherly nor atticlike—but what's in a name, anyway?

Address: *1106 W. Lake Dr., Detroit Lakes, MN 56501, tel. 218/847–1229 or 800/377–1229.*
Accommodations: *5 double rooms share 2 baths.*
Amenities: *Cable TV/VCR in living room; outdoor hot tub.*
Rates: *$55–$75; full breakfast, evening refreshments. MC, V.*
Restrictions: *Smoking in common rooms only, no pets.*

The Log House on Spirit Lake

A tornado put Lyle and Yvonne Tweten into the bed-and-breakfast business. Career Foreign Service officers who came home to retire in northern Minnesota, they bought 115 acres on Spirit Lake, built a house, and settled in. Then, in the summer of 1984, a tornado in McIntosh, Minnesota, hit Lyle's boyhood home, a by-then decrepit white clapboard farmhouse that had been in the family since 1889. Several boards were ripped off, revealing a surprise underneath: The house was made of square-hewn poplar logs. The Twetens moved the structure to their land, setting it on a hill a few steps from the lake, and restored it as a B&B.

Inside the three-story house are whitewashed walls, reproduction fir floorboards, and period furnishings; bathroom fixtures and kitchen appliances are modern touches. The upstairs bedroom has old-fashioned rag rugs on wide-plank wood floors and a thick, dark wooden ceiling beam. The basement bedroom is more modern and a bit frilly, but its private deck and porch are built from old silo wood.

Address: *Ottertail Rte. 4 (Box 130), Vergas, MN 56587, tel. 218/342–2318.*
Accommodations: *2 double rooms with baths.*
Amenities: *Air-conditioning, kitchenette.*
Rates: *$65–$70; full breakfast, evening refreshments. MC, V.*
Restrictions: *No smoking, no pets; closed Nov.–Apr.*

Nims' Bakketop Hus

Bakketop Hus means "Hilltop House" in Norwegian, and it's an appropriate name—the hillside views of rural Long Lake are perhaps the strongest asset of this large house, which Dennis and Judy Nims turned into a bed-and-breakfast when their kids grew up. (Judy is of Norwegian ancestry, hence for the inn's name.) While there are some antique items here, most notably the huge buffet that dominates the living room, the overall decor befits a house built in 1975. It's essentially a suburban split-level writ larger than usual, with some rustic touches.

The pink-and-black Master Suite, popular with newlyweds, offers a water bed, skylight, whirlpool bath, and a view of the garden and driveway. Another guest room, which opens onto a lakeview patio, has peach country French decor, with a draped canopy bed and a love seat.

Downstairs, a game room with pool table and player piano is available for guests, as well as a large outdoor deck facing the lake.

Address: *R.R. 2 (Box 187A), Fergus Falls, MN 56537, tel. 218/739-2915.*
Accommodations: *1 double room with bath, 2 doubles share 1 bath.*
Amenities: *Air-conditioning, cable TV and phones in rooms, whirlpool bath in 1 room.*
Rates: *$55-$85; full breakfast, evening refreshments. No credit cards.*
Restrictions: *No smoking, pets only by prior consent.*

Peace Cliff

While this bed-and-breakfast isn't a historic old house (David and Kathy Laursen built it in 1989), it takes advantage of its lovely Leech Lake location with sunset views from every room. And the house hearkens back in time, with half-timbered Tudor-style architecture.

The living room features an antique French tapestry; the dining room has Eastlake furniture. Upstairs in the tower, a Ralph Lauren–style library has tartan-covered rockers, leather wing chairs, and built-in bookcases. Two guest rooms are up here: the Belgian, with an immense 300-year-old walnut bedstead, and the Victoria, with an iron bedstead and floral wallpaper. In the bottom story are three other guest rooms, including the French Room, with its ornate French furnishings.

Perhaps the house is still too new for all these weighty antiques, but Peace Cliff has its most important assets: nature and the sunsets, serenading loons. Not a bad retreat.

Address: *HCR 73 (Box 998D), Walker, MN 56484, tel. 218/547-2832.*
Accommodations: *3 double rooms with baths, 1 single with bath, 1 suite.*
Amenities: *Cable TV/VCR in common room.*
Rates: *$37-$92; full breakfast, evening refreshments. AE, MC, V.*
Restrictions: *No smoking, no pets; 2-night minimum summer weekends.*

Prairie View Estate

T hank goodness for Norwegian bachelor farmers who throw nothing away. When sisters Phyllis Haugrud and Carol Moses, along with their cousin Janet Malakowsky, inherited the 800-acre family farm from their unmarried uncle in 1990, his will forbade them to sell it. Inside this Craftsmanesque gray stucco house, they found loads of old family furniture, and decided to turn the house into a B&B.

Exposed rafters and dark wood furnishings—some more than 100 years old—create a portrait not only of old Minnesota farm life, but also of Old Norway. The three guest rooms have solid, well-made antiques—not fancy pieces, but often beautiful.

Some restoration remains to be done. But it isn't difficult to ignore these details when you sit enjoying breakfast on the lovely long, enclosed porch with hardwood floors. At Prairie View Estate, the past is fighting back, and it usually wins.

Address: *Rte. 2 (Box 443), Pelican Rapids, MN 56572, tel. 218/863-4321.*
Accommodations: *1 double room with bath, 2 doubles share 1 bath.*
Amenities: *Air-conditioning.*
Rates: *$35–$45; full breakfast, evening refreshments. MC, V.*
Restrictions: *No smoking, pets only by prior consent.*

Stonehouse Bed and Breakfast

S tonemason Craig Nagel and his wife, Claire, built Stonehouse in 1988 on their wooded acreage a short walk from Lund Lake. The low-angled house somewhat resembles a rest-area building along an interstate highway, but the Nagels have emphasized a sense of nature. The exterior walls are made of cedar and stone that Craig prepared; the pine interior walls and floors came from trees right on the property. Craig also split the stones for the fireplace. Claire added decorations and crafted the stained glass that appears here and there throughout the house.

There's a double bed in the bedroom and a queen-size bed in the living area, so up to four people can stay here at a time. Though comfortable,

furnishings may remind some visitors of a good-quality motel—track lighting, nubby wall-to-wall carpeting, modern TV and kitchen appliances. One may wish that the Stonehouse were more eccentric and charming, like the Nagel's own house nearby, where breakfast is served. Still, this homemade (and well-made) cottage has the right location, nestled in a grove of pine trees, and its screened porch and stone-walled terrace are pleasant.

Address: *HCR 2 (Box 9), Pequot Lakes, MN 56472, tel. 218/568-4255.*
Accommodations: *1 cottage with 2 double beds.*
Amenities: *TV/VCR, kitchen.*
Rates: *$70–$120; full breakfast. MC, V.*
Restrictions: *No pets.*

Tianna Farms

Once a large, working dairy farm, this wooded 55-acre estate was opened as a bed-and-breakfast in 1991 by Peter Hawkins and Liza Vogt, grandchildren of the original dairy farmer. Though its outlines resemble a New England beach cottage, the 1920s-era house has an unadorned modernism that's part Prairie style, part Bauhaus.

Several details of the decor date from the mid-1970s, where the house underwent its last major redecoration, and they don't always work—the living room's handsome stone fireplace, for example, doesn't quite look right with the floral-upholstered sofas—but Frank Lloyd Wright himself would probably have approved of the library. The guest rooms are also a mixed bag. On the first floor, the twin-bedded Garden Room is country frilly. Upstairs, the Hunting Room looks heartily masculine, with maple floor, rifle collection, and woody-brown area rug.

The grounds include a tennis court, a greenhouse, and an elaborate wildflower garden with artificial waterfall.

Address: *Box 629, Walker, MN 56484, tel. 218/547–1306.*
Accommodations: *4 double rooms with baths, 1 suite.*
Amenities: *Air-conditioning, cable TV in living room and library; swimming dock, tennis.*
Rates: *$55–$110; full breakfast. D, MC, V.*
Restrictions: *No smoking indoors, pets only by prior consent.*

Walden Woods

It's not nearly as austere as Thoreau's famous cabin in Massachusetts, but Walden Woods has the same back-to-basics spirit. Ten years ago, Richard Manly, a Minnesota-trained forester who had worked many years for the Audubon Society in New York City, built his own log cabin near Mud Lake, a wooded pond about 17 miles east of Brainerd.

Though recently constructed, Walden Woods doesn't look raw or artificially rustic. The Manlys' quietly tasteful antique furnishings, in an eclectic mix of styles, work well inside these Norwegian pine walls. A porch faces the pond and the surrounding woods. Up the split-log staircase is a well-stocked library. The guest rooms all have hardwood floors, antique bedsteads, and subdued floral curtains, and Anne Manly, a straw-weaver and basket-maker, has accented them with her work.

The worthier elements of civilization are provided—bathrooms are up-to-date, though with older-style fixtures. There are many beautiful clocks here, but the Manlys don't bother to wind them. As for TV and air-conditioning, who needs them when you can listen to the loons serenade at dusk on Walden Pond?

Address: *Rte. 1 (Box 193), Deerwood, MN 56444, tel. 612/692–4379.*
Accommodations: *4 double rooms share 2 baths.*
Rates: *$55–$65; full breakfast. AE, MC, V.*
Restrictions: *No smoking, no pets.*

Wisconsin

Wisconsin

Madison and Environs

Home to both the state government and the University of Wisconsin–Madison campus, scenic Madison, with a population of 191,000, is a thriving center for business, government, education, and recreation. The ethnic and cultural diversity of the major university and the charged political atmosphere created by Madison's role as state capital add to the city's appeal.

Madison lies on the edge of Wisconsin's "driftless area"—a region bypassed by Ice Age glaciers some 10,000 years ago. Marked by deep, narrow valleys and steep, wooded hills, the region covers most of southwestern Wisconsin and was the scene of a major lead-mining boom in the 1830s. The city has been known since settlement times as Four Lakes, with Lakes Mendota, Monona, Wingra, and Waubesa lying within or just outside the city limits.

The city center is on an eight-block-wide isthmus between Lakes Mendota and Monona, with a skyline dominated (by ordinance) by the 285-foot dome of the state capitol. The city, filled with green spaces and conservation areas, includes more than 30 city parks. In addition, three state parks are within a 20-minute drive of downtown Madison. The university campus, stretching for more than a mile along the Lake Mendota shore, is considered to be one of the nation's most beautiful and acts as a backdrop for a number of feature films. Interesting nooks and crannies make the campus a perfect spot for a stroll. At the western edge of the campus sits the First Unitarian Society Meeting House, one of Frank Lloyd Wright's finest designs. Madison's wide variety of architectural styles, dating from the mid-19th century to the present, include a handful of private homes designed by Wisconsin's native son.

Madison is not a stranger to culture. There are several major cultural venues, including the University of

Wisconsin's Elvehjem Museum of Art, the Madison Art Center, and the State Historical Society Museum. The Madison Civic Center offers an extensive program of music, theater, and entertainment, including touring concerts and Broadway shows, and is home to the Madison Symphony and the Madison Repertory Theater. Downtown Madison hosts more than 100 annual events, including the Madison Symphony's outdoor summer concerts on the capitol square. In addition, the university's theatrical, musical, and film offerings add spice and variety to the cultural scene.

Madisonians are a sports-minded lot. University of Wisconsin's football, basketball, and hockey events draw large crowds. Badger football games are, in essence, an afternoon-long party where even mediocre teams attract upward of 70,000 red-clad fans to Camp Randall Stadium. The Madison Muskies, a Class A farm club for the Oakland Athletics, has sent players like Jose Canseco and Terry Steinbach to the A's. Softball is a summer passion; city leagues have some 400 organized teams. Boating, sailing, canoeing, and bicycling are also tremendously popular. In addition, over 100 miles of cross-country ski trails in the city and county offer a wide variety of terrain for winter sportmen.

For the most part, Madison is free of suburban sprawl, with green spaces and farms between the city and outlying communities such as Cross Plains. Middleton and Monona are separate entities, but only city-limits signs insulate them from Madison. East and south of Madison, the land smooths out into rolling hills and farm fields where herds of black and white cattle graze. To the east, Lake Mills and Oconomowoo are convenient to either Madison or Milwaukee. Aztalan, near Lake Mills, is a village where the Middle Mississippian Indian culture existed from 1075 to 1175. Oconomowoo was once known as the "Newport of the West" for its many palatial homes and beautiful lakes. Viroqua, in the western coulee country near the Mississippi

River, is marked by small town Victorian charm and neighborliness.

Places to Go, Sights to See

Blue Mounds. West of Madison, *Blue Mounds State Park* (tel. 608/437–5711) has hiking trails, picnic areas, a large campground, and viewing towers offering glorious vistas.

Elvehjem Museum of Art (800 University Ave., tel. 608/263–2246). The university's museum is one of the state's best, with a permanent collection of paintings, sculpture, and decorative arts dating from 2300 BC to the present.

Farmer's Market. Held on Capitol Square each Saturday from May through October, this extensive farmer's market has several hundred vendors offering baked goods, flowers, and fresh produce.

Henry Villas Park Zoo (702 S. Randall Ave., tel. 608/266–4732). Open from Memorial Day through Labor Day, the zoo exhibits nearly 200 species of animals and has a children's zoo where youngsters can pet and feed animals.

State Street. A lively pedestrian mall runs between the capitol and the college where coffeehouses, ethnic cafés, and shops vie for the attention of passersby.

University Arboretum (1207 Seminole Hwy., tel. 608/263–7888). Away from downtown, the arboretum has more than 1,200 acres of natural plant and animal communities, such as prairie and forest landscapes, and horticultural collections of Upper Midwest specimens. The large lilacs and apple-tree gardens are spectacular in spring.

University of Wisconsin. The college opened in 1849 with 20 students. Today, with an enrollment of 46,000, it occupies a 1,000-acre campus on the shores of Lake Mendota. Guided walking tours of the campus may be arranged at the visitor information center in the *Memorial Union* (800 Langdon St., tel. 608/262–2511)

Wisconsin State Capitol (tel. 608/266–0382). The city center, on an eight-block-wide isthmus, is anchored at one end by the State Capitol. Free tours of this magnificent Roman Renaissance structure take you through the Rotunda, Supreme Court Room, Senate and Assembly chambers, and Governor's Conference Room.

Bicycling

The 23-mile **Sugar River State Trail** (tel. 608/527–2334 for information and fees) runs from New Glarus to Brodhead, crossing the Sugar River and its tributaries 14 times. The **Military Ridge State Trail** (tel. 608/935–2315 for information and fees) traces the path of the Old Military Ridge Trail of the mid-1800s for 39.6 miles between Verona and Dodgeville.

Canoeing

The **Yahara River** runs from Lake Mendota into Lake Monona, then south to Lake Waubesa and Lake Kegonsa. From there, it continues south through farmland and the town of Stoughton, joining the **Rock River** at a point just below Fulton, some 25 miles from Madison. The Rock River meanders through more countryside, and the towns of Janesville and Beloit before entering Illinois, and eventually running into the Mississippi. The current of both rivers is slow; some dams will require portaging, and in low water additional portages may be necessary. Access is available at the lakes and towns that the rivers run through, as well as spots where roads cross over them.

Fishing

Northern pike, walleye, smallmouth and largemouth bass, bullheads, catfish, and a variety of panfish are found in southern Wisconsin's plentiful waters. Rainbow, brown, and brook trout are stocked in specially designated streams. Local bait and tackle shops or resorts can tell you where to look for fish, or recommend a professional guide.

Restaurants

Madison's Farmers' Market provides many of the ingredients for the dishes at **L'Etoile** (25 N. Pinckney St., tel. 608/251–0500), where regional food with a French flair is served in the shadow of the capitol building. **Ovens of Brittany** (305 State St., tel. 608/273–4900) is where to find hearty French-country fare, as well as the University of Wisconsin's intelligentsia, who've made this a hangout for the smart set. **Quivey's Grove** (6261 Nesbitt Rd., tel. 608/273–4900) dishes out sturdy Midwest cuisine in an 1855 farmhouse.

Tourist Information

Greater Madison Convention & Visitors Bureau (615 E. Washington Ave., Madison, WI 53703-2952, tel. 800/373–6376).

Collins House

This sturdy brick Prairie-style house, built for a lumber magnate in 1911, was divided into apartments, then used as an office building, and then abandoned. But it was on a prime corner lot in Madison's historic district, next to a small city park and overlooking Lake Mendota. So in 1985, Barb and Mike Pratzel bought it and dismantled its "modernizations," to reveal ceilings with oak and mahogany beams, decorative leaded-glass windows, and the clean geometric lines of Prairie design. Then they polished the rare red-maple floors, filled the house with a collection of vintage Mission and Arts-and-Crafts furnishings that complement the exquisite woodwork, and opened it as a bed-and-breakfast.

In the living room, a hassock, a low burgundy sofa, and armchairs are grouped around the straight-lined fireplace, which is bordered in large, moss-green unglazed tiles. The ceiling has beams, and an oakleaf frieze is stenciled on the cream-colored walls; moldings are dark mahogany. Twin leaded-glass fronted bookcases mark the entry to the library, whose frieze replicates one that was original to the house; inside, a plump upholstered armchair and sturdy rockers ring a well-worn Persian rug. Outside the library are three lakefront sun porches. Breakfast is served in one of them where guests can watch the sailboats and crew teams, and, in winter, ice skaters and ice fishermen. Barb and Mike,

who also own a gourmet catering firm, often serve Swedish oatmeal pancakes in the morning.

The light and airy guest rooms upstairs have handmade quilts, soothing color schemes, and striking Mission and Arts-and-Crafts furniture. The largest room affords views in three directions, over Lake Mendota and the capitol building's dome. A wooden screen with a stenciled butterfly motif separates two double beds; in the sitting area are a Mission rocker upholstered in brown leather, a tea cart filled with begonias, an immense oak breakfront, and a tall matching secretary.

The Collins House is a convenient, short walk from the capitol, the university, State Street shops, the Mendota's lakefront park, and Lake Monona.

Address: *704 E. Gorham St., Madison, WI 53703, tel. 608/255-4230.*
Accommodations: *4 double rooms with baths, 1 suite.*
Amenities: *Phones in rooms, TV in 1 guest room, TV and VCR in common room, video film library.*
Rates: *$65–$99; full breakfast. MC, V.*
Restrictions: *No smoking in guest rooms, inquire about pets.*

Fargo Mansion Inn

The Wells Fargo Company was doing rather well in 1890, so when E. J. Fargo bought himself this grand house, he set about making it even grander. To the already stately Queen Anne building Fargo added a gabled third floor, the cupola atop the showpiece octagonal turret, and an elaborate, gabled porte cochère. Over the years, however, the house fell into disrepair, and sat empty and condemned until it caught the eye of a developer who had driven past it after making a wrong turn: Barry Luce decided then and there to buy it. He completely renovated it, and the house became an inn, furnished with antiques from the town's Opera Mall Antiques Center, which the developer and his partner, Tom Bolks, also operates.

The sunny, spacious living room, a popular spot for weddings, is a Victorian confection full of sculpted moldings and other architectural furbelows. The focal point is the fireplace of laurel wreath–patterned tiles framed by an ornately carved wood mantelpiece; the shelves above are crammed with figurines and antique clocks. The music room holds a huge Federal dining table, two matching side tables, and two movable cabinets. The everyday dining room, wainscoted in oak, is no less elaborate, from its mirrored Victorian buffet and sideboard to the Corinthian columns that frame the doorway into the adjoining solarium.

The small library contains a Victorian pump organ, a sled filled with antique dolls and teddy bears, and a vintage toy ironing board.

Of the guest rooms upstairs, the Master Suite is the most popular because of its private balcony and its size: large enough to dwarf a bed with an 8-foot-tall headboard and to accommodate a teardrop chandelier and the plump velvet sofa by the white marble fireplace. A "secret" doorway, disguised as a bookcase, opens to reveal one of the inn's signature modern marble bathrooms; this one also has a Jacuzzi. The other rooms, of varying sizes, are decorated in late Victorian style and filled with antiques.

On the house's double lot, lovely gardens of shrubbery and banks of daffodils have replaced the bear pit in which Mr. Fargo staged battles between bruins for the entertainment of his guests.

Address: *406 Mulberry St., Lake Mills, WI 53551, tel. 414/648–3654.*
Accommodations: *5 double rooms with baths.*
Amenities: *Air-conditioning, TV in living room, Jacuzzi in 2 rooms, conference facilities.*
Rates: *$65–$130; full breakfast. MC, V.*
Restrictions: *No smoking, no pets.*

Mansion Hill Inn

Considered the height of opulence in Madison when it was built in 1858, this ornately carved sandstone Romanesque Revival mansion still upstages its neighbors in the historic district. Swagged with double tiers of delicate wrought-iron balconies, it would be more at home in New Orleans. Inside, a spiral staircase anchored by an immense, intricately carved newel post rises four stories from the jewel-box foyer to a turreted belvedere with sweeping views of the city. The tawny marble floor, flamboyant floral arrangements, elaborate gilt moldings, friezes, and rich detailing create the atmosphere of a small European hotel and set the tone for the entire inn.

The small front parlor is arranged with conversational groupings of Rococo-Revival style furniture: settees upholstered in rose damask, side chairs with velvet ottomans. Guests can warm up at the elegant marble fireplace, or sashay over to the Emerson square grand piano for a musical interlude. The carved walnut dining table, original to the mansion, holds plates and pitchers of refreshments and newspapers from near and far to which guests are welcome to help themselves.

Each of the guest rooms is individually and lavishly decorated, and most are embellished with ornate cornices and ceiling medallions and elegant, modern marble baths. In nine of the rooms, French doors open onto pleasant terraces. The Lillie Langtry Room has a white marble fireplace, veranda, wallpaper hand-painted in neo-Grecian patterns, Renaissance Revival furniture, and a bed draped in lace. The room known as the Turkish Nook recalls the 1890s craze for Orientalia: The wallpaper depicts the opening of the Suez Canal, and the bed, whose spread is a Near East–style tapestry, sits under a lacy sultan's tent. Velvet pouf ottomans complete the look. Rooms on the lower levels are smaller and not as elaborately decorated but have their own patios.

You can have breakfast delivered to your room, along with your choice of morning newspaper, or arrange to eat in the parlor.

Address: *424 N. Pinckney St., Madison, WI 53703, tel. 800/798–9070, fax 608/255–2217.*
Accommodations: *11 double rooms with baths, 6 with sitting areas.*
Amenities: *Air-conditioning, phones, TV, and stereo in all rooms; 9 rooms with terraces, whirlpools in 8 rooms; private wine cellar and catered dinners available, teleconference facilities; 24-hour valet service and valet parking, access to health club.*
Rates: *$80–$230 single, $20 additional person; Continental breakfast. AE, MC, V.*
Restrictions: *No pets.*

Middleton Beach Inn

In this country contemporary house, floor-to-ceiling windows frame spectacular views of Lake Mendota. But there's plenty to look at inside as well. The place is a showcase for the antique treasures that the peripatetic Dueslers collected during years of living in New England.

Antique sleds and sleighs are their particular weakness, and in the living room there's a sleigh parked by the window, covered with dolls and toys, and a sled that doubles as a coffee table. The room also holds a tavern table from the original Pabst Brewery, a pear-shaped oak Scandinavian grandfather clock, and a cabinet retired from the Wisconsin State Capitol (and now filled with collector marbles and four generations' worth of Duesler family teddy bears. By day sunlight pours through a skylight and the huge lake-view windows. A modern marble fireplace that takes up an entire wall warms winter nights.

The Victorian Suite's window wall and veranda also allows for sweeping lake views, and its red velvet Victorian settee is as curvaceous as the nude in the painting (posed for, says the owner, by none other than Marilyn Monroe). The huge, skylit bathroom has a whirlpool and a vanity mirror. The Carriage Room, also skylighted, has a 19th-century

country feel, with its Shaker-style bed, Jenny Lind trunk, cane-seat rocker, and drum table, fashioned from a vintage Baker's chocolate container. The blue-and-white Schoolhouse Room, smaller than the others, is enlivened by memorabilia from Mr. Duesler's pre-innkeeping career at Oscar Meyer, such as a toy Wienermobile. The hefty oak headboard of the queen-size bed in the Country Suite is embellished by intricate carving.

Two generations of Dueslers, outgoing, involved hosts, run this family business, and each morning father and daughter-in-law cook up crêpes, quiches, French toast, omelets, or bananas Foster, and urge their guests not to worry about the calories they consume—the many sports and athletic activities they can participate in nearby will help them work it off.

Address: *2303 Middleton Beach Rd., Middleton, WI 53562, tel. 608/831-6446.*
Accommodations: *4 double rooms with baths.*
Amenities: *Air-conditioning; phone and TV in room optional, TV and sound system in common room; free health club access, canoe and water sports.*
Rates: *$60–$125; full breakfast, afternoon refreshment. AE, MC, V.*
Restrictions: *No smoking, no pets.*

Jackson Street Inn

A retired Montana rancher built this foursquare clapboard house with oak and maple woodwork, cross-beamed oak ceiling, beveled glass windows, a glass-paneled pocket door, and Italian marble fireplace. That was in 1899. Now the house is an inn run by a retired couple who've lived here for more than 35 years. Its fine turn-of-the-century craftsmanship is diminished only by the homely gold shag carpeting and undistinguished furniture, except for the pair of huge Eastlake buffets with beveled-glass windows in the spacious, wood-paneled dining room and parlor.

The guest rooms are done in antiques and have delicately patterned floral paper on the walls and quilts on the beds. The color scheme of the largest bedroom takes its cue from a blue-and-white handmade Amish quilt, and the cushioned seats in the bay windows overlook a quiet, residential street.

Address: *210 S. Jackson St., Janesville, WI 53545, tel. 608/754-7250.*
Accommodations: *2 double rooms with baths, 2 doubles share 1 bath.*
Amenities: *Air-conditioning and ceiling fans in all rooms, TV in downstairs living room, telephone and refrigerator in upstairs hall sitting room; putting green, shuffleboard.*
Rates: *$55–$65; full breakfast. AE, MC, V.*
Restrictions: *No smoking in guest rooms.*

Lake House on Monona

T his stone house built in 1947 offers the best of both worlds: a lakeshore property and a location right in town. And, though it may look unremarkable, it has one more extra-charming feature—a screened porch that extends the length of the house, where guests can breakfast and linger in wicker chairs. They can also take in an expansive view of the wooded yard, the lake, and the Madison skyline on the opposite shore. A canoe, a sailboat, and the sun deck of the inn's boathouse are all at the guests' disposal, along with bikes to use for on-shore excursions. In winter, guests gather around the living room's fieldstone fireplace.

The suite is the only room with a lake view. It also has a private balcony, a vaulted ceiling with two skylights, a loft full of ferns, a wood-burning fireplace, and a refrigerator, TV, and whirlpool. The other rooms are sunny and decorated in casual weekend-house style, and the bathroom in one has a skylight. Breakfast choices range from hickory-nut pancakes to a Mexican quiche, plus fresh fruit.

Address: *4027 Monona Dr., Monona, WI 53716, tel. 608/222-4601 or 800/657-5147.*
Accommodations: *2 double rooms with bath, 1 double with half-bath, 1 suite.*
Amenities: *Air-conditioning; water sports.*
Rates: *$40–$115; full breakfast, evening sherry. D, MC, V.*
Restrictions: *No smoking, no pets.*

Past and Present Inn

irst came the gift shop, carrying quaint collectibles and dried floral wreaths made on the premises. Next, tired of watching shoppers go elsewhere for lunch, the owner opened a dining room that soon became legendary for its bacon-lettuce-tomato soup and cheesecakes. Then, two guest suites were added to this contemporary, colonial-style house to accommodate people hiking the nearby Ice Age Trail and anglers who wanted to fish for trout in adjacent Black Earth Creek. The two-bedroom suite, reached by an outside staircase, has private decks at each end. Inside is a mix of old and new furnishings and a kitchen, which makes this unit a good choice for those traveling with children. The other suite, on the ground floor, faces Black Earth Creek, and is done in country Victorian style with rattan furnishings and floral patterned wallpaper; a whirlpool takes up one corner of the bedroom. Another suite with a whirlpool is scheduled for early 1993 completion.

The breakfast menu offers omelets and other egg dishes, Belgian waffles, and specialty pancakes.

Address: *2034 Main St., Cross Plains, WI 53528, tel. 608/798–4441.*
Accommodations: *1 2-bedroom suite with bath, 1 1-bedroom suite with whirlpool.*
Amenities: *Phones, TV; restaurant, gift shop.*
Rates: *$75–$150; full breakfast (in restaurant). MC, V.*
Restrictions: *No smoking, no pets.*

Plough Inn

his recently renovated, handsome Greek Revival building from the 1850s started out as a stagecoach stop. Today, its sunny bedrooms are done in a clean, white, country-modern style, with Levelor blinds, gleaming wood floors covered with rugs, and new brass beds topped by down quilts. The Arborview Room looks out onto the university's arboretum, and guests can use the still-working stone fireplace. The nautical-theme Tap Room is full of sea charts, ships' models, and bugle lamps, and there's an old sea chest and a porthole window. The Parkside Room gets sunlight from two exposures and is filled with lace-trimmed linens and reproduction wing and Windsor chairs. The exposed brick-walled Studio on the top floor, with a large, separate dressing room, overlooks a wooded lot and has two skylights in its vaulted ceiling and another in its cedar-paneled whirlpool room.

Breakfast is served on an enclosed porch that overlooks the flower garden.

Address: *3402 Monroe St., Madison, WI 53711, tel. 608/238–2981.*
Accommodations: *4 double rooms with baths.*
Amenities: *Air-conditioning, radio in room, phone and TV in common room, refrigerator in one room, 2 rooms with whirlpool baths; bike path across street.*
Rates: *$59–$94; Continental breakfast weekdays, full breakfast weekends. MC, V.*
Restrictions: *No smoking, no pets.*

Victoria-on-Main

This high-style Queen Anne house, on a corner adjacent to the university campus, was built by Whitewater's mayor in 1895, and the pediments, pillared porch, and octagonal, cone-topped turret signal the residence of a prominent citizen.

Inside, all the rooms are decorated in Laura Ashley wallpaper and fabrics, and filled with antiques and bric-a-brac. Each guest room features a different Wisconsin hardwood. The Bird's Eye Maple room contrasts blue-and-white chintz against the golden-toned wood, and leaded-glass windows add a touch of elegance. In the Cherry Room, a 6-foot-tall cherry wood headboard stands out against the airy floral-print wallpaper. The Red Oak Room is furnished in, of course, red oak; its most striking feature is a fireplace of blue fleur-de-lis-patterned tiles, with a metal grate emblazoned with cavorting Grecian nymphs.

Breakfast, served at the kitchen table, may include caramel-baked French toast, quiche, baked eggs, or the inn's special puffed apple dish.

Address: *622 W. Main St., Whitewater, WI 53190, tel. 414/473-8400.* **Accommodations:** *1 double room with bath, 2 doubles share 1 bath.* **Amenities:** *TV in sitting room, kitchen available for guests' use.* **Rates:** *$43–$65; full breakfast. MC, V.* **Restrictions:** *No smoking, no pets.*

The Victorian Belle

The oak trees that shade this stately Victorian are almost as old as the house itself, which was completed in 1891. Although the exterior is restrained by the standards of the day, the rooms inside are faithful re-creations of the period's over-the-top decor. Furnishings are Victorian and the stained-glass windows, oak floors, pocket doors, and the fireplace, rimmed by vibrant blue-green glazed tiles and a mantelpiece full of floral carvings, are all original. The dining room, in which host Barb Jaeger serves such breakfasts as her signature deep-fried French toast or whole wheat pancakes with peaches and cream, is illuminated by a century-old brass chandelier; its corner china cabinet is filled with antique dishes.

Susanna's Room is most people's favorite guest room, for its hand-stenciled walls draped with antique clothing, its heirloom brass bed, its rolltop desk, and because of its private deck, which faces a sprawling yard filled with shade trees and perennials. Although the house is on the town's main street, it's in a residential neighborhood a few blocks from the business district.

Address: *520 W. Wisconsin Ave., Oconomowoc, WI 53066, tel. 414/567-2520.* **Accommodations:** *2 double rooms with baths.* **Amenities:** *Air-conditioning, TV in living room; picnic table.* **Rates:** *$60; full breakfast. MC, V.* **Restrictions:** *No smoking, no pets.*

Viroqua Heritage Inn

Restraint was the last thing the Boyle family had in mind when they built this Victorian extravaganza in 1890, and present owner Nancy Rhodes-Seevers has lovingly restored every last curlicue. This grand house rises in blue-shingled splendor, its porch embossed with a floral garland, and its corner tower topped with a conical cap.

More flowers bloom inside on the carved, ornately tiled fireplaces. Polished hardwood floors peep out from under the Oriental rugs in the parlor, and nearly outshine the brass and crystal chandelier; lace curtains, a pair of fringed settees upholstered in tapestry print fabric, and a globe gas lamp complete the mood. In the music room is another intricately carved fireplace, as well as a baby grand piano and a working victrola.

Each guest room is furnished with antiques; the largest has an 1840s four-poster bed and a sitting area in the turret, and shares a balcony that overlooks the garden. The upstairs bathroom has a claw-foot tub and pedestal sink.

Address: *220 E. Jefferson St., Viroqua, WI 54665, tel. 608/637–3306.*
Accommodations: *4 double rooms share 2 baths.*
Amenities: *Phones and TV available for rooms, robes, refrigerator and microwave available to guests.*
Rates: *$45–$65; full breakfast. AE, D, MC, V.*
Restrictions: *No smoking indoors, no pets.*

Milwaukee and Southeast Wisconsin

*With a population of about 636,000, Milwaukee is
Wisconsin's largest city and the nation's 24th largest; it
covers nearly 96 square miles and has more than 15
suburbs. Metropolitan Greater Milwaukee includes
a four-county area with a population of nearly 1.4 million.*

*Most Native Americans were gone by the mid-1840s, but
a few Potawatomi huts could still be found as late as 1854
in what is now downtown Milwaukee. The city's population
in 1845 was about 10,000, more than half of German
descent. Many Germans arrived in the 1850s, along with
Italians, Poles, Scandinavians, Serbs, and Irish. By the last
half of the 19th century, Milwaukee's German population
was so large that the city was often called the German
Athens. Only the Polish and Irish populations came close
in numbers, and English was rarely heard in some
neighborhoods. The German influence is still found
throughout the city in architecture, in language, and
especially in food, with a legacy of Old World restaurants.*

*A small-town atmosphere prevails in Milwaukee, which is
not so much a large city as a large collection of neighborhoods with respect for small-town values. Streets are clean,
homes are tidy, parks and green spaces abound. Modern
steel and glass high rises occupy much of the downtown
area, but the early heritage persists in the restored and
well-kept 19th-century buildings that share the city skyline.*

*Milwaukee is one of a handful of Midwest cities that has
a skywalk system, so downtown visitors can walk from
wherever they are staying to restaurants, shops, theaters,
and sporting events without having to step outdoors. The
Riverspan part of the system is the only skywalk in the
nation built over a navigable waterway, the Milwaukee
River.*

*The city claims more than 50 ethnic groups and celebrates
its "melting pot" origins with all kinds of ethnic and
cultural festivals, along with the annual State Fair.
Milwaukee has become known as the "city of festivals,"
stemming from the nationally known Summerfest, which
kicks off each summer's activities on the lakefront.*

*Another annual highlight is the Great Circus Parade,
a July spectacle that features scores of antique circus
wagons from the famed Circus World Museum in Baraboo.
More than a million people line the streets to watch it.*

*Milwaukeeans are proud of their festivals, their 137 parks,
the Brewers, the lakefront, the zoo, and the horticultural
domes in Mitchell Park. There are good art and natural
history museums. The Milwaukee Symphony plays at the
Performing Arts Center, and there are top-notch opera,
ballet, and repertory companies. Milwaukeeans will readily
admit their city doesn't dazzle like Houston, or charm you
like San Francisco. And they don't mind. At the same
time, the city lacks the hard edge of a Detroit or a Chicago,
and they don't mind that, either.*

Places to Go, Sights to See

Cedarburg. Restored to achieve the look of the 1840s, when German
immigrants first harnessed the nearby creek to power their new mills, the
entire downtown area of Cedarburg has been listed on the National Register
of Historic Places. One of those mills now houses the *Stone Mill Winery*
(tel. 414/377–8020), which offers tours, and the adjoining *Cedar Creek
Settlement,* a restored village jammed with restaurants, art galleries, and
shops. The *Ozaukee Art Center* (tel. 414/377–8230), in a former brewery,
displays the works of regional artists. Wisconsin's *oldest covered bridge*
spans Cedar Creek just 3 miles from town.

Lake Geneva. Ringing the lakeshore are the country houses of the 19th-
century wealthy, who could afford country quiet. Today's activities center
around the water. There are seven public beaches and boating is quite
popular. A 26-mile footpath circles the lake, and there are 10 public golf
courses and 10 hiking trails nearby, some of which are used for skiing in
winter. *Old World Wisconsin* (north on U.S. 67, tel. 414/594–2116),
a 50-building settlement comprising farmsteads and a village, is a short drive
away.

Milwaukee. Beer made this city famous, but there's more to it than breweries, bratwurst, and ballparks. Its true life and backbone are found in its pockets of German, Polish, Serbian, African-American, Irish, and other ethnic communities. Numerous festivals, parades, and restaurants celebrate the city's diversity. It has always had a lively arts scene; its reputation as a center of publishing and graphics design is growing. The new *Performing Arts Center* (929 N. Water St., tel. 414/273–7206) boasts a symphony orchestra, as well as ballet, opera, and theater companies. In an Eero Saarinen–designed lakefront building, the *Milwaukee Art Museum* (750 N. Lincoln Memorial Dr., tel. 414/224–3220) exhibits an impressive array of 19th- and 20th-century American and European artwork. The *Milwaukee Public Museum* (800 W. Wells St., tel. 414/278–2700) contains the fourth largest collection of natural-history exhibits in the United States.

Racine. This city's best-known attraction, the *S. C. Johnson Wax Building* (1525 Howe St., tel. 414/631–2154), was designed by Frank Lloyd Wright and set up in the 1930s, but it still looks like an office structure of the future. Tours are given Tuesday to Friday, and reservations are required.

Restaurants

One of the brightest stars in Wisconsin's culinary flag is **Sanford's** (1547 N. Jackson, tel. 414/276–9608), an upscale storefront restaurant serving Franco-Californian creations. But ethnic fare is what Milwaukee specializes in and the proof is there for the eating at longtime favorites like **Karl Ratsch's Old World** (320 E. Mason St., tel. 414/276–2720), which serves German food, and **Old Town** (522 W. Lincoln, tel. 414/672–0206), where Serbian dishes are on offer. In Kenosha, the place to eat is **Mangia** (5717 Sheridan Rd., tel. 414/652–4285), where inventive contemporary Italian dishes are served in an equally contemporary setting alongside the town square. **St. Moritz** (327 Wrigley Dr., tel. 414/248–6680), a Queen Anne summer cottage (read: mansion) on the shores of Lake Geneva, is proud of its *mesclún* salad, garlicky rack of lamb, and other dishes featuring Wisconsin veal and salmon. For wood-smoked ribs and prime rib in a casual setting in Lake Geneva, head for **Celebration** (422 Wells St., tel. 414/248–2555).

Tourist Information

Cedarburg Visitor Information Center (City Hall, W63N645 Washington Ave., Cedarburg, WI 53012, tel. 414/377–9620); **Greater Milwaukee Convention & Visitors Bureau** (510 W. Kilbourne Ave., Milwaukee, WI 53203, tel. 800/231–0903, fax 414/273–5596); **Lake Geneva Area Chamber of Commerce** (201 Wrigley Dr., Lake Geneva, WI 53147, tel. 414/248–4416).

Allyn Mansion Inn

When Alexander Allyn built this palatial mansion in 1885 with Milwaukee architect E. Townsend Mix, his motto might well have been "If you've got it, flaunt it—and do it in good taste." Current owners Joe Johnson and Ron Markwell followed that dictum when renovating Allyn's home, which for decades had served as a furniture store and nursing home. The house, listed in the National Register of Historic Places, is considered Wisconsin's best-preserved example of the Queen Anne style.

The duo filled the mansion's 23 rooms with American antiques that, along with six original gasoliers, French walnut woodwork, parquet floors, and 10 Italian marble fireplaces—four topped with grand Eastlake mirrors—create the very picture of late 19th-century elegance. The high, coved ceilings in each of the three parlors have been repainted with floral scrollwork, as in Allyn's day, following the designs that had been discovered in the basement. The front room glitters with gold French wallpaper, and green velvet portières dangle from walnut rings over the doorway. Shutters on the tall windows shield the room's stately grandfather clock, Victorian tufted-silk sofa, and matching chairs from sunlight, and a cribbage board made from a walrus tusk stands ready on the marble coffee table. In another parlor is an 1890 Steinway grand piano discovered in a convent (and now the focus of the inn's musicales). The dining room displays English china from Chicago's 1893 Columbian Exposition. In the library, floor-to-ceiling bookshelves accommodate a collection of books about the Windy City. The bathroom beyond has a galvanized tin tub dating from the 1880s, and the kitchen, anchored by a regal cream enamel stove manufactured in 1920, displays a calendar clock and a complete set of Flow Blue china.

The Empire Room is furnished completely in that period's antiques and dazzles guests with an 1830 canopy bed and the slipper sofa at its foot, a mirror, fireplace clock, game table, curvy settee, and marble-topped table. In the Mary Elizabeth Room guests can relax on the chaise longue before bedding down on the tall half-tester with velvet curtains.

Enormous trees and colorful flower beds surround the house, and the grand porte-cochère, a replica, will have you looking for carriages to drive up and complete the picture.

Address: *511 E. Walworth Ave., Delavan, WI 53115, tel. 414/728–9090.*
Accommodations: *8 double rooms share 7 baths.*
Amenities: *Air-conditioning.*
Rates: *$60 weekdays, $75 weekends; full breakfast. MC, V.*
Restrictions: *No smoking, no pets.*

The Manor House

When auto executive James Wilson became vice president of the Nash Motor Company, he had this grand estate constructed. Now listed in the National Register of Historic Places, Wilson's stately 1924 Georgian residence lives up to its new name. The present owner, Dr. Clifton Peterson, has furnished the house with 18th- and 19th-century American and European antiques, primarily Sheraton and Chippendale, along with furniture and decorative items that once belonged to the Rothschilds and the Shah of Iran. The interior's resemblance to the White House is intentional: The color scheme and key decorative elements are based on its design.

Among the parlor's most exquisite pieces are a pair of peony silk love seats from an Illinois mansion, a painting of Windsor Castle that once hung inside the building it depicts, and a gilt-frame, white silk-upholstered Louis XVI sofa that innkeeper Rikki Thompson encourages guests to sit on. "That's what it's here for," he says. To dispel undue reverence for the surroundings, Thompson plays the library's piano, invites guests to do the same, and provides a steady supply of fresh popcorn.

Breakfast is served in the guest rooms, in the upstairs sitting room, in the garden, or in the dining room at a large, Queen Anne–style table.

Upstairs in the vast, sunny, mauve room known as the Purple Room sit a hand-carved early-19th-century European farmhouse four-poster bed and a tall Eastlake standing mirror. The room has a view of Lake Michigan and two separate dressing rooms, each with countless drawers and compartments. The Rose Room, overlooking the garden, has a 1768 Sheraton canopy bed and Louis XVI side chairs upholstered in a rose motif. The vast dressing room opens onto a spacious rose-tiled bathroom. The large Yellow Room has a lake view, fireplace, and an aura of the 19th century, accented with wind-up Victrola. The smaller Green Room is also decorated in Victorian style, with floral-pattern lace curtains, a spinning wheel, and a rocking chair.

The grounds consist of a wonderful formal English garden, complete with rose beds, some 40 species of exotic trees and hedges, a fountain, gazebo, and even a lily pond.

Address: *6536 Third Ave., Kenosha, WI 53143, tel. 414/658–0014.*
Accommodations: *4 double rooms with baths.*
Amenities: *Air-conditioning, phones, cable TV in rooms, honor bar in library; access to tennis courts, bike trails, fishing wharf.*
Rates: *$100–$140; Continental breakfast. AE, MC, V.*
Restrictions: *No smoking in rooms, no pets.*

The Mansards on-the-Lake

This Second Empire–style house, built in 1867, sports a green mansard roof and neat rows of dormers. The structure has been occupied by a string of fascinating people: Its first owners, an inventor and his wife, a suffragette who worked as an editor, followed by a family of musicians and a circus acrobat whose wife, also a circus performer, did trick horseback riding. Today's owner is a retired teacher of Russian who inherited the house and many of its furnishings from her mother.

The second and third floors are now self-contained suites, each with living room, bedroom, bathroom, and kitchen. The high-ceilinged Polonaise Suite, on the second floor, is decorated with theatrical posters from Eastern Europe that the innkeeper collected during study tours. Its kitchen has a full-size refrigerator, stove, and microwave oven, and is stocked with the makings for breakfast, including cheeses and locally famous pretzel-shaped pastry known as Danish Kringle. The dining area, though small, has a view of Lake Michigan and contains a lively display of Polish circus posters, cut paper, and framed embroidery. Still other theatrical posters, these for European productions of *Romeo and Juliet* and *The Student Prince,* hang in the bedroom. A wicker table and chair sit beside the room's sunny bay windows. The crocheted bedspread was made by the innkeep-

er's mother while sitting in the very same wooden rocker you can relax in today. French doors open to a balcony with a lake view. The bathroom is "bigger than an airplane's," says the host—though not by much; it contains a tub and shower.

The third-floor Garret Suite has a Bohemian artist-in-residence ambience. Low dormer windows punctuate the sloped walls and the living room is full of books and magazines. The white reproduction French provincial–style furnishings do little to enhance the room's charm—the living room's sectional sofa does even less. But a 1950s-style chrome dinette gives the kitchen lots of character, and its terrific view of the lake doesn't hurt, either. Here, too, the refrigerator is stocked with breakfast fixings.

This inn is a good bet for those who are traveling with children or who will be in town for longish stays. The back yard leads straight to Lake Michigan, and Racine's historic district is a stroll away.

Address: *827 Lake Ave., Racine, WI 53403, tel. 414/632–1135.*
Accommodations: *2 suites.*
Amenities: *Air-conditioning on third floor, ceiling fan on second floor.*
Rates: *$55–$65; breakfast fixings stocked in kitchens; MC, V.*
Restrictions: *No smoking, no pets.*

The Ogden House

While shopping around for a house to run as a bed-and-breakfast, John and Mary Jane Moss made a list of names suitable for the gingerbread Victorian that they envisioned. Instead, says the genial couple, when they saw this stately, symmetrical, white-brick Federal-style building, the list was tossed, and the house christened for the original owner.

Carriage maker George Ogden had the house built for his daughter Marion in 1916, and hired the architect who designed Milwaukee's city hall. Listed on the National Register of Historic Places, the house features dual parapets projecting from the roof, and a seven-window facade with a central door and matching bay windows that flank the entrance.

Inside, the living-room walls and coved ceiling are soft green, and the mahogany woodwork a deep olive. The reproduction colonial furnishings enhance the home's genteel graciousness. Across the room is a grand piano, and a glass-topped colonial-style coffee table sits on a pastel Chinese rug. Under the dining room's coffered ceiling and teardrop chandelier, breakfast is served on antique Limoge china and Waterford crystal. Guests are impressd by the old-fashioned butler's pantry just off the kitchen, its cabinets now loaded up with china, and delighted by the call box once used to summon the servants.

Off a landing on the central staircase is a spacious sun room that overlooks the backyard's grape arbor. In the upper hallway stands the Mosses' furniture showpiece: a 100-year-old Welsh dresser, made in the Old Country by Mary Jane's great-grandfather and now filled with antique china. The master bedroom is a bright and spacious chamber with pale floral wallpaper and a butter-yellow trim. The room's canopied pencil-post bed is high enough off the floor to use the step stool to climb into it. The fireplace screen is elaborately hand-carved wood, and detail on the mantel is highlighted in gold leaf. Two easy chairs face the lake and catch the morning sun. The Tower Room overlooks the old stone watch tower, which is lit at night. Inside the cream-colored walls are trimmed in Williamsburg blue, and a queen-size four-poster bed is covered by hand-stitched patchwork quilts made by Mary Jane.

Address: *2237 N. Lake Dr., Milwaukee, WI 53202, tel. 414/272-2740.*
Accommodations: *2 double rooms with baths.*
Amenities: *Air-conditioning, family den with TV and VCR (VCRs available for rooms), copy machine, fax machine; off-street parking.*
Rates: *$75–$85; hearty Continental breakfast. No credit cards.*
Restrictions: *No pets.*

Riley House Bed and Breakfast

Built in 1903 as a wedding present for the future city attorney and his new bride, the Riley House is cute, tidy, and rather unassuming—every inch the embodiment of turn-of-the-century small-town America charm. You may have to remind yourself that this quiet South Milwaukee residential neighborhood, near the shore of Lake Michigan, is only a 15-minute drive from downtown Milwaukee.

Roberta—call her Bert—is the livewire of this innkeeping duo; her husband, Mark, is the resident chef and the hand behind the homemade chocolate truffles in every guest room. The couple uncovered the house's quarter-sawn oak woodwork and embossed wallcoverings. They also restored the double-decker oak mantels over the fireplace in the Gentlemen's Parlor, whose centerpiece is now a leather-upholstered Mission chair. The Greek Revival sofa nearby plays a comfy second. The upright piano in the Ladies' Parlor is the same age as the house—"which is why we *had* to have it." Bert can now look back with relief at the hours she spent stripping it of layer upon layer of blue paint. These days the piano is topped with a fringed shawl.

An antebellum cherry-wood armoire retrieved from Mark's family's attic dominates the Mary Riley Room, and both the white iron daybed and an ornately carved Victorian double bed are covered with floral comforters and heaped with pillows. The largest guest room is papered in a rich paisley print that complements the carved, queen-size cherry-wood bed and Duncan Phyfe drop-leaf table; the bathroom has the inn's only whirlpool tub. In another of the guest rooms is a full-size quarter-canopy bed made of walnut and an Eastlake-style dresser. The smallest room, originally the Riley family's nursery, holds a white iron double bed, a wicker rocking chair and desk, and cheery floral wallpaper.

You can expect a delicious breakfast here: an omelet or quiche, along with muffins and baked goods. Mark will deliver breakfast to your room if you like, or you can eat in the dining room, or on the shaded patio that looks out onto Oak Creek Parkway. Beyond, it extends to woodsy Grant Park and the Lake Michigan shoreline, where it hooks up with a 90-mile bike and hiking trail.

Address: *727 Hawthorne Ave., South Milwaukee, WI 53172, tel. 414/764–3130.*
Accommodations: *1 double room with bath and whirlpool, 3 doubles share 1 bath.*
Amenities: *Ceiling fans, turndown service, TV and VCR in parlor; off-street parking.*
Rates: *$48–$78; full breakfast. AE, MC, V.*
Restrictions: *No smoking, inquire about pets.*

Stagecoach Inn

After careful restoration by historian Brook Brown and his wife, Liz, this compact Greek Revival limestone inn once again welcomes travelers as it did when stagecoaches stopped in Cedarburg on their journey between Milwaukee and Green Bay in 1853, when the house was built. Restoring the corner pub was the Browns' first project. They uncovered the tin ceiling, set up a long, well-used wooden bar where the original had stood, refinished the rough plank floors, brought in some handsome tavern tables, and—in a place of honor behind the bar, next to the vintage silver cash register and grandmother clock—installed the original pub's wooden signpost depicting a fleet of white steeds. This is where the inn's guests gather for breakfast every morning and where, in the evenings, they congregate for draughts of Sprecher, a local root beer, and for cards, games, conversation, or a peek into the scrapbooks Liz kept of the restoration.

A prize wallflower bench from an old-time dance hall sits in the front-hall corridor, at the bottom of the steep, narrow cherry-wood staircase that leads to the guest rooms on the second and third floors. The rooms' sunny nooks and low dormers host a mishmash of rustic furniture, much of it 100-year-old pine purchased by the Browns during their previous careers as antiques dealers. Braided rugs warm the rough pine floors. One room has an exposed limestone wall, twin beds, and an oak dresser. Another, one of three that overlook Cedarburg's beautifully preserved old main street, has a hand-stenciled frieze on the walls and a cherry country Victorian bed, wardrobe, and dresser. The walls of the third-floor rooms are also stenciled, and the furniture is antique pine; one room has a whirlpool bath, another has two sleigh beds and is brightened by a skylight.

The only guest room on the ground floor is a suite. In it are an 1860 four-poster bed, a sturdy immigrant chest that still looks capable of transporting all your worldly possessions, and a well-worn Oriental carpet.

Across the hall from the pub is a branch of the Manitoac-based Beernstsen Candy Store, which sells chocolate candies shaped like computers, fish, and even costumed pigs named Green Bay Porker and Swine Lake.

Address: *W61 N. 520 Washington Ave., Cedarburg, WI 53012, tel. 414/375-0208.*
Accommodations: *13 double rooms with baths.*
Amenities: *Air-conditioning, TV and whirlpool in 5 rooms, pub, gift shop.*
Rates: *$65–$95; Continental breakfast. AE, MC, V.*
Restrictions: *No smoking, no pets.*

Washington House Inn

This cream-colored brick Victorian building, built on Cedarburg's main street in 1886, is actually the second hostelry to stand on this site; the first was established in 1846. Jim Pape, who restored Cedarburg's Stone Hill Winery (and spearheaded the town's historic-preservation movement), took on the task of returning the Washington House to its former glory. This was no small feat: The building had been used as offices and apartments since the 1920s, and the only original element inside that hadn't been modernized or covered up was the lobby's parquet floor. After removing decades' worth of "improvements," Jim and his wife, Sandy, decided to leave many of the building's broad supporting beams and rough limestone walls exposed, and set about filling guest rooms with regional period antiques. Some accommodations are Victorian, others country comfortable.

Guest rooms are named after the pillars of 19th-century Cedarburg society. The Frederich Hilgen Room, dressed in Bradbury & Bradbury wallpaper popular in the late 1800s, has a half-canopy bed draped in burgundy paisley print, a vintage marble-topped walnut table, and two reproduction wing chairs upholstered in burgundy flame stitch flanking the tall, narrow, shuttered windows. The bathroom is done in 1-inch white tile, and contains a marble sink and an antique dresser.

Dr. Friedrich Luening's Room is genteelly rustic with its tall South Carolina pencil-post bed and its plank floor strewn with rag rugs. Patchwork quilts decorate the walls, and a fire engine–red circular iron stairway from the old Pabst Brewery leads to the loft sitting area under the exposed-beam ceiling. Plants adorn the spa-like adjoining room, and there's a modern fireplace and a decidedly 20th-century double whirlpool bath.

Windows in the dining room, on the ground floor, overlook Washington Avenue, the town's main thoroughfare. But even when the comings and goings abate, there's plenty to look at inside, what with the pressed-tin ceiling, the farm tables, and the rustic Victorian chairs. On your way in or out, glance at the original hotel register on display in the spacious lobby.

Address: *W62 N573 Washington Ave., Cedarburg, WI 53012, tel. 414/375–3550 or 800/554–4717.*
Accommodations: *29 double rooms with baths.*
Amenities: *Air-conditioning, phone, cable TV, and HBO in rooms; whirlpool baths in 26 rooms, gas fireplaces in 9 rooms, social hour with local wine and cheese, elevator, sauna; bike and picnic basket rental.*
Rates: *$59–$139; Continental breakfast. AE, D, MC, V.*
Restrictions: *No pets.*

American Country Farm

Hams once hung from the ceiling beams of this snug fieldstone cottage, built in 1844 as a smokehouse for a country estate. Today, guests can toast their feet in front of the building's original broad fireplace. The cottage consists of a single room—with a tiny kitchen and bathroom—and is furnished with Wisconsin country antiques that include salt-glazed crocks set on the two-foot deep windowsill, a plump wing chair, and early 19th-century handwoven, two-tone coverlets. Murky oil paintings of farm scenes adorn the walls, and a large wooden cutout of a duck encircled by a wreath hangs over the fireplace.

Outside the cottage's two Dutch doors is a private patio facing a wooded wildflower preserve. Also on the 2-acre property are a grape arbor, kitchen garden, and the original white stone barn and farmhouse sheltered by tall pines. Every morning innkeeper and antiques dealer Donna Steffen arrives laden with hot baked goods for breakfast.

Address: *12112 N. Wauwatosa Rd., Mequon, WI 53092, tel. 414/242-0194.*
Accommodations: *1 double room with bath.*
Amenities: *Air-conditioning, TV, kitchen; outdoor barbecue grill.*
Rates: *$65 midweek, $85 weekends; Continental breakfast. MC, V.*
Restrictions: *No pets.*

Eleven Gables Inn on the Lake

Until 1965 this sprawling Carpenter's Gothic house and its grounds on Lake Geneva served as a private retreat for the rich and famous. Built in the 1850s, the white clapboard Victorian villa and adjacent coach house are only steps from the lake.

The rooms are individually decorated with a rainbow of fabrics and a mix of contemporary furnishings and antiques, such as the Wicker Suite's fainting couch and the Mildred Fasel Peach Room's 110-year-old brass and iron bedstead. In the Cornelius Vanderbilt, Jr., Room, the pair of barrel-backed velvet wing chairs are said to have been favorites of that frequent guest. Most of the rooms have a private balcony, veranda, or enclosed courtyard. There is a shortage of TLC here, however, especially in the breakfast room, which looks like a neglected coffee shop.

Address: *493 Wrigley Dr., Lake Geneva, WI 53147, tel. 414/248-8393.*
Accommodations: *6 double rooms with baths, coach house can be 2 or 3 rooms.*
Amenities: *Cable TV, fireplaces, kitchenettes in 3 rooms; private pier, bike and watercraft rentals.*
Rates: *$89-$119 midweek, $115-$140 weekends and holidays, packages available for cottage; full breakfast. AE, MC, V.*
Restrictions: *Inquire about pets; 2-night minimum weekends.*

Elizabethian Inn

As they say in real estate: location, location, location. Set on a long shady lot on the shore of Lake Geneva, two blocks from downtown, an hour's drive from Chicago, and 45 minutes from Milwaukee, this inn has it in spades. A gabled, 1903 Queen Anne clapboard with a square turret, a sun porch, and a deck, the inn looks—inside and out—like an archetypal "Grandma's house." The ivory-toned living room holds just a few of the inn's collection of English antiques and reproductions.

The largest of the guest rooms in the main house faces the lake and takes up the entire front upstairs. It's popular because of its spaciousness and lake view, its four-poster bed, and its tufted floral settee. Half of the inn's rooms are in the Kimberly House—originally a barn and converted to a residence at the turn of the century. The decor here is Laura Ashley/country style. A breakfast of omelets, quiche, corned beef hash, or waffles is served at a long trestle table in front of a fireplace.

Address: *463 Wrigley Dr., Lake Geneva, WI 53147, tel. 414/248-9131.*
Accommodations: *10 double rooms with baths.*
Amenities: *Air-conditioning, turndown service, TV in living room; private pier.*
Rates: *$95 weekdays, $115 weekends and holidays; full breakfast. MC, V.*
Restrictions: *No smoking, no pets, 2-night minimum weekends.*

Jeremiah Mabie House

Jeremiah Mabie made a fortune running Wisconsin's largest circus, but when it came to building a house, he didn't clown around. He plunked this aristocratic Italianate, Renaissance Revival mansion onto what was, in 1865, the city's most exclusive street, and today is near the historic district.

The building's large, wraparound front porch is still the place to see and be seen. The fireplace in the living room retains its original heavy, walnut mantel, and some of the room's windows feature beveled glass. Pocket doors lead to the first-floor guest room—a suite consisting of a living room, a bedroom, and a bath with a whirlpool, and a small refrigerator—which, when unoccupied, is made available to all guests.

A circular stairway leads upstairs. In one room are twin and double beds and an old-fashioned bathtub draped with a lace canopy. A massive Eastlake bed dominates another room.

Address: *711 Walworth Ave., Delavan, WI 53115, tel. 414/728-1876.*
Accommodations: *3 double rooms with baths, 1 suite.*
Amenities: *Air-conditioning, bedtime chocolates, TV in 2 rooms and in common room, whirlpool bath in suite.*
Rates: *$55 weekdays, $65 weekends, suite $95; full breakfast. MC, V.*
Restrictions: *No smoking, no pets.*

Lakeside Manor

From the living room's windows in this rambling, clapboard house, you can see the sandy beach of Delavan Lake. That is, if you can turn your gaze from the room's fireplace made of boulders and framed by an Eastlake mantel. This inn has the comfortable feel of a family weekend home, thanks, in part, to innkeepers Judy and Wayne Rolf's family heirlooms and the pieces that came with this turn-of-the-century house.

Guest rooms are decorated in a country Victorian style, and most have lake views. The octagonal, 700-square-foot Bridal Suite has lake views on three sides. Once the ballroom, it is now a roomy bedroom with a cherry-wood four-poster bed, a kitchenette, and a living room where a fold-out sofa allows for sleeping by the fireplace. A separate two-bedroom cottage sits at the water's edge. Its tongue-and-groove walls and wide, enclosed sleeping porch give it a cabinlike ambience.

Address: *1809 S. Shore Dr., Delavan, WI 53115, tel. 414/728-2043.*
Accommodations: *2 double rooms with baths, 3 doubles share 2 baths, 1 suite, and 1 cottage with bath.*
Amenities: *Air-conditioning, cable TV in suite and in living room, kitchenette in suite, full kitchen in cottage; dock, beach towels, canoe and bike rental.*
Rates: *$65–$85, suite $135, cottage $149; Continental breakfast weekdays, full breakfast weekends. MC, V.*
Restrictions: *No smoking, no pets.*

Lawrence House

Although this house, built in 1885, is one of the oldest in town, its owner and innkeeper, Larry Joseph, has opted for creature comforts over strict historical re-creation. Enjoy the luxurious double whirlpool baths in each room's sun-filled, oversize bathroom, loaded with towels and toiletries. Reached through French doors, these are a bit of heaven for those who love to soak and dawdle in the tub. Room decor ranges from the deep hunter green and burgundy tones of the walls, fabrics, and canopy bed of one first-floor room, to the softer peach and blue scheme and floral print wallpaper and fabrics in another. All the rooms have wide-screen TVs and VCRs concealed in reproduction Victorian armoires.

Guests can gather in the upstairs sitting room or around the living room's fireplace. Joseph's seven-course breakfast often features such dishes as eggs Benedict, soufflés, or waffles, and is served in the dining room, the enclosed wraparound sun porch overlooking the lake, or the screened-in porch.

Address: *403 S. Lake Shore Dr., Lake Geneva, WI 53147, tel. 414/248-4684.*
Accommodations: *5 double rooms with baths.*
Amenities: *Air-conditioning, whirlpool baths, TV, VCR video library.*
Rates: *$110–$140; full breakfast, afternoon refreshments. AE, MC, V.*
Restrictions: *No pets; 2-night minimum weekends in summer.*

William's

Filling most of its corner lot in a quiet residential neighborhood and a mere 10-minute walk from the lake and downtown is this small, 85-year-old, two-toned blue cottage. The smallish yard is big enough for two well-tended rock gardens, with benches for contemplation.

Inside, the furnishings are unassuming, with a few standout family antiques, such as the treadle sewing machine, and wedding china on display in the dainty dining room. The Victorian-style guest rooms have floral prints and light colors. One room has a curvaceous walnut bed, another a brass bed. The sunny octagonal room in the corner turret, with its low post bed and refinished hardwood floors, suggests an attic hideaway.

The innkeeper is a former chef, and his made-from-scratch gourmet breakfasts might include strawberry crepes or quiches, along with raisin bran muffins and cinnamon bananas.

Address: *830 Williams St., Lake Geneva, WI 53147, tel. 414/248–1169.*
Accommodations: *4 double rooms share 1 bath.*
Amenities: *Air-conditioning, TV and VCR in living room.*
Rates: *$60 weekdays, $80 weekends; full breakfast. MC, V.*
Restrictions: *No smoking, no pets.*

Hiawatha Valley

Wisconsinites owe their outdoorsy image to the year-round opportunities nature provides them. But you don't have to strap on snowshoes or float a kayak to appreciate what the residents of the rugged wedge of water, prairie, forest, and farmland take for granted. Instead, spend a couple of hours on the Great River Road (Route 35), which snakes along the east bank of the everwidening Mississippi River.

Navigating the rising and falling terrain is like riding the chest of a gently snoring giant, but the eye-popping scenery guarantees that you won't fall asleep at the wheel. This primeval nature show hasn't changed since the days of Cheif Red Wing and Princess Winona. Limestone bluffs fringed with fir trees rise dramatically around you, while hawks and eagles dip in and out of shadows. All along the way, old river towns such as Hudson, Prescott, Alma, Buena Vista Park, and Stockholm cling to coves and bluffs, each imparting its own unique personality.

Many things in this area look as it they've just jumped off hand-tinted postcards: vintage bandstands centered in shady parks, elegant mansions recalling the glory days of the lumber barons, red-and-white farmsteads sprinkled on the surrounding hills. Given this heady dose of Americana, it should come as no surprise that the village of Pepin was inspiration for Laura Ingalls Wilder's first book, Little House in the Big Woods.

The fur trade and logging industry shaped Eau Claire, which, at 50,000 people, is the largest town in the valley. Set at the confluence of the Eau Claire and Chippewa rivers, this former boomtown still has a young, visorous feeling about it, thanks to the branch of the University of Wisconsin located here. Many students consider Eau Claire the gateway to the state's rugged northern third, with hiking, biking, and cross-county paths radiating like so many spokes from it.

The calender is filled with antiques shows, arts and crafts fairs, and farmers' markets on warm-weather weekends, but autumn is the finest time of year in Hiawatha Valley. Be prepared. The trees start turning in early September, causing the valley's biggest tourist logjam and making film and accommodations premium items.

Places to Go, Sights to See

Hoffman Hills State Recreation Area (9 mi northeast of Menominee, north of U.S. 29/12 and west of U.S. 40, tel. 715/673–4725). If you're entranced by western Wisconsin's theater of ecology, here's a chance to see it all. Marshes, ponds, streams, prairies, meadowlands, and hardwood forests mingle on the 655 acres, which incorporate 8½ miles of trails. A 2-mile loop to the observation tower includes a nature trail.

Nelson Cheese Factory (U.S. 35, Nelson, tel. 715/637–4725). The fifth-generation family-owned shop produces 50 varieties of what the state's cows are best at.

Mabel Tainter Memorial Auditorium (205 Main St., Menominee, tel. 715/235–9726). This tribute to a lumber baron's daughter was built in 1980—an imposing Romanesque-style fortress harboring a jewel box of a theater done in Victorian Moorish style. Frequent performances range from jazz concerts to children's theater. Tours are also offered.

Red Cedar Trail (from Menominee at U.S. 29 south to Dunnville on Cty. Y). This limestone trail follows an abandoned railway right-of-way along the wooded banks of the Red Cedar River to its junction with the Chippewa River 15 miles south. Owls, eagles, deer, otter, and beaver share their habitat with hikers, bikers, and cross-country skiers.

Stockholm. This tiny hamlet shows many signs of its Swedish heritage, from the names in its romantic graveyard to the stores offering food and antiques, artwork from the old country in galleries, shops of Amish wares, and a charming old-time museum in the former post office.

Restaurants

The valley's specialty is its Friday fish fry, found in nearly every small town's bar and grill. **The Harbor View** (First and Main Sts., tel. 715/442–3893) in Pepin is one of those corner cafés, but with a twist. While it retains its "just folks" atmosphere, the place has become a destination for Twin

Citians, undaunted by a 90-mile drive and no-reservations policy when they're hungry for Swedish dumplings, coq au vin, or salmon with shiitake mushrooms. **The Creamery** (1 Creamery Rd., tel. 715/664–8354) in Downsville comes up with equally imaginative food, from lamb curry to fettuccine with morels, in a contemporary setting with a river valley view. Durand's **Cafe Mozart** (311 W. Main St., tel. 715/672–4103) ladles out *Gemutlichkeit* along with its Wiener schnitzel, while Prescott's **Steamboat Inn** (307 Lake St. N, tel. 800/262–8232) is a classic '50s supper club with the bonus of a riverside deck. **Corby's** (417 2nd St., tel. 715/386–1610) young British chef brings haute cuisine to Hudson with specialties like chicken Wellington, peppered walleye, and rack of lamb.

Tourist Information

Prescott Chamber of Commerce (Box 244, Prescott, WI 54021, tel. 715/262–3284); **Menominee Chamber of Commerce** (331 E. Main St., Menominee, WI 54751, tel. 715/235–9087); **River Falls Chamber of Commerce** (115 E. Elm St., River Falls, WI 54022, tel. 715/425–2533).

The Boyden House

P. Q. Boyden, mayor of Hudson, built this grand Victorian Gothic mansion in 1879 for $10,000, paid in cash. Nine owners later, Minnesota Orchestra violinists and innkeepers Julie Ayer and Carl Nashan treat guests to the kind of Sunday musical soirees in the music room that hearken back to the long-gone days of quieter pleasures. In one of the two adjoining parlors, separated by walnut-stained pine pocket doors, the innkeepers have awarded a place of honor to a 1926 Steinway Grand piano. An antique pump organ, Edison cylinder phonograph, and an old Victrola ensconced beside an ornately carved white marble fireplace are proudly displayed in the other. Performances are followed by sherry and pastries in the dining room, which guests share with a vintage Ayers teddy bear in a cane-seated high chair on wheels. All the rooms still have the woodwork, oak floors inlaid with walnut, and brass fittings that were picked out by Mayor Boyden.

Lace curtains filter sunlight onto the built-in butler's pantry resplendent with brass hardware. Carl's hobby, making Tiffany-style stained-glass lamps, is in evidence throughout the house. A particularly fine example of his work is the dragonfly-motif lampshade in the back parlor beside the antique backgammon table that awaits competitive guests. The dramatic black walnut staircase leads to the Buena Vista Room, furnished with a walnut dresser and white iron and brass bed, with a bay window that houses an antique wicker settee, rocker, and table. The Willow Room has two family-heirloom walnut beds, a vintage marble-top dresser, a nursing rocker, and a child's old sled piled high with well-loved dolls and stuffed animals from Julie's past. The rooms share a vast, sunny bathroom, whose centerpiece is—literally—an elegant claw-foot tub on a floral carpet. Guests in the Boyden Suite can sleep on a carved walnut bed and use a dresser that have been in the house from its beginning.

On some weekends, area innkeepers get together dressed in Victorian garb for a game of croquet on the double lawn that is still bound by an iron fence: Guests in modern attire are invited to join. The inn, amid the opulent residences of Hudson's former magnates, overlooks the St. Croix River just a short jaunt down the hill.

Address: *727 Third St., Hudson, WI 54016, tel. 715/386-7435.*
Accommodations: *2 double rooms share 1 bath, 1 suite.*
Amenities: *Air-conditioning, ceiling fans, silk robes, fireplace in parlor.*
Rates: *$75–$100; full breakfast, early morning juice and coffee. MC, V.*
Restrictions: *No smoking, no pets.*

The Franklin Victorian

W. G. Williamson, a prominent Sparta banker, personally inspected every piece of wood that went into the interior of this raspberry-red clapboard Victorian. His high standards are evident the minute you cross the white columned front porch. The floors are of glowing maple complemented by black ash and quarter-cut oak. Pocket doors of curly birch lead to a parlor where the mirror, russet ceramic tiles, beveled-glass window, and double-manteled fireplace with fluted Corinthian columns remind us of the late 1800s when Sparta, with its spas and mineral waters, was the hub of social life.

Cordial innkeeper Jane Larson has integrated her family heirlooms into the house. Set in the dining room's elaborate parquet floor with "braided" border is a buffet with floor-to-ceiling glass doors, showcasing china that's been in her family for three generations. In the parlor, her grandfather's Civil War–era miniature pump organ, an instrument he played at funerals, keeps company with a boxy Victorian velvet sofa trimmed in mahogany and its honor guard of stuffed velvet chairs that belonged to Jane's great-grandparents. The "sunset" stained-glass window gives a vivid late-afternoon glow to the stairway landing.

Forgo the somewhat out of place Plaid Room, with its Royal Stuart tartan wallpaper and green carpet, in favor of the master bedroom with another grand tiled and columned fireplace; an immense oak headboard Lloyd Larson, Jane's husband, crafted with wood from the wall of a judge's chamber; and a tall highboy of bird's-eye maple that belonged to Jane's parents. Its bathroom, with tongue-and-groove wainscoting, still boasts its marble-topped sink.

Guests can sit in rocking chairs and sip lemonade on the side and front porches while enjoying the corner lot of a quiet residential neighborhood, where trees loom taller than dormers and turetts.

Address: *220 E. Franklin Pl., Sparta, WI 54656, tel. 608/269-3894.*
Accommodations: *2 double rooms with baths, 2 double rooms share 1 bath.*
Amenities: *Air-conditioning, fireplace in 1 room and common room.*
Rates: *$60–$80; full breakfast, early morning coffee. MC, V.*
Restrictions: *No pets, no smoking.*

The Knollwood House

The comfortable atmosphere of the two-story Knollwood House and the warm hospitality of owners Jim and Judy Tostrud quickly transform guests into friends. Built in 1886 with red bricks from a local factory, the house, set on 85 acres in the rolling Kinnickinnic River Valley, draws people into its rich history. Jim farms the land, as his father did before him, and Judy, a horticulturalist, fills the landscape with perennials and hydroponic plants. Inside, you'll appreciate the Tostruds' personal touches, displayed in the plants that grace the window sills and the family heirlooms that furnish the rooms.

The Master Suite is filled with Tostrud family memorabilia. The queen-size bed with carved head- and footboards and matching dresser and armoire belonged to Jim's parents; the spinning wheel was his grandmother's. The suite includes an unusually spacious bathroom with tub and shower.

The Den, a smaller room with wainscoting and an antique brass bed, overlooks a miniature waterfall in the pond below the window. The aptly named Solarium Room on the first floor allows guests access to the plant-filled solarium, which has a hot tub, and to the Day Room, which features a piano kept in tune for visiting musicians.

The kitchen contains a double desk from the one-room school where Jim's mother taught, a glazed pottery water cooler, and a farmhouse pie cabinet with glass doors to tempt the hungry. Judy prepares a down-home breakfast featuring muffins made with the strawberries and raspberries she grows herself. The meal is served in the dining room, in the solarium, or in the flower garden beside the swimming pool.

There is no lack of activities at Knollwood: Just about everything is found right outside the door. Badminton, croquet, basketball, softball, shuffleboard, boccie, a swimming pool, an in-ground trampoline, and a 180-yard par-three golf hole are found within the 3½-acre yard. The more ambitious athlete can try the 2 miles of well-maintained hiking and cross-country ski trails nearby.

Address: *N. 8257 950th St., Knollwood Dr., River Falls, WI 54022, tel. 715/425–1040 or 800/435–0628.*
Accommodations: *2 double rooms share 1 bath, 1 suite.*
Amenities: *Air-conditioning, robes, fireplace in common room; hot tub, pool.*
Rates: *$55–$75; full breakfast. No credit cards*
Restrictions: *No smoking, no pets.*

The Oak Street Inn

Prescott's city founders, William Copp and Orrin Maxson, built this graceful Italianate clapboard mansion back in 1854 to demonstrate how civilized the river settlement, where the St. Croix joins the Mississippi, had become. The house's many metamorphoses include service as a church and parsonage, a hospital annex, and a piano-melodeon factory before the Johnsons undertook its renovation as, they now recall with amusement, "a lark."

The small parlor, dressed in warm tones of yellow and green, with small-paned windows, gleaming hardwood floors, and framed by severe Italianate arches, is home to a plush Italianate settee, a pendulum clock that ticks stridently, and a low, marble-top table that's been in young innkeeper Ann-Marie Johnson's family "forever." But the showpiece is a working old melodeon that she ably demonstrates for willing listeners. Corinthian pillars define the adjoining dining area, whose buffet is filled with her grandmother's china.

The feminine Elizabeth Room, done in cream, pink, and blue, has a four-poster bed, Breuer-style rocker, a dressing room, and a bathroom equipped with what Ann-Marie deems essential: a great reading light thoughtfully positioned over the claw-foot tub. A small library where early morning coffee and Continental breakfast are served unites the Elizabeth Room with the Avery Room, a vast, blue and rose "special occasion" chamber with queen-size, trundle, and alcove beds; private bath; and dining area lit by large windows.

Guests also may relish the Scandinavian breakfasts on the front porch, which is furnished with wicker furniture, or on the sprawling, shady lawn.

On a quiet street that's a bit of a hike from Prescott's historic main street, the Oak Street Inn overlooks the river bluff a few blocks away. Ann-Marie supplies directions to nearby Carpenter Nature Center and Kinnickinnic State Park and, as president of the city's Chamber of Commerce, stories of early Prescott as well.

Address: *506 Oak St., Prescott, WI 54021, tel. 715/262-4110.*
Accommodations: *2 double rooms with baths, 1 suite.*
Amenities: *Air-conditioning, turndown service.*
Rates: *$65–$85; full breakfast, refreshments on arrival. MC, V.*
Restrictions: *No smoking, no pets.*

The Phipps Inn

This Queen Anne house has remained virtually untouched since its debut in 1884. From the octagonal tower under the witch's-cap roof to the wraparound veranda with scrolled friezes and pedimented gables, the house is the showplace of the river town.

William Phipps, a prominent Hudson banker, politician, and philanthropist, moved to town to serve as land commissioner for the railroad, and certainly wasn't averse to living well. The interior of his former house is equipped with six fireplaces flamboyantly carved, guarded by Ionic columns, and set with Italian tiles. Ornate brass hardware, stained-glass windows, and parquet flooring in intricate geometric designs add to the "got it, flaunt it" look.

Innkeepers John and Cyndi Berglund bought the mansion intact but empty. This gave them the mandate of filling it with antiques from the St. Croix River Valley, including an 1890s pump organ and tufted Victorian sofas and chairs in the two parlors. In the music room, they've installed a snazzy 1920 baby grand piano that's set these days with afternoon snacks.

Guests linger over breakfast in the dining room, warmed by sun streaming through the stained-glass windows and by one of the fireplaces.

The Bridal Suite boasts an 1880 walnut half-canopy bed, a fireplace with Italian ceramic tile, and a wicker table. The Master Suite has a canopied pine four-poster bed, another fireplace, and a large, climb-through window that leads to a private balcony. Victoria's Room, a more intimate hideaway done in a black-and-gold Victorian floral motif, highlights a brass bed and antique armoire; the Garden Suite features hand-stenciled walls, a wicker four-poster canopy bed, and windows that capture the afternoon sun.

Above all looms the third floor's grand ballroom. Once the sight of the Phipps's elegant gatherings, it has been converted into the Willow Chamber, and the Peacock Chamber. Guests will find Jacuzzis in all the bathrooms, except that of the Garden Suite, which still has an original claw-foot tub.

Address: *1005 Third St., Hudson, WI 54016, tel. 715/386–0800.*
Accommodations: *6 double rooms with baths.*
Amenities: *Air-conditioning, fireplaces in 3 rooms and in common rooms, whirlpool tubs in 5 rooms; bikes, dinners and picnics available with advance notice and extra charge.*
Rates: *$95–$159; full breakfast, champagne and cookies on arrival. MC, V.*
Restrictions: *No smoking, no pets.*

The Arbor Room

For those seeking the ultimate in romantic, the Arbor Room is the answer. On a hill above the St. Croix River, it adjoins a turn-of-the-century house that is reminiscent of an English country cottage. Owned by landscape architect Steve Schmitz, who practices his talents on the spacious yard, the guest room, with its own private entrance, is approached through a rose arbor. The landscape is an arrangement of stately trees, flowering shrubs, and perennials—some more than 75 years old. Inside, pastels, plush carpeting, a maple Victorian-style bed with down comforter and intricately stitched patchwork quilt all spell relaxation (if not antiquity). The ultimate luxury, breakfast in bed, is served on his grandmother's china. If anything can lure guests from such comfort, it's the wide array of activities available in the area. The Arbor Room is within walking distance of the St. Croix and Mississippi rivers and is 30 minutes from the Twin Cities. Local diversions include boating, golfing, biking, skiing, and antiques-hunting.

Address: *434 Court St. N, Prescott, WI 54021, tel. 715/262–4166.*
Accommodations: *1 double room with bath.*
Amenities: *Air-conditioning, flowers and chocolates, robes; bikes, shuttle service from marinas.*
Rates: *$75; full breakfast. No credit cards.*
Restrictions: *No smoking, no pets.*

Cedar Trails Guesthouse

This was a working farm until 1984. These days, there's a new deck—big enough to hold a hoedown—surrounding the comfy, 80-year-old farmhouse, where city folk can watch cattle marching to the barn and horses entering the paddock. Proprietor Barb Anderson also invites guests to mosey over to her second farm nearby, "where she raises sweaters." Her sheep provide wool for the handmade comforters and mattress pads that warm the guest beds in the six-level house.

The furnishings are an eclectic mix ranging from art-deco squatting peacock chairs to framed needlework pillow shams. One guest room features an antique rooming-house washstand with drawers, while another has a modern sleeping loft complete with a futon set by a window. The overall effect is informal. "It's like visiting relatives, without the relatives," Barb claims, inviting guests to raid the cookie jar. The living room has a welcoming overstuffed couch and chair and turn-of-the-century rocker, and the picture window in the parlor offers lovely views of the pines beyond the long driveway.

Address: *Cty. U.S. C, Downsville, Rte. 4 (Box 175), Menominee, WI 54751, tel. 715/664–8828.*
Accommodations: *2 double rooms with baths, 2 doubles share 1 bath.*
Amenities: *Air-conditioning.*
Rates: *$45–$65; full breakfast. MC, V.*
Restrictions: *No smoking, pets allowed outside only.*

The Creamery

Although the redbrick building began life in 1904 as a co-op creamery turning local cream into butter, today, thanks to a tasteful renovation by a family of hands-on proprietors, the building has a clean, contemporary look. The windows of its bright, white dining room frame a garden terrace sloping to a wooded lake. The Creamery is known for imaginative American cuisine, and the wine list is excellent. From the lounge, which is lined with old milk bottles, wildlife can frequently be spotted beyond the adjoining open deck.

Upstairs, guest rooms with the same bucolic view are done in cherry woodwork and modern walnut furnishings. Handmade pottery lamps and bathroom tiles—including a mosaic mural in the suite's bathroom—originated in the resident pottery shop. The tiny town of Downsville is a quarter-mile down the road, where the 14-mile Red Cedar Bike Trail sails by. A friendly crew of college kids augments the family staff.

Address: *Cty. C, Box 22, Downsville, WI 54735, tel. 715/664–8354.*
Accommodations: *3 double rooms with baths, 1 suite.*
Amenities: *Air-conditioning, phone, TV, and whirlpool tub in rooms, fireplaces in common rooms, bar, lounge, restaurant.*
Rates: *$70–$105; Continental breakfast. No credit cards.*
Restrictions: *Closed 2 wks in Mar. and some holidays, restaurant closed Mon.*

The Gallery House

This neat 1861 mercantile brick building has served as a store with a family residence above it ever since its Civil War–era beginnings. The general merchandise and post office trappings have been replaced by innkeeper and watercolor artist John Runions's gallery of his local scenes and wildlife. His wife, Joan, sells spices, teas, and gifts in the shop. Guests share their home above, where bedrooms open off a wide, hotel-like hall that's also lined with the artist's work. The inn features standard reproduction furnishings, but the rooms overlook a broad, white-spindled veranda, ideal for viewing barges chugging toward the nearby Mississippi River locks.

John serves his touted eggs Benedict in the Early American–style family room, which is crammed with bookcases and lots of games. It's a lot like visiting Grandma's—old-shoe comfort with few frills.

Address: *215 N. Main St., Alma, WI 54610, tel. 608/685–4975.*
Accommodations: *1 double room with bath, 2 doubles share 1 bath.*
Amenities: *Air-conditioning, ceiling fans.*
Rates: *$40; full breakfast. No credit cards.*
Restrictions: *No smoking, no pets.*

The Harrisburg Inn

Grandmotherly Carol Crisp calls her place "a view with a room"—not an understatement when used to refer to this century-old, small-town house perched high on a bluff above Lake Pepin in the Mississippi River Valley. Actually, there are four rooms lining the upper hallway, all with valley views and homey, turn-of-the-century rustic furniture, and a country look accented by colorful quilts. The two end rooms, each with old-fashioned clawfoot tubs, are the most coveted because they sport roomy balconies good for watching towboats and soaring eagles on the river and listening for the whistle of passing trains—or even for enjoying a sunrise breakfast. Just beyond the common rooms, the front porch, with its cache of rockers, catches the last of the evening sun. Guests can also enjoy the view from the large windows of the living room while listening to the tapes from Carol's classical and jazz library.

Address: *W3334 U.S. 35, Maiden Rock, WI 54750, tel. 715/448–4500.*
Accommodations: *4 double rooms with baths.*
Amenities: *Air-conditioning.*
Rates: *$48–$88; full breakfast, refreshments on arrival. D, MC, V.*
Restrictions: *Smoking on porches only, no pets.*

The Jefferson-Day House

The Miller family's pre–Civil War Italianate house is full of details that give it a gracious air. The inn's bedrooms combine historic flavor with modern luxury. The Captain's Room contains a brass bed and lace curtains; the Harbor Room sports stenciled walls and matching quilt; and the Hudson Suite holds a display of antique dolls. Guests will also find the decidedly modern addition of whirlpool baths for two. The more luxurious three-room St. Croix Suite has soft rose-and-blue accents on ivory walls and a sitting room; the bedroom features a queen-size bed and double Jacuzzi. The suite also includes a full private bath and a sun porch on which guests can enjoy a specially delivered four-course breakfast.

The inn is within walking distance of downtown Hudson and the St. Croix River. Favorite recreations include river cruises, visits to local museums, and taking in concerts and plays at the Phipps Center for the Arts.

Address: *1109 Third St., Hudson, WI 54016, tel. 715/386–7111.*
Accommodations: *2 double rooms with baths, 2 suites.*
Amenities: *Air-conditioning, champagne, double whirlpool baths, fireplaces in 3 rooms.*
Rates: *$89–$149; Continental breakfast weekdays, full breakfast weekends, afternoon refreshments. No credit cards.*
Restrictions: *No smoking, no pets.*

The Kaleidoscope Inn

Guests neglect to ask which sights to see in the little Dutch village of Baldwin because they're glued to innkeeper Chris Jacobson's kaleidoscope collection—70 and growing—supplemented by curio cabinets crammed with antique tin wind-up toys. Guests also won't be swayed from the foyer's nickelodeon (which feeds on quarters these days) with its unique stained-glass panels.

Any excess seems right at home in this turn-of-the-century house, guarded by concrete lions at the entrance. Here Victoriana runs rampant, from carved sofas curvaceous as a Gibson Girl to the dolphin base of the ornately carved dining room table. Guests are summoned to breakfast by the antique chimes on the wall. More carved vines and love-birds twine on the oak bedroom set in the Rose Room, while the Blue Room's bed boasts oak columns and carved capitals. Aside from fruit carvings on the grandiose bedroom set of the Gold Room, there's a melodeon for anyone inclined to play.

Address: *800 11th Ave. (Box 648), Baldwin, WI 54002, tel. 715/684–4575.*
Accommodations: *1 double room with bath, 3 double rooms share 1 bath.*
Amenities: *Air-conditioning, TV in rooms.*
Rates: *$55–$65; Continental breakfast. MC, V.*
Restrictions: *No smoking, no pets; closed weekdays Oct.–Apr.*

The Katy May House

College sweethearts Kari and John Dahl started collecting antique treasures for their dream house even before they got married, and their finds fit in beautifully after the renovation of this early 1900 brick farmhouse. The guest rooms are a perfect combination of period pieces and tasteful decor. One room, colored an airy light blue and white, features a high queen-size bed with a mosquito-netting canopy and a sitting area with an inviting stuffed chair and rocker. Another room, done in rust and navy, has an adjoining sun-filled reading room with a bound collection of *National Geographics* from 1915 to 1922. All the guest rooms include small tables and chairs for those who wish to enjoy a private breakfast.

Guests congregate in the living room, whose furnishings include a Mission-style couch, chair, and cabinet, or on the white wicker-filled wraparound veranda, where breakfast is served when weather permits. Many guests come to try out the Red Cedar State Bike Trail, play golf, or visit the nearby museums, cheese factories, and antiques shops.

Address: *2013 Wilson St., Menominee, WI 54751, tel. 715/235–1792.*
Accommodations: *2 double rooms with baths, 2 doubles share 1 bath.*
Amenities: *Air-conditioning, turn-down service.*
Rates: *$49–$69; full breakfast, afternoon refreshments. AE.*
Restrictions: *No pets.*

The Ryan House

In 1870, Patrick Ryan, an accomplished carpenter, built this stately home—a farmhouse like no other for miles around—for his bride, Emma, on 12 acres of Bear Creek Valley farmland miles from town. The yellow house with green shutters, capped by an elegant mansard roof, became the talk of the county.

Inside, the indistinct living room's strong suit is its original oak woodwork, pocket doors, and stained-glass windows. The dining room boasts an elegantly carved fireplace that was found in the attic: It has been restored to its rightful place of honor, warming guests breakfasting on the homemade cinnamon rolls.

Upstairs is the Hat Room where the Ryans traditionally boarded teachers. In fact, innkeeper Lorena Weiss can recall visiting her teacher here as a little girl. The Garden Room holds Lorena's old dressing table and the four-poster bed her husband built. There's a nice view out the window of the flower garden below.

Address: *U.S. 10 and Cty. V (Rte. 2, Box 28), Durand, WI 54737, tel. 715/672-8563.*
Accommodations: *1 double room with bath, 2 doubles share 1 bath.*
Amenities: *Fireplace in common room.*
Rates: *$35–$40; full breakfast, afternoon refreshments. MC, V.*
Restrictions: *No smoking, no pets; closed Jan.–Mar.*

Hidden Valleys
*Including La Crosse
and Prairie du Chien*

*The rumpled rural terrain known as Hidden Valleys hugs
the eastern edge of the Mississippi River as it flows
southward from La Crosse to the Iowa border, rolling
inland in some spots for 40 or so picturesque miles. As
viewed from the window of a plane, the land is a pincushion of church steeples and grain silos, towers of
strength that neatly summarize what this somnolent slice
of small-town America is all about.*

*Faith first arrived in these parts in the person of Jesuit
priest Jacques Marquette, who busily converted Native
Americans even as he and explorer Louis Jolliet searched
for the Mississippi in the 17th century. Agriculture
appeared not to long afterward, as successive waves of
immigrants from several European nations literally set
down roots in the rich topsoil.*

*Many of these communities proudly maintain their Old
World character, a task made easier by their relative
isolation. The region has the Midwest's largest concen-
tration of hardwood forests and is unblemished by an
interstate, allowing the Norwegian heritage to survive in
Westby and helping Hillsboro to keep its distinctive Czech
culture. In New Glarus, founded in 1845 by immigrants
from Glarus, Switzerland, many of the residents are still
bilingual—a pleasant discovery for visitors to such annual
events as the Heidi Festival in June, the Volksfest in
August, and the Wilhelm Tell Festival on Labor Day
weekend. Like the other festivals in the area, these are
genuine ethnic celebrations that have so far resisted being
cloying.*

*Another ethnic enclave is Mineral Point, just south of
Dodgeville along U.S. 151. Here Cornish miners in the*

*1830s sat out winters in underground dwellings called
badger holes. The lead and zinc mines contributed to
Wisconsin's admittance to the Union in 1848, and the
prospectors' dugouts accounted for its nickname as the
Badger State. Mineral Point today is a growing artists'
colony featuring a wide variety of influences, but its
English history is still very much in evidence, from the old
stone houses to the formidable meat pies called pasties.
A rewarding side trip is the historical village of Pendarvis,
with its collection of restored limestone and log Cornish
cottages from the 1840s.*

*The two largest towns in the region, La Crosse and Prairie
du Chien, were both settled by French traders looking to
exploit their locations on the Mississippi River. The
distance between these ports can be leisurely traversed via
steamers or Route 35. The latter, part of the Great River
Road, is a 55-mile drive that offers a succession of scenic
vistas; it's particularly spectacular in October, when the
statewide "Colorama" autumn festival is in full swing.*

Places to Go, Sights to See

Cassville. Visit *Stonefield Village* (north on Cty. VV, tel. 608/725–5210),
home to the State Agricultural Museum and a replica of an 1890s village,
complete with costumed guides. Across the road, *Nelson Dewey State Park*
(tel. 608/725–5374) is a perfect place to catch the drama of river-bluff vistas.

Elroy-Sparta Bike Trail (tel. 602/463–7109). The first abandoned railroad
grade to be converted to a recreation trail winds through 32 miles of wooded
valleys, small towns, and railroad tunnels, with interpretive stops, parking,
and picnic facilities. The valley's six biking trails include the *Great River
State Park Trail* (tel. 608/534–6409), 22½ miles along the Mississippi Valley,
and the 23-mile *Sugar River State Park Trail* (tel. 608/527–2334).

La Crosse. The *Convention and Visitors Bureau* in Riverside Park (tel.
608/782–2366) is also the home of *Riverside USA*, an animated exhibit
describing life on the Mississippi. The bureau also provides maps for a *Heritage Tour*, which details 42 historic buildings throughout the town, beginning
at the *Hixon House* (429 N. 7th St.), now the County Historical Museum, and
including the G. Heileman Brewery and Christina Winery. Nearby, *La Crosse
Queen* (tel. 608/784–2893 or 608/784–8523) and *Island Girl* (tel. 608/784–
0556) offer paddleboat river excursions. *Granddad's Bluff* towers 530 feet

above the city; the summit offers a panoramic view of three states and three rivers.

New Glarus. "Little Switzerland" honors the Alpine life of its founders in the pastoral *Swiss Historical Village* (612 7th Ave., tel. 608/527–2317), where twelve reconstructed buildings depict the homes, trades, and skills of the Swiss who first settled here, including a tour of a 19th-century cheese factory. Events such as the Wilhelm Tell and Heidi festivals, and the Volkfest, Polkafest, and Winterfest take place throughout the year and include arts-and-crafts fairs, outdoor music, and historical plays.

Norskedalen (Cty. P1 west of Westby, tel. 608/452–3424). "The Norwegian Valley," as it translates, has grown from an arboretum to a 400-acre expanse that includes log farmsteads. Maps guide hikers past corn and tobacco fields, oak and spruce forests, prairies, ponds, and springs. Cross-country skiers use the trails in sunny weather.

Prairie du Chien. Remains of the American Fur Trading Company's stone warehouses and fort survive on St. Feriole Island. In 1870, fur fortunes built opulent *Villa Louis Mansion* (531 N. Villa Louis Rd., tel. 608/326–2721), home of Wisconsin's first millionaire. Today, tours are offered daily from May through October. Along the river behind the mansion, the St. Feriole Island Railroad's restored railroad cars are filled with shops. Nearby, *Lawler Park* has swimming beaches and marinas.

Restaurants

In Monroe, you have your choice between **Baumgartner's Cheese Store & Tavern** (1023 16th Ave., Monroe, tel. 608/325–6157), in the town's historic square, serving bulky cheese sandwiches and a local brew, or a fancier meal at the century-old **Idle Hour Mansion** (1421 Mansion Dr., Monroe, tel. 608/325–1200), where the Sunday champagne brunch is popular. You're back in history once more at the **Westby House** (200 W. State St., Vernon, tel. 608/634–4112), where, in a Victorian tea-shop setting, you can order Wisconsin cheeses, a classic filet mignon, crab Mornay casserole, and on Fridays, fresh local trout. In New Glarus, the **New Glarus Hotel** (100 Sixth Ave., New Glarus, tel. 608/527–5244) no longer accommodates guests overnight but does serve authentic Alpine dishes such as fondue and raclette. The **Chalet Landhaus** (801 U.S. 69, New Glarus, tel. 608/527–5234), housed in a town landmark, has a similar menu. In Mineral Point's Chesterfield Inn, another 19th-century site, **Ovens of Brittany** (20 Commerce St., Mineral Point, tel. 608/987–3682) serves its legendary baked goods, along with quiche and other light entrées.

Tourist Information

La Crosse Convention & Visitors Bureau (Box 1895, Riverside Park, La Crosse, WI 54901, tel. 608/782–2366); **Mineral Point Chamber of Commerce** (Box 78, Mineral Point, WI 53565, tel. 608/987–3201); **New Glarus Chamber**

of Commerce (Box 713, New Glarus, WI 53574, tel. 608/527–2095); **Prairie du Chien Chamber of Commerce** (Box 326 H.V., Prairie du Chien, WI 53821, tel. 800/732–1673); **Sparta Chamber of Commerce** (101 S. Water St., Sparta, WI 54656, tel. 800/354–2453).

The Duke House

Even though it is in the Midwest, this 1870 Federal-style house—one of the oldest in Mineral Point—feels like a New England Victorian. Darlene Duke and her husband, Tom, packed up their antiques collection and drove out of the East Coast fast lane in search of a more pleasant way of life. One of the reasons Darlene loves the light and airy house is that there are so many windows you can do your needlework even on a gloomy day. The living room, painted creamy white, centers on a working fireplace, and a plush pastel Chinese rug that warms the broad-planked floor. An old brass trunk serves as a coffee table, and there's a Colonial drum table under the newel post. These and a few reproduction pieces give the room a lived-in, homey atmosphere, perfect for the early evening social hour that the Dukes feel is the best time of the day.

The house is built on the area's highest point of land so the views from the upstairs bedrooms capture most of the small city, which is almost untouched by time. The four-poster bed in the Canopy Room is covered with a crocheted string spread and a canopy, and the finials are shaped like pineapples, the symbol of hospitality. With its pierced-tin lamp, its low, wooden Colonial-era rocker, the steamer trunk in the huge walk-in closet, and the copper warming pan affixed to the wall, the room is comfortable but not precious. Across the

hall, in Grandma's Room, more pineapples appear on the four-poster bed, complemented by floral wallpaper, a white rug covering well-polished floorboards, a decorative kerosene lamp, and bookcases filled with tomes of area history and lore. Other pieces find their way here from Duke's Antiques only a short stroll away, close to the artisans' shops that occupy the former miners' dwellings.

Address: *618 Maiden St., Mineral Point, WI 53565, tel. 608/987-2821.*
Accommodations: *2 double rooms share 1 bath.*
Amenities: *Air-conditioning, fireplace in common room.*
Rates: *$42–$55; full breakfast, morning coffee and Cornish appetizers delivered to bedroom doors. MC, V.*
Restrictions: *No smoking, no pets; closed Mar.*

The Inn at Wildcat Mountain

All tall white pillars, with a classic Georgian air, this inn looks like the White House of woodland Wisconsin. A Greek Revival mansion on the edge of tiny Ontario, it was built in 1908 with high hopes: Its builder expected to make a fortune by planting ginseng and shipping it to Oriental buyers in Chicago. But the proposed railroad never made it this far, and the interior of the gorgeous house was carved up into apartments.

After undergoing a monumental restoration, the building is the dream come true of innkeeper Pat Barnes. With her children grown and gone, turning her home into a bed-and-breakfast seemed natural: "How else could I justify buying a house like this?" she laughs. She says she enjoyed restoring the building and likes entertaining people who appreciate the cherry, oak, and bird's-eye maple woodwork she spent years of her life refinishing.

Pat describes her former life as "collecting things," an understatement once you see the period pieces and acres of vintage clothing hung everywhere on walls, clothes trees, and mannequins. A fan revolves on the parlor's lofty ceiling, and lace-curtained windows rise even higher than the dignified grandfather clock. The focal point of the room is a 1905 oak secretary. The dining room, connected to the parlor by an archway, is set with silver candelabra whose lights flicker on the walnut-stained buffet.

Of the four upstairs rooms, the most asked for is Scarlett's Room, which has a turn-of-the-century brass bed and its own curved balcony. The back room, called Shady Rest, boasts the house's only closet, as well as a four-poster bed and bare wood floor. Those who choose it are rewarded with a view a rolling pine-dotted lawn where guests play badminton or look on from the comfort of deck chairs.

The 5-acre woodland setting, in the lap of the forested Wildcat Mountain Park, makes the inn especially popular with outdoor-sports enthusiasts. Guests can bring their own horses or canoes here or rent both at nearby outfitters. Or they can just loll on Pat's wide, inviting front porch and watch the butterflies flit by.

Address: *U.S. 33 (Box 112), Ontario, WI 54651, tel. 608/337–4352.*
Accommodations: *3 double rooms and 1 single room (¾-sized bed) share 1 bath.*
Amenities: *Air-conditioning, ceiling fans.*
Rates: *$45–$85; full breakfast, afternoon refreshments. MC, V.*
Restrictions: *No smoking, pets in kennels outside only.*

The Jones House

This regional showcase looks as grand as the day it was built; oddly enough, it was almost never lived in. William Jones, once commissioner of the Bureau of Indian Affairs for President McKinley, erected the 16-room redbrick mansion in 1906 as a homecoming present to himself after his stint in Washington. He died soon after and his will forbade its sale until the death of his wife and children. Boarded up intact, a housekeeper religiously dusted it twice a week until 1986, when June and Art Openshaw learned that it was to be sold at last. Having eyed it covetously for years, they were first in line with an offer.

A grand, boxy staircase winds around one of the seven unusual fireplaces. The stairs rise from the foyer to a stained-glass skylight that casts patterns on the entrance carpet. The mahogany-beamed dining room is graced by forest-green woodland scenes painted above the wainscoting. A green-tile fireplace warms guests during breakfast. Twin sideboards topped by graceful arches glint with beveled glass, and padded velvet window seats on either side of the fireplace overlook the broad side lawn. To complete the *après la chasse* feel, the hardwood floor is covered in a moss-green carpet.

The Persian rugs, dark patterned wallpapers, and brass light fixtures, which came with the house, create a decidedly masculine atmosphere. The small Ladies' Parlor overlooking the front walk, however, provides respite with its garlands of roses painted on its high, pale walls.

The front bedroom, with a bricked-up, white-tile fireplace, the original needlepoint chairs, and floral coverings on both bed and daybed, also has a more feminine air. A screen door leads to a porch-top balcony that overlooks the town. The adjacent front bedroom, with a view of the spreading side yard as well as the avenue. A Colonial-reproduction rocker and pineapple finials on the four-poster bed give the room a pleasantly formal air. The back bedroom, in contrast, has a country-antique look.

There are traces of Mr. Jones still in the house: Outside the Master Suite, which includes a bathroom and sitting room, stand the master's antique golf clubs; his leatherbound books still line the library's shelves; and his walking stick hangs on the door of the vestibule.

Address: *215 Ridge St. (Box 130), Mineral Point, WI 53565, tel. 608/987–2337.*
Accommodations: *2 double rooms share 1 bath, 2 suites.*
Amenities: *Fans in rooms, 7 fireplaces in common rooms.*
Rates: *$45–$75; full breakfast. No credit cards.*
Restrictions: *No smoking, no pets.*

Just-N-Trails

sk Don and Donna Justin why they added a bed-and-breakfast to their 213-acre working farm and they just laugh, "We'd been doing it free for 15 years anyway for all the relatives." The accommodations are "all things to all people," claim the friendly, laid-back couple, who delight in welcoming guests. Their 50 head of Holstein often provide visitors with a late-night show (no cover charge)—the birth of a calf. An athlete's nirvana, their spread has 10 miles of groomed and mapped hiking and ski trails, six nearby cycling trails (the area calls itself "the bike capital of America"), and five rivers close at hand where guests can fish or go canoeing. The farm is also a romantic getaway spot with two private cabins and Laura Ashley–decorated rooms upstairs in the farmhouse.

Each cabin has a front porch with Amish hickory rockers from which you can watch the sun sinking past the fields and wooded hills. The cabin decor is on the kitschy side—plastic pine boughs with twinkling lights, lots of cows and teddy bears—but each has its own whirlpool bath. The beds are invitingly comfortable with an abundance of pillows that make reading a pleasure. Unfortunately, the bathrooms, with curtains instead of doors, are dark and tiny. The new log cabin, Little House on the Prairie, has a whirlpool bath in the loft under skylights.

Guests in the farmstead's upstairs rooms—such as the Maple Room with a green, pink, and white floral scheme and double sleigh bed of bird's-eye maple—get the same nine-pillow treatment as those in the cabins. In the evening, everyone gathers for games on the sun porch or around the old upright piano in the parlor for the nightly sing-alongs. The wake-up call is a wren's warble or perhaps a moo, followed by Donna's hearty, farm-style breakfast on the glassed-in sun porch. There's also a microwave guests can borrow when the hungries hit, as sometimes happens after a ramble on the hills up to the tiny lake and down again via the Bambi trail—so named to reassure novice skiers.

Address: *Rte. 1 (Box 274), Sparta, WI 54656, tel. 608/269-4522 or 800/488-4521, fax 608/269-3280.*
Accommodations: *3 double rooms with baths, 2 doubles share 1 bath, 2 cabins.*
Amenities: *Air-conditioning, fireplaces and whirlpool tubs in cabins; hammocks, picnic tables, "traditional agrarian fitness center with pitchfork and hay bales."*
Rates: *$65–$175; full breakfast. MC, V.*
Restrictions: *No smoking, no pets.*

Martindale House

W hen Anita Philbrook opened the Martindale House in a quiet residential section of La Crosse, she was concerned that bed-and-breakfast establishments "were a fad, like the vitamin craze." But repeat guests—from as far away as England, Spain, and Scandinavia—have proved there's no cause for concern. "I offer not just a bed, but an experience," Martindale's polished hostess maintains. Luckily, it includes a hearty Swedish breakfast served on the fifth-generation family china patterned in wedding-ring gold, with antique silver coffee spoons, in the white, bright Scandinavian-style dining room lined with a traditional collection of family portraits.

The imposing green-shuttered house is a grand architectural mélange of Italianate cupola and Colonial clapboard, with an Indian bungalow–style wraparound porch to boot. Combatting years of disrepair, Anita restored moldings and chandeliers discovered in the basement to their proper places and resurrected the iron fence, unearthed in the carriage house. Then she replanted the entire garden.

Inside, the parlor is a historian's delight. There is a stately grandfather clock, an antique chess table, antique Oriental rugs on the blond-oak floors, floor-to-ceiling windows flanked by their original shutters,

and a piano that's been in her husband's family for five generations.

The white staircase in the foyer leads to four bedrooms. The Martindale Room features an 1800 cannonball bed, a warming pan, porcelain dolls in cradles, and quilts from the nearby Amish community. The French Room derives its name from the carved Louis XVI bed that came from a castle in Lyons; its other highlight is the carved-wood chest made by Anita's Swedish grandmother. The English Room offers a fireplace, a garden view, and a lace-canopied four-poster bed. This room has the advantage of a vast, soothing bathroom, dubbed by guests "the rub-a-dub." Honeymooners prefer the sunny yellow Scandinavian Room, whose 1740 antique beds, their hostess warns them, came from a nun's convent. The well-loved Lappland dolls on display there belonged to Anita's grandmother. Plans are in the works to convert the carriage house to a private suite. Obviously, Martindale House is here to stay.

Address: *237 S. 10th St., La Crosse, WI 54601, tel. 608/782-4224.*
Accommodations: *4 double rooms with baths.*
Amenities: *Air-conditioning, use of portable phones, several languages spoken.*
Rates: *$80–$135; 4-course breakfast. MC, V.*
Restrictions: *No smoking, no pets.*

Westby House

Pat Smith is not a native of these parts—indeed, she claims she's here to "add a little variety to Westby's sturdy Norwegian mold," but she knows the territory. She grew up in St. Louis, and Westby was traditionally the halfway stop en route to Madeline Island, where her family spent summers.

In 1984, Pat purchased a country manor–style house built in the 1890s by a successful Norwegian immigrant. The mansion's signature Queen Anne witch's turret caught her eye, and as luck would have it, no paint marred the fine oak woodwork, and the light fixtures, stained glass, and imposing pillared fireplaces were still in place.

Upstairs in an otherwise undistinguished hallway, the original dining-room buffet stands guard over a pair of spacious front bedrooms. The Tower Room has a tiny bathroom and a down-quilt-covered brass bed set into an alcove of bay windows. The Firepalce Room has a tiled fireplace and a rocking chair; a TV and lots of magazines help compensate for a lackluster view of storefronts just off the town's main street. The two rooms are connected by double doors and can be rented as a suite. The Anniversary Room is almost a suite, with reproduction wing chairs and a sofa forming a conversation group in its bay window. Its brass bed merits the handmade quilt and white eyelet comforter. The Greenbriar Room's caned chairs, rag rugs, marble-top washstand, and old-fashioned white iron bed, topped with another antique quilt, has the look of Grandma's house—comfortable but not fancy.

When Pat bought the house, she vowed never to cross the kitchen door. Ironically, she now runs a public restaurant in the three adjoining dining rooms. Polished wood floors, bare wooden tables, and ice-cream-parlor chairs mingle with an old pump organ and a fireplace replete with ceramic tiles and a mirror over the mantel.

This very Norwegian town is especially lively during the Settendai Mai festival in May, when rooms are spoken for well in advance; the Old World Norskedalen Village, 6 miles away, attracts Pat's Scandophile guests year-round.

Address: *200 W. State St., Westby, WI 54667, tel. 608/634-4112.*
Accommodations: *2 double rooms with baths, 4 doubles share 2 baths.*
Amenities: *Air-conditioning, TV in bedrooms, fireplaces in common rooms, restaurant, gift and antiques shops.*
Rates: *$55–$65; Continental breakfast weekdays, full breakfast weekends, refreshments on arrival. MC, V.*
Restrictions: *No pets.*

The Country Manor

German pancakes have long been the specialty of Berlin-born, Milwaukee-bred Ursula Henke, but she never dreamed of whipping up a fresh batch every day. Nor did she and her husband, Eugene, picture themselves retiring to a small town in Wisconsin to run a bed-and-breakfast—until they stayed a night in one. Its owner knew of a deserving restoration project nearby—a solid 1860s brick farmhouse set in the wooded hills on the edge of town. Now the house is a candidate for the National Register of Historic Places. The Hinkes added a modern fieldstone fireplace to the sunny, white living room, which they've furnished with a collection of family pieces and antiques. Next they refinished the French doors that connect it to the bright dining room, where they've situated their pride and joy, a Civil War–era rocker.

Upstairs, each bedroom is sparkling and white from the walls to the German coverlets, china washing sets, and chamber pots. There are also Amish wicker rockers to sit in while taking in the view of shady elms and furrowed fields.

Address: *W5456 Boma Rd., La Crosse, WI 54601, tel. 608/787–1719.*
Accommodations: *1 double room with bath, 3 doubles share 1 bath.*
Amenities: *Air-conditioning, fireplace in common room.*
Rates: *$60–$75; full breakfast, afternoon and evening snacks. MC, V.*
Restrictions: *No smoking, no pets.*

The Geiger House

Marcus and Penny Neal searched far and wide until they discovered a sleepy river town where time seemed to stand still. Then they combed it for a house that could hold their collection of antique furniture. The stately Greek Revival home they finally settled upon, now in mid-renovation, is on a spacious corner lot just steps from the Mississippi River. A trim white picket fence marks the spot.

Many of the rooms have vintage country-Victorian furniture from the front bedroom with a rough-hewn table, to the antique upright piano that anchors the sitting room.

All bedrooms have access to the grand veranda above the front porch—box seats for Cassville's annual Twins Parade, where Penny, a twin herself, is always front and center. A sun porch in the back faces a grove of cherry, apple, and plum trees, which is a cloud of blossoms in spring. In winter, the dining room's fireplace makes a cozy gathering spot for breakfast.

Address: *401 Denniston St., Cassville, WI 53806, tel. 608/725–5419.*
Accommodations: *1 double room with bath, 2 doubles share 1 bath.*
Amenities: *Air-conditioning, fireplace in common room; bikes, gift shop, shuttle to river ferry.*
Rates: *$40–$50; full breakfast, morning coffee, afternoon refreshments. No credit cards.*
Restrictions: *No smoking, no pets.*

Nathaniel Treat House

In 1881, Nathaniel Treat, a captain in Sherman's army during the Civil War, came back to Monroe, his hometown, to build this neo-Jacobean house. Nathaniel's portrait presides over the lofty living room that, along with the dining room, has a 12-foot ceiling. Photographs of his daughter, Nellie, married here in 1907, adorn the marble-top Victorian table set under a teardrop chandelier that dangles from a sculpted plaster rose on the floral-bordered ceiling.

Captain Treat's Room, with another portrait of Nellie, has a private bath and his-and-hers upholstered rockers drawn up to a bricked-in white marble fireplace. The room glows with the light from the courthouse clock tower, ablaze all night. Helen's Room features a hanging painted-china gas lamp, a brass bed, a white metal trundle bed, as well as lots of morning sun.

Guests may sit on the two porch swings and enjoy the marble urns full of flowers. In addition, Monroe is Wisconsin's Swiss cheese capital and the home of Huber and Berghoff breweries, both of which are on the Old World Town Square two blocks from the inn.

Address: *1222 11th St., Monroe, WI 53566, tel. 608/325-5656.*
Accommodations: *2 double rooms with baths, 2 doubles share 1 bath.*
Amenities: *Air-conditioning, TV in one room; pool.*
Rates: *$37–$73; full breakfast. MC, V.*
Restrictions: *No smoking, no pets.*

Oak Hill Manor

First a word about breakfast: *Gourmet* magazine has asked for the eggs Benedict recipe. Lee and Mary De Wolf used to own a restaurant, and it shows in the wonderful assortment of eggs, crêpes, sausages, and the fresh-baked bread. The couple's other passion is their acre-long terraced garden, which guests can enjoy from an old-fashioned swing on a porch that spans the 1908 American four-square house.

The proud farmwife for whom the house was built insisted on being able to survey the comings and goings from both directions, so the inn sits diagonally on its corner. The house showcases some of the lady's upscale tastes: ivory-embossed wallpaper in the entry hall and the dining room appointed with oak pocket doors, rich oak woodwork, and built-in buffet, as well as a fireplace with tall wooden Ionic columns and a shiny brass grate. Upstairs, off a wide, sunny hall that leads to a cheery gathering room, are the two most popular bedrooms: Sylvia's, with a white-tiled, pillared fireplace, and Josephine's, with a private sun porch filled with wicker furniture.

Address: *401 E. Main St., Albany, WI 53502, tel. 608/862-1400.*
Accommodations: *4 double rooms with baths.*
Amenities: *Air-conditioning, fireplace in one room and common rooms; bikes.*
Rates: *$35–$55; full breakfast, snacks of local cheese. MC, V.*
Restrictions: *No smoking, no pets.*

The Parson's Inn

The cross on the rooftop is the clue that you've found the Parson's Inn—a 12-room, turn-of-the-century brick rectory that once served the church right across the street.

Just off the wraparound porch overlooking the wooded river valley and the hills beyond town is the original priest's office. "It's where I signed my marriage papers," says the mother of proprietor Julie Cull. She grew up and then raised her children in this secluded pocket of the state. Together, Julie and her mother peppered the eclectic furnishings with family antiques such as the rolltop desk in the living room; the dining-room set that was her grandmother's wedding present—where Julie serves her mom's melt-away pecan rolls and homemade jellies for breakfast; and her great-grandmother's bird's-eye maple bed with ruffled half-canopy, now in Granny's Room.

The Belle Suite's fireplace has been bricked over, but there's a rag rug on the floor, a handmade basket-pattern quilt on the bed, and a dresser and chest built into an alcove; from its awning-shaded deck the nearby bluffs spread out before your eyes.

Address: *Rock School Rd., Glen Haven, WI 53810, tel. 608/794-2491.* **Accommodations:** *2 double rooms share 1 bath, 1 suite.* **Amenities:** *Air-conditioning.* **Rates:** *$45-$80; full breakfast, afternoon refreshments. No credit cards.* **Restrictions:** *Closed Dec.-Mar.*

Sugar River Inn

The Sugar River is the source of many pleasures for the Albany community and its visitors. The inn's backyard is on the river shores, so guests can linger in the gazebo and watch canoes drift by or enjoy the view from the windows of the inn's country-style bedrooms—the Oak Room even has a small balcony.

Jack and Ruth Lindberg have furnished their 1920s brick home with Colonial-reproduction furniture, but it is their unique touches that give the rooms charm. The quilt in the Country Room's four-poster Shaker-style bed depicts the same farm scene you see on the room's wallpaper border. The Rose Room's antique dolls and toys fit in perfectly with its pink walls and white lace.

The Twin Room is home to a small library.

Ruth sends her guests off with a hearty breakfast featuring her "golden treat," a mélange of granola, golden raisins, bananas, vanilla yogurt, and honey, while a full cookie jar awaits guests at the end of every afternoon.

Address: *304 S. Mills St., Albany, WI 53502, tel. 608/862-1248.* **Accommodations:** *1 double room with bath, 2 doubles share 1 bath.* **Amenities:** *Air-conditioning, fireplace in parlor, turn-down service, wake-up coffee.* **Rates:** *$45-$55; full breakfast. No credit cards.* **Restrictions:** *No smoking, no pets.*

Trillium

These two tiny, three-room cottages are nestled amid 85 acres of rolling hills in the heart of Amish farm country. "They're my dollhouses," exclaims young innkeeper and farmwife Rosanne Boyett, who lives in the nearby frame house. The shingle cottages probably feel a bit larger to Roseanne's husband: to keep the houses identical, he laboriously hauled sandstone from the banks of the nearby Kickapoo River to build a huge fireplace in one.

The cottages can be shared because each has a sitting room that doubles as a bedroom. The sitting room's humble and well-used look comes from overstuffed and antimacassared armchairs and treadle sewing machines. There's a patchwork quilt folded on the double bed in the cor-

ner and a sofa bed for yet another pair. Beyond an arched doorway is a cozy inner bedroom with a neatly folded double wedding ring quilt at the foot of the bed. An old wood stove dominates the kitchen (with a 1950s electric range as backup). The cottages' spacious covered porches are complete with rocking chairs. Paths lead to a brook and waterfall in the woods and circle fields of grain.

Address: *Rte. 2 (Box 121), La Farge, WI 54639, tel. 608/625-4492.*
Accommodations: *2 2-room cabins, each shares 1 bath.*
Amenities: *Fireplace, kitchen, telephone in cottages.*
Rates: *$65; full breakfast. No credit cards.*
Restrictions: *No pets.*

Victorian Garden

Trees shade the arched front porches of this 110-year-old Victorian belle located on a quiet street in Monroe. But what makes you catch your breath is the double lot's gardens, crossed by meandering brick pathways.

The guest rooms are named after the garden's flowers, which can be seen from the rooms' windows. In the spacious Sweet Jasmine Room is a king-size bed, an antique loveseat, and a bay window that affords a particularly lovely view. The Rosebud Room has an antique double bed and a private bath.

The large shared bath is spectacular: roses bloom on its black wallpaper and its folding screen. Live plants twine around the claw-foot tub and

antique pedestal sink, and French doors overlook the garden.

Privacy is foremost in the Secret Garden dormer suite, with its own white staircase, skylights, and television alcove; the breakfast area has a refrigerator and microwave, and the sunny bathroom comes complete with a rubber duck in the whirlpool.

Address: *1720 16th St., Monroe, WI 53566, tel. 608/328-1720.*
Accommodations: *2 double rooms with bath, 2 doubles share 1 bath, 2 suites.*
Amenities: *Air-conditioning; whirlpool tub, microwave, and refrigerator in suite; robes.*
Rates: *$45-$150; full breakfast. MC, V.*
Restrictions: *No smoking, no pets.*

Door County

Jutting into Lake Michigan like the thumb on a mitten, Door County is a 70-mile-long, 13-mile-wide peninsula that is often called the Cape Cod of the Midwest. And not without reason: Quaint coastal villages dot 250 miles of shoreline, with the waters of Green Bay on the west and Lake Michigan on the east. Lighthouses, wide sand beaches, apple and cherry orchards, quiet backroads, commercial fishing boats, and offshore islands complete the picture. Fishing, sailing, bicycling, and cross-country skiing are popular Door County sports, and most visitors at some point sample the region's famous fish boil—a 100-year-old traditional way of cooking whitefish steaks in a caldron over a wood fire (boiled red potatoes, coleslaw, and cherry pie are the de rigueur *side dishes). Nearly 2 million people flock here each summer, many of them repeat summer visitors. Substantial crowds also come to view the brilliant leaf colors in autumn.*

Door County was named after Portes des Morts *("Doors of Death"), a strait of water separating the peninsula from Washington Island, at the mitten-thumb's tip. French explorers more than 300 years ago gave the strait this name because its currents are so strong that sailing vessels sometimes could not make headway against it, and there have been numerous wrecks here over the years. Door County nowadays is also separated from the Wisconsin mainland by a ship canal dug across it at Sturgeon Bay, the sixth-largest shipbuilding port in the nation.*

First-time visitors often make a circle tour via U.S. 57 and 42. The Lake Michigan side of the peninsula is somewhat less settled and the landscape more rugged. It is not uncommon for the Lake Michigan side to be foggy and stormy, with choppy waters, while just a few miles across the peninsula, the bay is calm, and the skies are blue and sunny. The Green Bay side also offers another advantage:

The many bluffs along its shoreline offer breathtaking sunset views to the west.

Sturgeon Bay is more or less the gateway to the peninsula; U.S. 42 and 57, the main roads leading to and around Door County, converge in Sturgeon Bay. Heading up the Green Bay side of the peninsula on U.S. 42, you'll pass first through Egg Harbor, then Fish Creek, full of gingerbread Victorian houses that today house several bed-and-breakfasts and boutiques. Just north of Fish Creek lies Peninsula State Park, where you can marvel at the views from atop Eagle Bluff.

Two miles north of Fish Creek is the picturesque town of Ephraim, known as the "White Village" because its tiered hills rising from the bay are heavily covered with white wooden houses and churches. Founded in 1853 by a group of Moravians of Norwegian heritage, the town remains "dry" to this day. A short distance up U.S. 42 from Ephraim is Sister Bay, whose early settlers were mostly Scandinavian or German immigrants. Farther north is Ellison Bay, founded in 1870; the quiet backroads around here make for particularly good biking and hiking (nearby Newport State Park is a good camping spot). The fishing village of Gill's Rock is the next town north; the passenger ferry to Washington Island leaves from here, while the car ferry leaves from Northport, at the very tip of the peninsula.

Washington Island has nearly 100 miles of roads and is a popular cycling spot. Its population of 600 inhabit the oldest Icelandic settlement in the United States. Ferries from Washington Island take visitors on to remote Rock Island, once the private estate of millionaire inventor Chester Thordarson and now a primitive state park permitting only backpacking and cycling.

Back on the mainland, retrace your route along U.S. 42/57 until U.S. 57 branches east to follow the Lake Michigan shore. The chief town to stop in along this side of the peninsula is Baileys Harbor, founded in the 1840s by Captain Justice Bailey, who landed here during a storm en route to Buffalo. A boatload of immigrants traveling with Bailey found the area so charming that they decided to stay right here. Many a present-day tourist has been tempted to do the same in Door County.

Places to Go, Sights to See

Al Johnson's Swedish Restaurant and Butik (702–712 Bay Shore Dr., Sister Bay, tel. 414/854–2626). Tourists wait in line for hours to feast on Swedish pancakes, meatballs, and all manner of Swedish delights. To keep them occupied while they wait, diners are invited to go outside and watch the goats grazing on the sod roof.

Bjorklunden Chapel (7603 Chapel La., Baileys Harbor, tel. 414/839–2216). A replica of an ancient Norwegian church, this beautifully decorated chapel demonstrates the fine handiwork of the region's early Scandinavian settlers.

Cana Island Lighthouse (Rte. Q, northeast of Baileys Harbor). Connected to the mainland by a low stone causeway often covered with water, this 1851 lighthouse is still in use.

Cherryland Brewery (341 N. Third Ave., Sturgeon Bay, tel. 414/743–1945). Located in the former train station, this lively microbrewery is open daily 11–5; guided tours run from May through October.

The Clearing (just off U.S. 42, Ellison Bay, tel. 414/854–4088). This 128-acre oasis is the home of a summer residential school studying the Danish folk tradition. Designed in 1935 by landscape architect Jens Jensen, the retreat can be visited by the public on weekends, when guides will show you through the rustic buildings built to fit the peaceful blufftop site.

Door County Historical Museum (18 N. Fourth Ave., Sturgeon Bay, tel. 414/743–5809). Indian relics, pioneer items, and an early firehouse are displayed here, daily from May through October.

Door County Maritime Museum. There are two branches of this museum, one in Sturgeon Bay (Third Ave. and Sunset Park, tel. 414/743–8139) and the other in Gills Rock (12590 U.S. 42, tel. 414/854–2860). The Sturgeon Bay location, right next to the city's extensive modern-day shipyards, exhibits a refurbished ship's pilothouse, antique engines, turn-of-the-century sailboats, and artifacts from sunken ships; in Gills Rock you'll view nautical paintings and items illustrating the history of commercial fishing. The museum is open from Memorial Day through October.

Door Peninsula Winery (5806 U.S. 42, Sturgeon Bay, tel. 414/743–7431). Wine tastings and guided tours are offered here.

Fishing Tours. Charters available up and down the Green Bay shore include those at *Eagle Harbor Charters* (South Shore Pier, Ephraim, tel. 414/854–4324) and the *Shoreline Resort* (12747 U.S. 42, Gills Rock, tel. 414/854–2606). For Lake Michigan fishing, try *Baileys Harbor Charter Fishing* (Box 72, Baileys Harbor, tel. 414/839–9111).

Maple Grove Gallery (County Rd. F between Fish Creek and Baileys Harbor, tel. 414/839–2693). It's worth a drive to visit this crafts store, featuring traditional Door County pottery and handwoven clothing, throws, pillows, and wall hangings.

Miller Art Center (107 S. Fourth Ave., Sturgeon Bay, tel. 414/743–6578). Painting and graphics by Door County artists and others from the Midwest are featured in this gallery, in the Door County Public Library.

Peninsula State Park (U.S. 42, just north of Fish Creek, tel. 414/868–3258). The state's busiest park, Peninsula offers miles of bike trails, beaches, an 18-hole golf course (tel. 414/854–5791), and the Peninsula Players (W4351 Peninsula Players Rd., tel. 414/854–9938), the oldest professional summer-theater troupe in the country, performing from late June to mid-October. In summer you can tour the park's 19th-century Eagle Bluff Lighthouse, which is still in use.

Pioneer School House (Moravia St., Ephraim). Amid period furnishings, local artists' work is on display from May to October in this 1869 schoolhouse.

The Ridges Sanctuary (Rte. Q, ½ mi north of Baileys Harbor, tel. 414/839–2802). Hiking trails wind through this beautiful 800-acre nature and wildlife reserve.

Sailing Cruises. Try *Bella Sailing Cruises* (South Shore Pier, Ephraim, tel. 414/854–4324) or the *Schooner Friendly* (Sturgeon Bay, tel. 414/743–1592).

Uncle Tom and Aunt Marge's Candy Shop (Europe Bay Rd. and Timberline Rd., Ellison Bay, tel. 414/854–4538). Uncle Tom passed away recently, but Aunt Marge still welcomes visitors eager for her sublime fudge or peanut brittle.

Washington Island Tram Tours. Two operators—*Washington Island Ferry Train* (tel. 414/847–2546) and *Viking Tour Train* (tel. 414/854–2972)—run narrated tram tours of Washington Island from Memorial Day to mid-October, leaving from the ferry dock (purchase ticket with your ferry ticket at Northport or Gills Rock).

Restaurants

Don't go to Door County looking for nouvelle cuisine. Instead, look for good, hearty food that will keep you going during long bike rides, hikes, or days spent on the lake fishing and boating. In Sister Bay, **Al Johnson's Swedish Restaurant and Butik** (702–712 Bay Shore Dr., tel. 414/854–2626), a Door County tradition, has fans coming as much for the sight of goats grazing on the thatched roof as they do for the Swedish pancakes and meatballs. Just down the road, in Ephraim, **Wilson's Ice Cream Parlor and Restaurant** (U.S. 42, tel. 414/854–2041) is a favorite for its giant ice-cream cones with jelly beans at the bottom and old-fashioned sundaes and sodas; the menu also features breakfast and bakery items as well as more substantial sandwiches and salads. **Paulson's Old Orchard Inn Restaurant and Bakery** (U.S. 42, Ephraim, tel. 414/854–5717) offers complete breakfasts that include biscuits, Swedish pancakes, and fresh-baked caramel pecan rolls. Whether you enjoy a lunch of soups, salads, or sandwiches or a dinner from their extensive fish and foul menu, be sure to save room for one of Paulson's famous desserts.

To enjoy a traditional Door County fish boil head for the **White Gull Inn** (4225 Main St., Fish Creek, tel. 414/868–3517). The boils are presided over by Russ Ostrand, who carefully cooks up Lake Michigan whitefish and potatoes in a giant outdoor kettle over an open fire while he entertains guests with songs and stories. On evenings when the fish boil is not offered, the inn is a nice spot for a candlelight dinner. It also serves hearty breakfasts including its famous stuffed French toast.

Slightly off the beaten path in Ellison Bay is the **Wagon Trail Resort, Restaurant and Meeting Center** (1041 U.S. 22, tel. 414/854–2385). The well-known restaurant at the resort offers a number of Scandinavian favorites. Buffets, a coffee shop, and a formal dining room make this a good spot for a variety of occasions.

Tourist Information

Baileys Harbor Business Association (Box 31, Baileys Harbor, WI 54202, tel. 414/839–2366); **Door County Chamber of Commerce** (U.S. 42/57, just south of Sturgeon Bay; Box 406, Sturgeon Bay, WI 54235; tel. 414/743–4456); **Fish Creek Civic Association** (Box 74, Fish Creek, WI 54212, tel. 414/868–2275); **Sister Bay Advancement Association** (Box 351, Sister Bay, WI 54234, tel. 414/854–2812); **Sturgeon Bay Area Advancement Group** (Box 212-C-1, Sturgeon Bay, WI 54235, tel. 414/743–3924); **Washington Island Chamber of Commerce** (RR1, Box 22, Washington Island, WI 54246, tel. 414/847–2225).

The Ephraim Inn

I n the picture of his son that inn owner Tim Christofferson carries in his wallet, another man is included—the Wal-Mart photographer who took the picture. Tim just wanted to make sure he remembered the guy. That's the kind of good humor Tim exudes, and inn guests feel it from the time they walk in the door. A former McDonald's marketing executive, Tim had always wanted his own business; he and his wife, Nancy, moved to Door County in 1979 when they bought Wilson's Ice Cream Parlor, overlooking the harbor in Ephraim's charming historic district. Then, in 1985, the big white house next door, where the town doctor, Dr. Sneeberger, had lived and practiced for 40 years, went up for sale. Tim and Nancy bought it and built a large addition that turned it into a sprawling horseshoe-shape inn with a center cupola. Much to the dismay of their sons, Tim and Nancy sold Wilson's in 1987 (but it's still in operation next door) to concentrate on the inn.

The Christoffersons live in most of the old main house; all of the 17 guest bedrooms are in the new addition, where such modern essentials as soundproofing, air-conditioning, and private baths were easy to install. Each room has its own motif; often Shaker inspired, it shows up on the room's wooden key tags, the painted symbol on its door, and the hand-stenciled border on its ceiling. Shaker-style peg rails around the

walls hold such decorative touches as dried flowers, grapevine wreaths, straw hats, and even chairs. The furniture is a mix of reproductions and antiques, with the couple's preference for the simple, clean lines of country furniture.

The large, harbor-view common room brings guests together around a large fireplace or in a well-stocked library nook. Full breakfasts, served in three small dining areas, may include homemade granola, fresh-baked pastries, and an Ephraim Inn omelet, a quiche-like dish of baked eggs, cheese, and spices.

The shorefront location, a decided asset, gives the inn wonderful water views and puts guests within walking distance not only of Ephraim's historic sights but also of an unspoiled beach just around a curve of the road. Not much farther up the road are Peninsula State Park and its fine 18-hole golf course.

Address: *Rte. 42 (Box 247), Ephraim, WI 54211, tel. 414/854-4515 or 800/622-2193.*
Accommodations: *17 double rooms with baths.*
Amenities: *Air-conditioning, TV in rooms; beach across street.*
Rates: *$75-$135; full breakfast. MC, V.*
Restrictions: *No smoking, no pets; 2-night minimum weekends.*

The Griffin Inn

onverted from a private house to a summer hotel in 1921, the Griffin Inn is quite a retreat, situated on 5 acres of rolling lawn shaded by maple trees. Long verandas with porch swings and a gazebo give guests plenty of places to sit and enjoy the breeze. Besides the main building, a Dutch reform–style house built in 1910, there are two cottages on the property, each with two guest units.

Innkeepers Jim and Laurie Roberts, who took over from Paul and Joyce Crittenden (now of the Church Hill Inn in Sister Bay; *see below*), added some of their own touches—on the dining-room wall hang two quilts, one made by Laurie and one by her grandmother. Handmade quilts cover the antique double beds in the guest rooms as well, and each room's decor centers on the colors of the quilts. Though the bedrooms are fairly small, they have been comfortably furnished in a collection of pieces that reflect the tastes of the various owners of the inn throughout the years.

Common rooms include the dining room, a downstairs living room with a large fieldstone fireplace where guests gather for popcorn every night, and a small library where guests can curl up on a love seat with a book.

The cottages, which are open only in the summer, are a bit more rustic,

with open-beam ceilings, rough cedar walls, and ceiling fans. Cottage guests can either pick up a breakfast basket each morning or make arrangements to join the main-house guests for the full family-style breakfast Laurie serves in the dining room. Laurie, who is quite a cook—she wrote two cookbooks, which are for sale at the front desk—bakes her own muffins and tea breads.

Only two blocks from downtown Ellison Bay, the inn is within walking distance of Green Bay. It sits directly on a well-traveled bike route, and is not far from Newport State Park, which has a fine Lake Michigan beach. Guests play badminton or croquet on the inn grounds, a sight that conjures up images of the inn's long past as a summer retreat.

Address: *11976 Mink River Rd., Ellison Bay, WI 54210, tel. 414/854–4306.*
Accommodations: *8 double rooms and 2 triple rooms share 2 baths; 2 cottages each sleep 4 people.*
Amenities: *Air-conditioning, TV in cottages only.*
Rates: *$73–$83; full breakfast for inn guests, Continental breakfast for cottages. No credit cards.*
Restrictions: *No smoking, no pets; 2-night minimum weekends, 3-night minimum holidays.*

The White Gull Inn

One of the oldest lodging establishments in Door County, the White Gull Inn was founded in 1896 by a Dr. Welcker as a lodging for wealthy German immigrants who came to Fish Creek by steamer. Its current owner and manager, Andy Coulson, is a former journalist who was traveling in Australia when a friend contacted him and asked if he wanted to join a group of investors to buy the White Gull. Andy said yes—with the condition that he could run the place. The other partners happily agreed. One of Andy's first managerial decisions was to hire a new housekeeper, Jan, who proved such a prize that five years later he married her. Today Andy and Jan also own the nearby Whistling Swan (*see below*). The Coulsons, have worked hard to maintain the original feel of the white-frame inn, with its inviting front porches (upstairs and down), gleaming hardwood floors covered with braided rugs, and country-style antiques.

The main entry is the focus of activity; it's here that guests watch television or gather around the large fieldstone fireplace. Besides overnight guests, crowds of people visit the inn's restaurant, famous throughout Door County for its traditional fish boils, conducted on Wednesday, Friday, Saturday, and Sunday nights in summer (Wednesday and Saturday in winter). The restaurant serves three meals a day;

breakfast may include eggs Benedict, hash browns, or buttermilk pancakes.

The inn is perfectly situated: To the left is Sunset Beach Park; to the right, the charming shops of Fish Creek and then Peninsula State Park. Accommodations are spread around a number of buildings. The main house has several guest rooms, each with a comfortable wrought-iron or carved-wood bed, and each decorated with antiques, some of them once owned by Dr. Welcker himself. Behind the inn is the slightly more luxurious Cliffhouse, whose two suites have fireplaces and lush furnishings; the inn also owns three nearby cottages that make wonderful little vacation homes for families.

Address: *4225 Main St. (Box 160), Fish Creek, WI 54212, tel. 414/868–3517.*
Accommodations: *4 double rooms with baths, 4 double rooms and 1 single room share 2 baths; 6 cottages each sleep 2–8 people.*
Amenities: *Air-conditioning, TV in 4 bedrooms and cottages, complimentary coffee and newspaper in rooms each morning, restaurant.*
Rates: *$46–$121; cottages $102–$205; breakfast extra. AE, D, DC, MC, V.*
Restrictions: *No pets; 2-night minimum weekends, 3-night minimum holidays.*

White Lace Inn

In 1982, a bed-and-breakfast was born when Bonnie and Dennis Statz purchased a run-down Victorian house that had been built in 1903 for a Sturgeon Bay attorney. They renovated the house outdoors and in, painting the exterior rose and cream and restoring the intricate wood paneling inside. Then in 1983, they bought the 1880s-vintage Garden House for $1 and had it moved to the grounds of their inn, right beside the flower gardens. Soon after, they bought the Washburn House, on an adjacent lot around the corner, and converted it to extra guest quarters.

"Whimsical Victorian" is the Statzes' description of the White Lace Inn's distinctive style. Massive antique Victorian furniture—not perhaps innately whimsical—has been toned down by the use of floral fabrics, fluffy pillows, and, of course, white lace. Whether it's a framed doily, lace curtains, or pillowcases, there is at least one piece of white lace in each room. Bonnie, who holds a degree in interior design, was responsible for decorating this growing inn, and she has given each room in the three buildings its own look. All bedrooms in the Garden House and Washburn House have fireplaces; all Washburn House rooms also have whirlpool baths, as do three of the Main House rooms. Bonnie personally shops at outlet stores to find thick towels for her guests; the rooms are brightened with books

of poetry and photographs; and little hand-painted rocks rest on the bed pillows, gently reminding guests to remove pillow shams before retiring.

The Main House's parlor, sitting room, and dining room serve as common areas for the entire inn complex. Guests are encouraged to mingle here; cookies and other treats are served. Walk out through the white picket fence and you're on a quiet residential street, with tall shade trees and stately old houses, two blocks away from Sturgeon Bay's historic downtown district.

For Bonnie and Dennis, the inn is the realization of a dream shared since college days—owning a business. "We didn't know what kind of business we wanted, so we explored different things and came up with this," Bonnie said. "It's perfect because we like this kind of thing and we like people."

Address: *16 N. Fifth Ave., Sturgeon Bay, WI 54235, tel. 414/743-1105.*
Accommodations: *14 double rooms with baths, 1 suite.*
Amenities: *Air-conditioning, whirlpools in 7 rooms, guest phones, TV in 4 rooms.*
Rates: *$66–$146; Continental breakfast. AE, MC, V.*
Restrictions: *Smoking in 5 rooms only, no pets; 2-night minimum weekends, 3-night minimum holidays.*

The Barbican Guest House

Don't expect to get to know your fellow guests if you stay at the Barbican Guest House—there are no common areas here for mingling—but if your aim is a romantic getaway, this is the place. All accommodations are two-room suites, decorated with thick carpets, floral-print wallpapers, and English country-house-style antiques. Each suite has a queen-size bed, double whirlpool, its own fireplace, cable TV, stereo, refrigerator, and room-service breakfasts, so guests don't have to leave their rooms at all if they don't want to.

The Barbican, right in Sturgeon Bay's historic district, one block from the water, is actually two houses, both built by local lumber baron L. M. Washburn. The larger main house has a welcoming wraparound porch. Brothers Jim and Mike Pichette and Mike's wife, Cherie, bought the houses in 1986 and turned them into a bed-and-breakfast, painting them the same color: a soft mauve-like pink that perfectly communicates the romantic spirit of the inn.

Address: *132 N. Second Ave., Sturgeon Bay, WI 54235, tel. 414/743–4854.*
Accommodations: *11 suites.*
Amenities: *Air-conditioning, cable TV, whirlpools, stereos, in-room refrigerators.*
Rates: *$95–$130; Continental breakfast. MC, V.*
Restrictions: *No pets; 2-night minimum weekends, 3-night minimum holidays.*

The Church Hill Inn

Built in the late 1980s, the Church Hill Inn isn't a historic property, but owners Paul and Joyce Crittenden—who formerly owned the Griffin Inn in Ellison Bay and the White Apron Inn in Sister Bay—have done their best to re-create the feeling of a secluded old inn. The guest rooms are not dissimilar to what you might find in a luxury hotel, but they still are individually decorated with English antiques (many of the beds are four-posters) collected by Joyce on travels abroad. The two-story white-railed veranda that runs the length of the inn's front gives several rooms private balconies, and each of the building's five wings has its own cozy parlor with a fireplace. At the same time, the inn offers modern amenities such as an outdoor pool, exercise room, sauna, and a whirlpool/spa (11 rooms have their own double whirlpool baths as well).

Breakfasts are served in a two-level dining room under a skylight; drinks and complimentary hors d'oeuvres are offered in a pub in the main parlor each evening.

Address: *425 Gateway Dr., Sister Bay, WI 54234, tel. 414/854–4885 or 800/422–4906.*
Accommodations: *35 double rooms with baths.*
Amenities: *Air-conditioning, cable TV, phone in rooms, hot tub, fitness room; outdoor pool.*
Rates: *$104–$134; full breakfast. MC, V.*
Restrictions: *No pets; 3-night minimum weekends.*

The Eagle Harbor Inn

Set well back from the main road, U.S. 42, and surrounded by birch and cedars in peaceful seclusion, this Cape Cod–style inn is the focal point of a complex of 12 vacation cottages built in the 1920s, except for No. 9, a century-old log cabin. The inn itself is the newest building on the property, having been built in the 1950s as a residence for the cottages' owners. Ronald and Barbara Schultz bought the inn in 1986.

Full breakfasts are the rule here—homemade scones and granola are Barbara's specialties, but Ron does most of the cooking—served in a sunny enclosed porch. Most of the cottages, convenient for families, have their own kitchens, but cottage guests can have breakfast in the inn for an extra charge. The property is within walking distance from a boat ramp and a sand swimming beach on the shores of Green Bay.

Address: *9914 Water St. (Box 72), Ephraim, WI 54211, tel. 414/854–2121.*
Accommodations: *9 double rooms with baths; 12 cottages (9 one-bedroom, 2 two-bedroom, 1 three-bedroom).*
Amenities: *Air-conditioning, cable TV, whirlpool in 1 room; children's playground, basketball court, grills.*
Rates: *$56–$140; full breakfast. MC, V.*
Restrictions: *Smoking in cottages only, no pets; 2-night minimum weekends, 3-night minimum holidays.*

48 West Oak

Growing up in Sturgeon Bay, Henry Isaksen always loved this 1896 Italianate redbrick house on a quiet residential street, and when it came on the market in 1989, he knew he had to buy it. He and his wife, Jean, took the plunge, using the first floor for Henry's office (he's an architect) and turning the top floor into a small but top-notch bed-and-breakfast. There are two rooms, both with beautifully restored woodwork, hardwood floors, and turn-of-the-century antiques. The smaller one, wallpapered in plush green, has a cherry mantel over the fireplace and a stained-glass window over the double whirlpool bath. The larger room is a suite, with a good-size parlor and dining area, a separate bedroom, and a bathroom with raspberry-colored tile around the whirlpool. The furniture and original mantels over the fireplaces blend with such up-to-date features as a microwave, refrigerator, and VCR.

Henry still works in his downstairs office, and on Tuesday nights, his barbershop quartet rehearses there. Wander downstairs to listen, and maybe they'll take a few requests.

Address: *48 W. Oak St., Sturgeon Bay, WI 54235, tel. 414/743–4830.*
Accommodations: *1 double room with bath, 1 suite.*
Amenities: *Air-conditioning, cable TV, whirlpool baths, phones.*
Rates: *$90–$135. No credit cards.*
Restrictions: *No smoking, no pets; 2-night minimum weekends, 3-night minimum holidays.*

The French Country Inn of Ephraim

Architect Walt Fitzpatrick immediately was drawn to this square, white-frame house in the Door County village of Ephraim. Built in 1912 for a Chicago family with 10 children, it was a classic summer beach house, with deep eaves and large casement windows to catch breezes off Green Bay, just down the road.

Like many summer houses, this one has many large open areas, which have been turned into comfy common rooms. Striving to give their inn a European ambience, Walt and Joan encourage guests to mingle. One room has a bed from an old French hotel; in another, a whole wall is covered with hats that Joan, a former teacher, once kept in her classroom to amuse students. The

two-bedroom cottage, built from the house's original outside kitchen, is best for families. The inn's country garden, with scattered flower beds and meandering paths, is Joan's pride and joy. Walt says that guests love to watch Joan mow the lawn—using, of course, an old-fashioned push mower.

Address: *3052 Spruce La. (Box 129), Ephraim, WI 54211, tel. 414/854-4001.*
Accommodations: *2 double rooms with baths, 5 doubles share 2 baths; 1 2-bedroom cottage.*
Rates: *$49–$74; cottage $465 per week; Continental breakfast, evening refreshments. No credit cards.*
Restrictions: *No smoking, no pets; 2-night minimum weekends, 3-night minimum holidays.*

The Gray Goose Bed and Breakfast

Wicker furniture awaits guests on the large front porch; the Civil War–era dining table is already set for breakfast. John Burkhardt, a former advertising executive, and his wife, Jessie, a former nurse, are innkeepers who enjoy chatting with their guests, especially when the topic is the inn itself: an 1862 frame house, now painted red, with huge dormer windows overlooking the bay. They live on the inn's first floor, right under the porch, and are always ready to offer popcorn, cocoa, or some other treat.

In each of the bedrooms, look for Jessie's special touch—old cookie cutters hung as a ceiling border in one room, dried flower bouquets draped across the rafter in another,

a border of hand mirrors around the top of one of the shared bathrooms, and, of course, a goose motif carried out in every room. Comforters and quilts accompany country-style antique furniture. It all adds up to a casual atmosphere, in keeping with the inn's quiet, wooded setting a few miles north of the town of Sturgeon Bay.

Address: *4258 Bay Shore Dr., Sturgeon Bay, WI 54235, tel. 414/743-9100.*
Accommodations: *4 double rooms share 2 baths.*
Amenities: *TV in guest lounge.*
Rates: *$65–$75; full breakfast. AE, MC, V.*
Restrictions: *Smoking in lounge on porch only, no pets; 2-night minimum holidays.*

The Harbor House Inn

Else Weborg laughingly tells visitors that she never really wanted to be an innkeeper—still doesn't, as a matter of fact. But it's hard to believe this charming Danish woman, since she runs Harbor House Inn with such vigor. The house itself, a gray-blue frame structure with touches of Victorian gingerbread, was built by Else's husband's ancestors in 1904. In the mid-1980s, Else and her husband, David, a general contractor, restored the house and turned it into a bed-and-breakfast.

Guests rooms in the main house preserve a Victorian look, with turn-of-the-century furnishings. Ground-floor bedrooms have bay windows, while those upstairs have private balconies.

In 1991, Else and David added a new wing of four one-bedroom suites with floral-print fabrics and blond furniture. A carriage house tucked away in the pine trees behind the main house has been turned into Troll Cottage, which preserves the stovewood construction used by the region's early Scandinavian settlers.

Address: *12666 U.S. 42, Gills Rock, WI 54210, tel. 414/854–5196.*
Accommodations: *7 double rooms with baths, 4 doubles share 2 baths; 1 cottage sleeps 2.*
Amenities: *Air-conditioning, TVs; sauna, hot tub; private beach.*
Rates: *$39–$85; Continental breakfast. AE, MC, V.*
Restrictions: *2-night minimum weekends, 3-night minimum holidays.*

The Inn at Cedar Crossing

Pressed-tin ceilings, stenciled walls, secluded balconies, and a TV room just like Mom used to have are features that make the Inn at Cedar Crossing charming. The setting is convenient, if not secluded—right in Sturgeon Bay's downtown historic district, at the corner of Third Avenue and Louisiana Street, which used to be Cedar and Cottage streets (hence the inn's name). Downstairs is a restaurant, also operated by the inn's owner, Terry Wulf; upstairs are nine guest rooms furnished with antiques (most beds are four-posters or canopies), plus the "gathering room."

Terry bought the brick vernacular-style building in 1985, when it was just 101 years old, and restored it carefully. Each room has its own look: golden oak in one, hand-carved mahogany in another, painted Scandinavian furniture in another. Terry also installed oversize whirlpool tubs in half of the rooms, understanding how sore muscles can be after a day of hiking, skiing, or cycling around Door County.

Address: *336 Louisiana St., Sturgeon Bay, WI 54235, tel. 414/743–4200.*
Accommodations: *9 double rooms with baths.*
Amenities: *Air-conditioning, whirlpools in 4 rooms, restaurant.*
Rates: *$75–$125; Continental breakfast. D, MC, V.*
Restrictions: *Smoking only in designated areas, no pets; 2-night minimum weekends, 3-night minimum holidays.*

The Scofield House

Fran and Bill Cecil believe in letting life take them where it will. In 1987, it took them down a street in Sturgeon Bay, where they saw a gabled Victorian frame house built in 1902 by Herbert Scofield, Sturgeon Bay's mayor. They promptly bought the house, then refinished its parquet floors and massive carved mantelpieces, and gave the exterior a distinctive paint job that layers the three stories in colors of bittersweet, mustard gold, and olive green.

Special touches in the guest rooms include embossed wall coverings from England, stained-glass windows, hand-crocheted lace curtains, vintage photographs taken by the house's original owner, heirloom quilts, marble-topped dressers and washstands, and roomy antique armoires. The most impressive (and most expensive) room is the third-story suite, which has skylights, Oriental rugs, a double whirlpool, golden oak wainscoting, and a pressed-tin ceiling.

Address: *908 Michigan St. (Box 761), Sturgeon Bay, WI 54235, tel. 414/743-7727.*
Accommodations: *6 double rooms with baths.*
Amenities: *Air-conditioning, cable TV and VCR in 4 rooms, whirlpools in 4 rooms.*
Rates: *$65-$175; full breakfast. No credit cards.*
Restrictions: *No smoking, no pets; 3-night minimum holidays.*

Thorp House Inn and Cottages

Unlike many historic bed-and-breakfasts, the Thorp House Inn actually began life as a boardinghouse. When the original owner was killed in a shipwreck in 1903, his widow completed construction on their house and supported herself by renting rooms to tourists. In 1986, Christine and Sverre Falck-Pedersen restored it and made it a B&B again. Besides the main house, where the Falck-Pedersens live in the ground floor, there are seven cottages (circa 1940) tucked into the cedar woods behind the inn. Like the main inn's guest rooms, they are furnished mostly with country antiques, worn and comfortable. The Falck-Pedersens expanded their complex by buying Beach House, a four-year-old condominium down the street, whose suites are more modern and luxurious. Christine considers remodeling an ongoing project—she's constantly looking for new additions. But homeyness, not fussiness, is the keynote here.

Address: *4135 Bluff Rd. (Box 490), Fish Creek, WI 54212, tel. 414/868-2444.*
Accommodations: *4 double rooms with baths; 3 2-bedroom suites; 7 2-bedroom cottages.*
Amenities: *Air-conditioning, ceiling fans in guest rooms, cable TV in cottages, whirlpool in 1 room and 1 cottage; bicycles.*
Rates: *$70-$150; Continental breakfast. No credit cards.*
Restrictions: *No smoking in main house, no pets; 3-night minimum holidays.*

The Whistling Swan

A sister property to the White Gull Inn (*see above*), one block away, the Whistling Swan is Jan Coulson's baby. A fastidious innkeeper, she has fussed over every detail of the smaller inn's decoration and operation, down to the bed linens that match the wall coverings, the fresh flowers on nightstands beside each bed, and the bottles of imported spring water she leaves for guests. Pastels, floral prints, and white-painted woodwork give the inn a bright, clean look. Continental breakfast is served on the sunny porch, and in cold weather, Jan also serves afternoon tea in front of the fireplace in the inn's parlor.

Originally located across Green Bay in Marinette, this white frame 1887-vintage house was towed across the frozen bay one winter to its present Fish Creek location, right on Main Street. The neighborhood is full of cottages that have been converted into shops, so Jan's boutique, downstairs in what used to be the house's music room, fits right in.

Address: *4192 Main St. (Box 193), Fish Creek, WI 54212, tel. 414/868–3442.*
Accommodations: *5 double rooms with baths, 2 suites.*
Amenities: *Air-conditioning, cable TV in common room.*
Rates: *$90–$121; Continental breakfast. AE, D, DC, MC, V.*
Restrictions: *No smoking, no pets; 2-night minimum weekends, 3-night minimum holidays; closed weekdays Nov.–Apr. (except open all of Christmas week).*

The White Apron

G uests arriving at the White Apron might think they are about to check into an old country store, with its storefront windows, pink awnings, and rockers on the front walk. The stovewood building was in fact a combination private home and meat market in the 1890s, but it has been an inn for several years now, thanks in large part to its location, just off U.S. 42. The present owners, Jim and Mary Werner, took over in 1991, stripped the floors, scrubbed it, and renamed it The White Apron.

The downstairs restaurant, open to nonguests as well, serves a dinner menu of "uncomplicated food"—lake fish, chicken, beef, and pasta, along with its own special blend of coffee. Inn guests are served full breakfasts here each morning, featuring fresh-baked coffee cakes, muffins, and crusty baguettes. In keeping with the restaurant's style, the goal of the little bed-and-breakfast upstairs is to keep things simple, according to innkeeper and cook Barbara McCarrier. Guest rooms here are quaint, though small, furnished with sturdy old beds, inviting linens, ceiling fans, and a few carefully chosen accessories.

Address: *414 Maple Dr., Sister Bay, WI 54234, tel. 414/854–5107.*
Accommodations: *5 double rooms with baths.*
Amenities: *Restaurant.*
Rates: *$65; full breakfast. MC, V.*
Restrictions: *No smoking, no pets; 3-night minimum holidays.*

Wisconsin River Country
Including Baraboo and Spring Green

*Running north to south, the Wisconsin River wiggles
through the center of the state before suddenly veering west
to join the Mississippi. At times there is a distinct herd
mentality here, from the Holsteins munching on the grassy
banks to the armada of out-of-state vans and mobile homes
making their way down U.S. 51 (which parallels the river)
to Wisconsin Dells and other tourist meccas.*

*There's a sharp contrast between the original Winne-
bagos—the Native American tribe that just three centuries
ago silently canoed the river's course—and their 4-wheel
namesakes, especially during the summer crush. That's
when small towns up and down the river host a stream of
history pageants, arts festivals, crafts fairs, band concerts,
fireworks displays, athletic competitions, and other
weekend happenings.*

*The state's most-visited attraction, Wisconsin Dells, is
where the Wisconsin River twists through walls of
castellated sandstone. Originally called Kilbourn, the town
officially changed its name in 1931 in an unabashed
attempt to draw more visitors to the picturesque region,
which had garnered national renown through the
stereoscopic photographs of H. H. Bennett. It may have
succeeded too well. Outside of a museum dedicated to early
photography in the H. H. Bennett Studio and an exciting
15-mile boat ride through the gorge, the overall experience
for some has become homogenized. It doesn't help that the
roads leading in and out of the dells are lined with
hundreds of "family fun" venues and neon-laced motels
that wink at passersby like so many painted ladies.*

*These pressures have not yet reached Baraboo, the original
winter quarters of several circuses, including the five
Ringling brothers. This pleasant community, which took its*

name from an early French trader, Baribault, is home to the Circus World Museum and other Big Top–related attractions. When you're tired of circuses, take in the International Crane Foundation. This fascinating center for the study and preservation of endangered cranes is 5 miles north of town on U.S. 12.

As circus performers first learned, Wisconsin can be very hospitable in winter. There is the lure of groomed Alpine and cross-country ski trails, of course. But most of the credit for the state's reputation as a winter playground belongs to the snowmobile, which evolved from a mechanical creature of necessity in the 1940s into a recreational toy by the 1970s. Today, Wisconsin leads the country in the production and use of snowmobiles, and there are racetracks and tours galore.

If you can ride a bicycle, the natives say, you can ride a snowmobile. Technology has progressed to the point where today even a rank amateur from Florida can feel comfortable his first day in the woods. Today Wisconsin offers sledders 13,000 miles of state-funded groomed trails that cut through parks and fields and often end at some scenic overlook. In fact, for many regular visitors to Wisconsin, the annual vacation photo doesn't involve a beach or cabin. It's a snowsuited family hoisting steaming cups of hot chocolate, enjoying a vrooom with a view.

Places to Go, Sights to See

Baraboo. *Circus World Museum* (426 Water St., tel. 608/356–0800), the original Ringling Bros. winter home, re-creates the razzle-dazzle era with an outstanding collection of circus wagons and big-top performances featuring today's circus stars. Both *Devils Lake State Park* (3½ mi south on U.S. 123, tel. 608/356–8301), featuring Devil's Lake and several prehistoric Native American mounds, and the *International Crane Foundation* (5 mi north on U.S. 12, ¼ mi east on Shady Lane Rd., tel. 608/356–9462), a preserve for endangered crane species, offer guided and self-guided tours.

Portage. This river town's historic district has a cache of elegant homes worth touring; one of them is author *Zona Gale's* (804 MacFarlane Rd., tel. 608/742–4959), now the public library. The *Old Indian Agency House* (Hwy. 33E, tel. 608/742–6362) of 1832, the *Surgeon's Quarters* (Hwy. 33E, tel. 608/742–2949) from the 1820s, and the adjoining 1850s *Garrison School* recall the pioneering era with their period furnishings.

Spring Green. Frank Lloyd Wright chose this farming community on the Wisconsin River for his home *Taliesin* and his school for architects, *Hillside Home* (3 mi south on U.S. 23, tel. 608/588–2511), both of which can be toured from May through October. *The House on the Rock* (9 mi south on SR23, tel. 608/935–3639), eccentric builder Robert Jordan's tour de force perched atop a chimney-like rock 450 feet above the Wyoming Valley, is an architectural wonder of a different stripe. The complex, begun in 1940, includes waterfalls, massive fireplaces, and the millionaire's eclectic collections of dolls, paperweights, mechanical banks, and armor.

Stevens Point. A branch of the *University of Wisconsin* (tel. 715/346–4242) is situated here, and campus tours can be arranged. A planetarium and observatory in the Science Building are open year-round, as is the world's largest computer-assisted mosaic mural. The *Museum of Natural History* (Albertson Learning Resources Center, University of Wisconsin, tel. 715/346–2858) features one of the country's most comprehensive collections of preserved birds and bird eggs.

Wausau. The *Andrew Warren Historic District* (3rd St. and surrounding area) encompasses 10 blocks of historic homes built between 1868 and 1934. You can pick up maps at the Visitors Council (300 3rd St., Suite 200, tel. 800/236–9728) in Washington Square, the center of Wausau's historic Third Street pedestrian mall. *The Grand Theater* (415 4th St., tel. 715/842–0988) was recently restored to its 1926 splendor at a cost of over $2 million; the Greek Revival structure is now home to the performing arts in the area.

Wisconsin Dells. The scenic dells of the Wisconsin River are one of the state's foremost natural attractions. Created over thousands of years by the river cutting through soft limestone to a depth of 150 feet, the Upper and Lower Wisconsin Dells are nearly 15 miles of fantastic soaring rock formations. While the sandstone cliffs, majestic pines, and gently flowing waters are still popular, man-made attractions nearly overshadow the region's natural wonders. Virtually everything in the dells is casual; shorts and T-shirts are allowed nearly everywhere, and swimsuits, tanning lotion, and comfortable shoes should be considered standard equipment. For more information on dells attractions, dining, and lodging, contact *Wisconsin Dells Convention and Visitors Bureau* (701 Superior St., Wisconsin Dells, WI 53965, tel. 800/223–3557).

Restaurants

The **Spring Green Restaurant** (U.S. 23 and County Hwy. C, Spring Green, tel. 608/588–2571), the only restaurant Frank Lloyd Wright designed, provides a Continental menu more traditional than its surroundings, which are embellished by a view of the Wisconsin River. The town's **Round Barn** (⅛ mi west of U.S. 23N and 14, Spring Green, tel. 608/588–2568), only a little more formal than when the cows ate here, segues from sandwiches to giant Wisconsin steaks. The **Silver Coach** (38 Park Ridge Dr., Stevens Point, tel. 715/341–6588), a railroad car that once streaked through Stevens Point, now turns out a "fish fry" as upscale as its Art Deco quarters with salmon, garlic shrimp, and tuna. **The Cottage** (1502 Post Rd., Plover, tel. 715/341–1600), where dining is in the comfy rooms of an 1860s house, does a signature beef Wellington. Beef is also the popular choice in **Field's Steak 'n' Stein** (U.S. 13, 2 mi north of Wisconsinville, tel. 608/254–4841), the Wisconsin Dells's classic, family-owned supper club.

Tourist Information

Portage Chamber of Commerce (301 W. Wisconsin Ave., Portage, WI 53901, tel. 608/742–6242); **Spring Green Travellers Guide** (Box 3, Spring Green, WI 53588, tel. 608/588–2042); **Stevens Point Convention & Visitors Bureau** (660 Main St., Stevens Point, WI 55481, tel. 800/236–4643); **Wausau Convention & Visitors Council** (Box 6190, Wausau, WI 54402–6190, tel. 800/236–9728); **Wisconsin Dells Visitors & Convention Bureau** (701 Superior St., Wisconsin Dells, WI 53965, tel. 800/223–3557).

Dreams of Yesteryear

Designed in 1901 by architect J. H. Jeffers (who was also the architect for the Wisconsin Pavilion for the 1904 St. Louis World's Fair), Dreams of Yesteryear was singled out from among its Victorian peers by Bonnie and Bill Maher, a couple determined to save the attractive, grande old Queen Anne from destruction. Bonnie, an antiques collector, recognized the value and potential in the oak woodwork, hardwood floors, leaded glass windows, and footed tubs that had been preserved in the house. She replaced a rotting roof with wood shingles and restored the Queen Anne lines of "a chimney you could watch the sunset through." Then, with the major overhaul completed, she began "gathering" Victoriana. One of her early finds, a hope chest, graces the Isabella Room. The voluptuously carved parlor sofa became theirs when a stranger telephoned to say, "Aunt Minnie just died at 93—could you use it?"

Today that sofa, along with a revolving library table discovered at a church bazaar, faces the fancy fireplace with its Victorian cascade decorations and surrounding tools. Sheet music for "Lola" sits on the vintage upright piano, alongside a 1904 phonograph that still has its wood needles. Bonnie's lavish breakfasts, which feature local cranberry juice and pecan-stuffed French toast, are served on the inn's original dining-room set.

Upstairs, it's hard to choose between Gerald's Room, done in French blue, with a pineapple-post bed and tiny balcony; Isabella's Room, with an elaborately carved headboard, an ivy-filled bay window, and a cozy reading nook; Florence Myrna's Room, with gardenia wall coverings and its own deep green ceramic-tiled bathroom, lit by antique wall sconces; and the cozy Maid's Quarters, done in peach, with telephone access and a desk that appeals to business travelers.

If you ask Bonnie what she does in her spare time, besides keeping up the three different gardens that surround the house, chances are she'll invite you to come and see for yourself: She's the town's square-dance caller.

Address: *1100 Brawley St., Stevens Point, WI 54481, tel. 715/341-4525.*
Accommodations: *2 double rooms with baths, 2 doubles share 1 bath.*
Amenities: *Fan in rooms, fireplace in common room.*
Rates: *$55–$75; full breakfast. MC, V.*
Restrictions: *No smoking, no pets.*

Historic Bennett House

Historic Bennett House is a pleasant alternative to the many hotels and resorts in the Wisconsin Dells. A handsome 1863 Greek Revival mansion, the inn takes guests back to a gentler era. It was here that Civil War veteran Henry Bennett became a pioneer photographer noted for the first stop-action pictures that are displayed today in the Smithsonian Museum. Gail and Richard Obermeyer, a former stage actress and a university drama teacher, are running it in their retirement years. "We wanted the change of seasons. We'd vacationed here in the Dells and loved it; when we consulted a psychic, she divined that we were people-people and suggested, 'Why not open a B&B?' " The couple knew exactly what they wanted: the intimate atmosphere of a European bed-and-breakfast, "A recognizable home, not a historic museum," Gail said.

First they found the perfect house, complete with a white picket fence and only a block from downtown and the Wisconsin River. Then they waited for it to come on the market—which it soon did.

Guests from as far away as Germany and South Korea have come to this casually elegant inn. Visitors relax with a drink before dinner on the floral-patterned sofa or in a pair of wing chairs drawn up to the white, wood-burning fireplace in the living room. Breakfast is served at the communal table in the other half of the long room, which has a reproduction walnut-toned china cabinet and buffet and, on cool days, an open fire. Here Gail brings out the house specialty, eggs Bennett. There's a screened porch that doubles as a summer breakfast room where guests can sit and admire the Obermeyers' rose garden.

The compact ground-floor suite has a bedroom with Eastlake furniture, a Chinese-accented small parlor with a VCR and film library, and a tiny bathroom. Upstairs, the English Room has the original black floors, a walnut canopy bed, and an antique armoire from Britain. It shares a bathroom with the snug Garden Room, fitted with a brass bed and wicker furniture. The bathroom, with its gold fixtures, hand-painted Italian sinks, and candlelit claw-foot tub, is so seductive that some guests call it therapy.

Address: *825 Oak St., Wisconsin Dells, WI 53965, tel. 608/254–2500.*
Accommodations: *2 double rooms share 1 bath, 1 suite.*
Amenities: *Air-conditioning, TV and VCR in suites, fireplaces in common rooms; off-street parking.*
Rates: *$60–$85; full breakfast, early morning coffee. No credit cards.*
Restrictions: *No smoking, no pets.*

Mascione's Hidden Valley Villas

Phil and Mary Ann Mascione, as Italian as Chicagoans can get, do not come across at first as isolated rancher types. In fact, the fellow with the big grin and hearty handshake was the sports photographer for the *Chicago Tribune* for years. But when their kids grew up and moved away, the couple came here—to a hidden valley reached by a back road that weaves through stands of pine along the bluffs of the Kickapoo River.

All by themselves, the Masciones built an Alpine-style guest retreat. Phil scoured the countryside for weathered boards from fallen barns while Mary Ann collected American crafts. They created a minivillage of chalet-type guest villas that front the paddock where Windy City Dancer, their prize-winning racehorse, gambols among the grazing cattle.

The Golden Antler villa follows a hunting-lodge motif and comes complete with mounted stags' heads, skis, snowshoes, and antlers used as racks for an antique gun collection. The Camelot villa's decor has a medieval theme. Both villas have two bedrooms in a loft space. The first floors have wagon-wheel chandeliers, fireplaces made of local fieldstone that Phil collected, complete kitchens including microwaves, dining areas, and a shared bathroom. They also have decks with umbrella tables and barbecue grills.

Three new two-person chalets have been added. The snug living room of each has a fireplace and in the corner, a small minikitchen. Upstairs, under the slanting ceiling, Phil built impressive pine beds that Mary Ann carved and painted in keeping with the theme of each chalet: the Cheyenne, the Aztec, and the Eagle's Nest.

Mary Ann cooks a hearty breakfast of eggs Benedict or soufflé with local bratwurst and serves it in a separate, pink-shingled cottage, whose entryway houses a gift and antiques shop.

Set back in the pines on a hill is an Olympic-size pool surrounded by a deck and umbrella tables. The 80-acre property has two trout ponds, a croquet court, and a baseball field, as well as miles of meticulously tended walking trails.

Address: *Rte. 2 (Box 74), Hillsboro, WI 54634, tel. 608/489-3443.*
Accommodations: *2 2-bedroom villas and 3 1-bedroom villas, each with bath.*
Amenities: *Air-conditioning, coffee maker and microwave, and fireplace in villas; hiking trails, pool.*
Rates: *$80–$150; full breakfast, snacks stocked in rooms. No credit cards.*
Restrictions: *Smoking limited, no pets; closed Nov. 2–Apr. 30.*

Rosenberry Inn

T he Artzes' innkeeping career started one day when they went antiques-hunting and strayed too far from home. "We'll stay in a B&B," Pat informed her dubious husband. Next thing they knew, they were renovating a mansion of their own in a community "where people didn't have to lock their doors."

The good news about their choice, a 1908 Prairie schoolhouse built for Judge Rosenberry in Wausau's Andrew Warren Historic District, was that they could afford it if they did the renovation work themselves. The bad news was that there was plenty to do; back in the 1940s, the place had been turned into efficiency apartments.

Today, each guest room contains a tiny kitchen, eating nook, bath, and rustic Victorian furnishings— patchwork quilts, wooden rockers, and braided rugs. The four first-floor bedrooms still have tiled working fireplaces; rooms with western exposure are the sunniest and most spacious. In the romantic Hat Room, on the eastern side, antique headpieces adorn the walls, an old record cabinet now holds books, and there's an antique grapevine-canopy bed. On the second floor, where pressed-tin ceilings have been added, the bedrooms are filled with more attractive furniture—a calliope horse, a stencilled bed, and a wicker settee.

You won't find a dining room or parlor; instead, guests congregate in the third-floor common room for breakfast served on an old farmhouse trestle table. The imposing staircase that leads there is crammed with vintage teddy bears and lined with mannequins showcasing the couple's collection of antique clothing.

Across the street the Artzes converted the DeVoe House, the oldest home in Wausau, into two guest suites; both the downstairs and upstairs accommodations contain whirlpool tubs, fireplaces, and open-to-view kitchen appliances, all in one large room with partitions. Throughout the house are collections of antique hope chests, patchwork quilts, and, in the room under the rafters, a rope-suspended porch swing.

Both establishments on this quiet, almost aristocratic residential street have porches and gardens for relaxation. They are also only a quick walk from downtown.

Address: *511 Franklin St., Wausau, WI 54401, tel. 715/842–5733.*
Accommodations: *8 double rooms with baths, cottage with 2 double rooms with baths.*
Amenities: *Air-conditioning, fireplace in 4 bedrooms.*
Rates: *Rosenberry Inn $50, DeVoe House $90; Continental breakfast. MC, V.*
Restrictions: *No pets.*

Bettinger House

Marie Neider's hilltop brick home, built in 1904, has been in her family since 1913, when her grandfather moved in. Today, it's a walk-in album of family history: Vintage photos line the walls of the house where her grandmother, a midwife, delivered more than 300 of Plain's babies.

Relatives' names are scrolled in brass on the doors of the four guest rooms. Uncle Edmund's Room has an heirloom handknit bedspread, white ruffled curtains, and floral stenciling. The front room, named for Grandma Elizabeth, looks like a schoolgirl's bower, complete with dainty wicker dresser.

The common rooms are more modern and have less personality than the rest of the house. Breakfast is informal; guests gather around the maple kitchen table. A swing on the front porch catches the action in this small town, but don't let the relaxed atmosphere fool you: the Bettinger House fills up fast in the summer because of its proximity to Frank Lloyd Wright's Taliesin, the American Players Theatre, and The House on the Rock.

Address: *855 Wachter Ave., Hwy. 33, Plain, WI 53577, tel. 608/546-2951.*
Accommodations: *2 double rooms with baths, 4 doubles share 2 baths.*
Amenities: *Air-conditioning.*
Rates: *$45-$55; full breakfast. MC, V.*
Restrictions: *Smoking limited, no pets; 2-night minimum weekends.*

Breese Waye

Portage, Wisconsin's third-oldest city, sits where the Fox River, flowing north toward the waters of Green Bayou, comes within a mile of the Wisconsin River. It was here, in 1880, that banker Llewellyn Breese built the Breese Waye—a Queen Anne mansion, once the belle of the neighborhood.

In the front foyer, a fireplace with sculpted tiles of classic Grecian profiles catches your eye immediately. The rest of the family rooms are less distinctive, unless you're after velvet swivel chairs and reproduction Early American hutches.

Guest rooms, however, have a lot to offer. The Surgeon's Quarters has a collection of antique physicians' instruments, two rocking chairs, and an extra-large bathroom with bright white tiles. The young, or perhaps the young at heart, may prefer the Toy Room, full of owner Gretchen Sprecher's collection of huggable dolls and stuffed animals. Don't let the toys keep you from noticing the room's gorgeous parquet floors, spoolback rocker, and metal-bound steamer trunks.

Address: *816 MacFarlane Rd., Portage, WI 53901, tel. 608/742-5281.*
Accommodations: *2 double rooms with baths, 2 doubles share 1 bath.*
Amenities: *Air-conditioning, fireplace in common room.*
Rates: *$45-$55; full breakfast. No credit cards.*
Restrictions: *Smoking limited.*

Enchanted Valley Garden

Guests are lured to Ken and Marcia Helgerson's inn by its natural surroundings, which offer days full of outdoor pursuits. Located in a farming community 30 minutes east of Spring Green, the modest house sits on 5 acres of woods and fields, perfect for long walks and bird-watching. It's just 4 miles from Indian Lake Nature Preserve, a 442-acre park with hiking and natural cross-country ski trails.

Guests who stay closer to home will enjoy the iris that bloom in early summer. Bounty from the Helgersons' herb and vegetable garden goes into the farm-style breakfast, served in a sunny kitchenside nook with broad picture windows, or on a deck that commands panoramic views of the trees, wildflowers, and hills. Any surplus from the garden makes its way to Madison's Farmers' Market each Saturday.

The two guest rooms, both with queen-size beds, are anonymously modern, with tiny windows. Guests would do better to relax in the central den, which has floor-to-ceiling windows, an old-fashioned iron stove, and, if all else fails, a TV.

Address: *5554 Enchanted Valley Rd., Cross Plains, WI 53528, tel. 608/798-4554.*
Accommodations: *2 double rooms share 1 bath.*
Amenities: *Badminton, croquet.*
Rates: *$50–$60; full breakfast, snacks. MC, V.*
Restrictions: *No smoking, no pets.*

Hill Street

All the woodwork in this Queen Anne house is hand-carved, making Doris Randall's Hill Street one of the nicest bed-and-breakfasts in Spring Green. The grand central staircase has a striking design, and throughout the main floor you'll find, mixed with more contemporary furnishings, an antique piano, treadle sewing machine, and console radio.

Guest rooms, named after prominent settlers of the town, are each decorated differently. Most attractive is the Harry Gray Room, banded by four windows in a turret alcove, with wicker furniture, a ceiling fan, and a coat tree. Dr. Bossard's Room looks more feminine than its namesake might have wished, with straight-back chairs dressed in powder-blue slipcovers and a pink fabric swag above the bed. In the basement are unprepossessing guest rooms and the TV lounge.

Before setting out, guests can breakfast on Doris's giant pancakes with home-grown raspberries or the house specialty, French toast stuffed with pecans and cream cheese.

Address: *353 Hill St., Spring Green, WI 53588, tel. 608/588-7751.*
Accommodations: *5 double rooms with baths, 2 doubles share 1 bath.*
Amenities: *Air-conditioning, robes in rooms that share baths.*
Rates: *$50–$70; full breakfast. MC, V.*
Restrictions: *No smoking indoors, no pets; 2-day minimum weekends.*

M. Plank House

They literally "raised the roof" here in the good old days. Hancock merchant Melvin Plank built this classically proportioned clapboard house in 1885. As his business prospered and his family grew, he had the roof lifted and a story added. The house has been gracefully restored by German-speaking Clarence and Alma Vogelsang, who moved here to retire. No flounces, no knickknacks, no overdose of antimacassars—instead, the sunny rooms exude a tasteful less-is-more allure.

Small accents enhance the parlor, done in deep green with fresh white trim. In the bedrooms, plants figure prominently. Maidenhair fern in a bay window and a cart of African violets freshen the Rose Room, whose white iron bedstead shows off the alabaster crocheted bedspread Clarence's grandmother made. The Blue Room, also graced with ferns, has a delicate white writing table. In the Violet Room, a cherrywood chest of drawers and washstand fit comfortably amid the antique flower prints on the walls. The rooms share an immense bathroom, a deep red from floor to ceiling. Don't miss the kitchen with its cache of enamel coffeepots.

Address: *123 W. Brown St. (Box 193), Hancock, WI 54943, tel. 715/249-5411.*
Accommodations: *3 double rooms share 2 baths.*
Amenities: *Ceiling fan in rooms.*
Rates: *$45; Continental breakfast. No credit cards.*
Restrictions: *No smoking, no pets.*

Nash House

The Nash House, in Wisconsin Rapids, recalls some of the state's historic past. Built in the early 1900s, it was home to Guy Nash, father of Philleo Nash, special assistant to President Harry S. Truman and head of the Federal Bureau of Indian Affairs. When Phyllis and Jim Custer bought the house in 1987, their love of historical homes prompted them to draw the Nash family past into the inn's future by naming the rooms after Philleo and his siblings.

The beds in the three guest rooms are covered with antique quilts; Philleo's Room, decorated in mauve and white, features one crafted by a local Amish woman. Jean's Room displays hand-stenciled furniture, while Tom's Room has an antique brass bed and walnut highboy. Each sunny bedroom has floor-to-ceiling windows and all rooms offer the comfort of a private bath (Jean's and Tom's have claw-foot tubs).

Breakfast is usually served on the screened back porch, giving guests a chance to appreciate the array of daylilies, phlox, and impatiens blooming in the inn's garden.

Address: *1020 Oak St., Wisconsin Rapids, WI 54494, tel. 715/424-2001.*
Accommodations: *3 double rooms with baths.*
Amenities: *Air-conditioning, ceiling fan in rooms, fireplace in common room; tandem bike.*
Rates: *$40–$45; full breakfast, afternoon refreshments. AE, D, MC, V.*
Restrictions: *No smoking, no pets.*

Parkview

Tom and Donna Hofmann used 43 rolls of wallpaper and 35 gallons of exterior paint to turn this Queen Anne Victorian into a bright, homey place. A few steps from downtown on a corner in Reedsburg's historic district, Parkview is surrounded by other Victorian homes and churches. But Parkview is different. Built in 1895 by a local hardware merchant, the house has an abundance of ornate hinges and doorknobs. The yard behind the house is just as fanciful, crowded with a playhouse, goldfish ponds, stone flower pots, trellises, and a windmill, built of pebbles, that lights up.

The guest rooms upstairs are furnished with antiques bought at local auctions. One room has a high-top bed with carved head- and footboards; another, a deal dresser with swinging mirror; another features a brass bed.

Address: *211 N. Park St., Reedsburg, WI 53959, tel. 608/524-4333.*
Accommodations: *4 double rooms share 2 baths.*
Amenities: *Air-conditioning, ceiling fan in rooms, fireplace in common room.*
Rates: *$45–$55; full breakfast, popcorn, fresh strawberry pie, and cider on arrival. AE, MC, V.*
Restrictions: *No smoking, no pets.*

Pinehaven

Enjoy the ride between the twin columns of pines lining the drive of the 80-acre Pinehaven retreat. Overlooking a private pond on the edge of Baraboo, the house is the dream of a farm couple who began its construction in 1971.

In the living room, sliding glass doors frame bucolic vistas, a wall of white luma stone surrounds a dramatic modern corner fireplace, and there's a baby grand piano that accompanies many sing-alongs. There are two levels of guest rooms, all with private baths and three with queen-size beds. Of the four rooms, the Victorian, done in white wicker, has the most dramatic views.

You can sit in the screened porches or outside on shady decks, swim, row, or lounge on rafts. Other activities include strolling to the nearby Baraboo River, or riding one of Pinehaven's nine sturdy Belgian draft horses. The horses team up in the summer for wagon rides and in the winter for sleigh rides.

Address: *13083 Hwy. 33, Baraboo, WI 53913, tel. 608/356-3489.*
Accommodations: *4 double rooms with baths.*
Amenities: *Air-conditioning, fireplace in common room; small private lake, free use of paddleboat and rowboat.*
Rates: *$55–$65; full breakfast, Wisconsin apple cider on arrival, candy in rooms. MC, V.*
Restrictions: *No smoking, no pets.*

The Swallow's Nest

Although the Swallow's Nest bed-and-breakfast, a modern cedar-shingled lake house, is nestled among tall timbers and wildflowers of the forest, you can catch a glimpse of the lake's sparkling water from the house's windows. This scenery is the inspiration for the photography and paintings innkeeper Rod Stemmo.

The house is built around a sunny, two-story atrium. An open staircase leads to a bridge that overlooks the plant-filled atrium and connects the four guest rooms. In the Tamarack Room, blue-gingham-covered walls and lace curtains offset an antique mirrored dressing table. Paintings and floral plates grace the soft pink walls of the Wild Rose Room, complementing the room's heirloom English walnut furniture. Twin knotty pine beds, pine paneling, and green and rust accents make the Whispering Pine Room quite masculine. The suitably named Sunburst Room is done in pale yellows, with a queen-size brass bed.

After a breakfast on the deck, guests can take a woodland walk or rent a boat to explore the lake.

Address: *141 Sarrington St., Lake Delton, WI 53940, tel. 608/254–6900.*
Accommodations: *4 double rooms with baths.*
Amenities: *Air-conditioning, fireplaces in common rooms, pool table.*
Rates: *$55–$65; full breakfast. MC, V.*
Restrictions: *No smoking, no pets.*

Victorian Swan on Water

Jean Ouelette's Victorian Swan on Water, appropriately named for its Water Street address, is easy to find—the town's water tower looms behind it. A grove of giant pines screens the tower from the 100-year-old blue clapboard house, which is flanked by a beautiful garden of annuals and perennials.

Ivy trails through the home's sunny dining room where the daily three-course breakfast is served. Before retiring to one of the four bedrooms, guests can relax in the garden's double porch swing or in the Victorian drawing room, with distinctive black walnut–inlaid floors and elaborate crown moldings.

In the peaches-and-cream Newport Chaney Room, Jean turned an alcove into a sitting area with a skirted table and two antique chairs. The Rothman Room features a hand-carved antique dresser. Its bathroom has a claw-foot tub, pedestal sink, and cabinets made to match the walnut and maple floor. The Balcony Room, romantically decorated in rose and lilac chintz, has a canopy-draped wrought-iron bed; a small balcony affords views of the surrounding pines.

Address: *1716 Water St., Stevens Point, WI 54481, tel. 715/345–0595.*
Accommodations: *4 double rooms with baths.*
Amenities: *Air-conditioning, fireplace in parlor.*
Rates: *$45–$65; full breakfast. AE, D, MC, V.*
Restrictions: *No smoking, no pets.*

Directory 1
Alphabetical

Directory 2
Geographical

Michigan

Alden
Torch Lake Bed & Breakfast 75
Ann Arbor
The Reynolds House at Stonefield Farm 12
Au Train
Pinewood Lodge 41
Bay City
William Clements Inn 15
Bay View
The Gingerbread House 74
Beulah
Brookside Inn 62
Big Bay
Big Bay Point Lighthouse 40
Brooklyn
Chicago Street Inn 16
Champion
Michigamme Lake Lodge 39
Charlevoix
The Bridge Street Inn 73
La Bergerie 71
Clinton
Clinton Inn 17
Detroit
Blanche House Inn 16
Dundee
Dundee Guest House 18
Eagle River
Eagle's Nest Bed & Breakfast 40
Ellsworth
The House on the Hill 69
Fennville
Crane House 24
Kingsley House 25

Grand Blanc
The Country Inn of Grand Blanc 17
Harbor Springs
Kimberly Country Estate 70
Main Street Bed & Breakfast 74
Holland
Parsonage 1908 30
Lake Leelanau
Centennial Inn 58
Lake Village
Walloon Lake Inn 75
Lakeside
Pebble House 31
Laurium
Laurium Manor Inn 38
Mackinac Island
Bay View at Mackinac 47
Bogan Lane Inn 51
Cloghaun Bed & Breakfast 51
Haan's 1830 Inn 48
The Inn on Mackinac 49
Metivier Inn 50
Murray Hotel 52
1900 Market Street Inn 52
Maple City
Leelanau Country Inn 63
Marshall
National House Inn 26
Northport
Birch Brook 61
North Shore Inn 60
Old Mill Pond Inn 64
Petoskey
Bear River Valley 73
The Benson House 68
Stafford's Bay View Inn 72
Port Huron
Victorian Inn 14

Saginaw
Montague Inn 10
St. Joseph
Snow Flake Hotel 32
South Cliff Inn 27
Sanilac
Raymond House Inn 11
Saugatuck
Fairchild House 29
Maplewood Hotel 30
Wickwood Country Inn 28
Sault Ste. Marie
Water Street Inn 41
South Haven
Yelton Manor 32
Suttons Bay
Lee Point Inn 63
Tecumseh
The Stacy Mansion 13
Traverse City
Bowers Harbor Bed & Breakfast 61
Cherry Knoll Farm 62
Linden Lea 59
Neahtawanta Inn 64
Union Pier
The Inn at Union Pier 29
Pine Garth Inn 31

Minnesota

Alexandria
Carrington House 142
The Robards House 140
Blue Earth
Fering's Guest House 131
Cannon Falls
Quill & Quilt 109
Crosby
Hallett House 136
Deerwood
Walden Woods 146

Notes

Notes

The Upper Great Lakes Region

Please help us evaluate B&Bs and country inns for the next edition of this guide. Mail your response to Fodor's Travel Publications, Inc., 201 E. 50th St., New York, NY 10022.

B&B or Inn

City/State

Comments

B&B or Inn

City/state

Comments

General Comments

Your Name *(Optional)*

Number/Street

City/State/Zip

Fodor's Travel Guides

U.S. Guides

Alaska

Arizona

Boston

California

Cape Cod, Martha's
Vineyard, Nantucket

The Carolinas & the
Georgia Coast

Chicago

Disney World & the
Orlando Area

Florida

Hawaii

Las Vegas, Reno,
Tahoe

Los Angeles

Maine, Vermont,
New Hampshire

Maui

Miami & the Keys

New England

New Orleans

New York City

Pacific North Coast

Philadelphia & the
Pennsylvania Dutch
Country

San Diego

San Francisco

Santa Fe, Taos,
Albuquerque

Seattle & Vancouver

The South

The U.S. & British
Virgin Islands

The Upper Great
Lakes Region

USA

Vacations in New York
State

Vacations on the
Jersey Shore

Virginia & Maryland

Waikiki

Washington, D.C.

Foreign Guides

Acapulco, Ixtapa,
Zihuatanejo

Australia & New
Zealand

Austria

The Bahamas

Baja & Mexico's
Pacific Coast Resorts

Barbados

Berlin

Bermuda

Brazil

Budapest

Budget Europe

Canada

Cancun, Cozumel,
Yucatan Penisula

Caribbean

Central America

China

Costa Rica, Belize,
Guatemala

Czechoslovakia

Eastern Europe

Egypt

Euro Disney

Europe

Europe's Great Cities

France

Germany

Great Britain

Greece

The Himalayan
Countries

Hong Kong

India

Ireland

Israel

Italy

Italy's Great Cities

Japan

Kenya & Tanzania

Korea

London

Madrid & Barcelona

Mexico

Montreal &
Quebec City

Morocco

The Netherlands
Belgium &
Luxembourg

New Zealand

Norway

Nova Scotia, Prince
Edward Island &
New Brunswick

Paris

Portugal

Rome

Russia & the Baltic
Countries

Scandinavia

Scotland

Singapore

South America

Southeast Asia

South Pacific

Spain

Sweden

Switzerland

Thailand

Tokyo

Toronto

Turkey

Vienna & the Danube
Valley

Yugoslavia

Fodor's Travel Guides

Special Series

Fodor's Affordables

Affordable Europe

Affordable France

Affordable Germany

Affordable Great Britain

Affordable Italy

Fodor's Bed & Breakfast and Country Inns Guides

California

Mid-Atlantic Region

New England

The Pacific Northwest

The South

The West Coast

The Upper Great Lakes Region

Canada's Great Country Inns

Cottages, B&Bs and Country Inns of England and Wales

The Berkeley Guides

On the Loose in California

On the Loose in Eastern Europe

On the Loose in Mexico

On the Loose in the Pacific Northwest & Alaska

Fodor's Exploring Guides

Exploring California

Exploring Florida

Exploring France

Exploring Germany

Exploring Paris

Exploring Rome

Exploring Spain

Exploring Thailand

Fodor's Flashmaps

New York

Washington, D.C.

Fodor's Pocket Guides

Pocket Bahamas

Pocket Jamaica

Pocket London

Pocket New York City

Pocket Paris

Pocket Puerto Rico

Pocket San Francisco

Pocket Washington, D.C.

Fodor's Sports

Cycling

Hiking

Running

Sailing

The Insider's Guide to the Best Canadian Skiing

Fodor's Three-In-Ones (guidebook, language cassette, and phrase book)

France

Germany

Italy

Mexico

Spain

Fodor's Special-Interest Guides

Cruises and Ports of Call

Disney World & the Orlando Area

Euro Disney

Healthy Escapes

London Companion

Skiing in the USA & Canada

Sunday in New York

Fodor's Touring Guides

Touring Europe

Touring USA: Eastern Edition

Touring USA: Western Edition

Fodor's Vacation Planners

Great American Vacations

National Parks of the West

The Wall Street Journal Guides to Business Travel

Europe

International Cities

Pacific Rim

USA & Canada